WOMEN'S LANGUAGE

Women's Language

An Analysis of Style and Expression in Letters before 1800

Edited by
Eva Hættner Aurelius, Hedda Gunneng
& Jon Helgason

NORDIC ACADEMIC PRESS

Nordic Academic Press
P.O. Box 1206
S-221 05 Lund
Sweden
www.nordicacademicpress.com

© Nordic Academic Press and the authors 2012
Typesetting: Stilbildarna i Mölle, Frederic Täckström
Translation: Lena Olsson
Copyediting: Charlotte Merton
Expertise in mathematical statistics: Mats Brodén and Tobias Rydén
Adaptation of diagrams: Fugazi form
Jacket design: Maria Jörgel Andersson
Printed by ScandBook AB, Falun 2012
ISBN: 978-91-87121-87-6

Contents

This research project was funded
by Riksbankens Jubileumsfond.

Introduction

Women's language—a separate culture?

Eva Hættner Aurelius, Hedda Gunneng & Jon Helgason

The subject of this study is the notion that there was a silent, female culture, understood here as being expressed through language. The idea is that when women addressed women their language was different than when women spoke to men, or when men alone spoke. In order to test this theory empirically, we have selected a corpus of letters from the twelfth to the eighteenth centuries between women, between men, and by women to men and men to women: a total of 1,250 letters written in Latin, Swedish, French, German, and English, divided between five subprojects. The reason we chose written correspondence as our source material reflects the fact that this was a genre much used by women, and in the period studied was associated with the idea of a particularly female mode of expression, to wit a specific 'femininity'.[1] In order to test the notion that there was a distinctively female idiom—a female mode of expression used in a given genre—we have studied the style used, but we have also partly contextualized the ideals associated with the letter-writing genre, looking at whether (and if so, how) each piece of correspondence satisfies the standard criteria for how women ought to write letters.

The question addressed is whether women used a different language when they wrote to women. According to Elaine Showalter, the idea of a female language that only women have at their command is impossible, for 'all language is the language of the dominant order, and women, if they speak at all, must speak through it.' On the other hand, women's language should 'be considered … in terms of styles, strategies, and contexts of linguistic performances'.[2] We have taken women's language to be a 'double discourse', so that the variation in language is our choice of methodological starting-point.

Historically speaking, these ideas are closely related to the notion of a 'female' epistolary style, with its distinctive characteristics. Ever since antiquity, letters have been associated with attributes such as spontaneity and intimacy, and it was primarily in seventeenth-century France that this view of the letter genre became linked to the concept of the feminine, in the sense that the ideas relating to the nature of women were amplified in the ideas of the letter genre, for instance in (generally stylistically defined) concepts such as *'négligence'*, *'bagatelle'*, and *'spontanité'*.[3]

Our analysis of the style was so designed that each sub-corpus was analysed stylistically in much the same manner (although for methodological reasons certain studies cannot be performed in all languages) in order that the results of each analysis might be comparable with one another. This comparison is designed to test the hypothesis that there is such a thing as a women's language in what one might term an essentialist sense—a womanliness that transcends time and place. On the other hand, the stylistic analysis of each language tests a more constructivist view of the term 'woman', here as a question of letter-writers of the same class, date, and language. The differences observable here in letters between women, between men, and from women to men or vice versa ought to show if women were construed in a different way than the men—that they were at least in part located in a different culture.

The stylistic analysis required that we chart a series of stylistic variables on various linguistic levels—lexical, syntactic, and textual—including the relative proportions of concrete and abstract substantives, emotive and neutral adjectives, and dynamic and static verbs. Further, the analysis comprises syntactic complexity and stringency, the use of rhetorical figures, the number and nature of appeals to the reader, and code-switching.

Syntactic depth

The syntactic depth of a text is considered to be an important stylistic variable, as the greater the syntactic depth the more difficult a text is to understand. Syntactic depth can be measured in a number of ways. Two of the commonly used methods are to count the number of words in each macrosyntagm (sentence) or to count the number of levels of subordination in the same unit. We have done both. In all the subprojects, the two methods produced the same result, namely that there seems to be a positive correlation between the number of words in a macrosyntagm and the number of levels of subordination. A comparison of the syntactic depth found by the subprojects does not give a similarly consistent picture, however, leaving it impossible for us to conclude that syntactic depth might be greater in letters written and/or received by men, regardless of time and place. One can take as examples the letters between women in the German and Latin corpora, which have a lower syntactic depth, while the equivalent group shows greater syntactic depth in the Swedish letters, and in the French letters no difference at all.

Here one must strike a note of caution, however, for all subordinate clauses have been taken to be equivalent, regardless of their semantic content. In reality, subordinate clauses that demand two or more logical operations in order to be understood—for example, concessive and conditional clauses—complicate the reader's assimilation of the text far more than, say, nominal and attributive subordinate clauses might. Macrosyntagms can be extended considerably by the adding on of such clauses without becoming any more difficult to understand. In other words, the measurement of syntactic depth as a stylistic variable in a text needs to be differentiated and refined if it is to serve as an instrument of stylistic analysis.

Recipient adaptation

That a letter-writer's message is in part determined by her or his notion of the recipient is a well-known phenomenon in human communication, and such addressee adaptation may explain some of the results of the present study. Throughout the period in question, men had an education that was very different to women's, primarily because it included Latin. In the Latin letters, tropes are much in evidence, while other stylistic figures are used more sparingly. Despite this economy of style, they are to be found far more often in letters from women to men than in letters between women. The use of different stylistic figures was an accomplishment that was learned by reading the classical authors in school.

In the Swedish sources, one sees clearly that the number of subordinate clauses increases when women write to men instead of to other women. Long sentences with large numbers of sub-ordinate clauses were also one of the stylistic ideals taught along with Latin itself. In a similar fashion, the women who wrote the French-language letters studied here seem to have used longer bases (p. 33) when writing to men than to other women. Even rhetorical questions feature more frequently in women's letters to male recipients. The fact that women used metaphor more when they wrote to men than when they wrote to women, while the men generally used metaphor far more than the women did, is evident in both the Swedish and German letters. This can also be understood as a form of recipient adaptation.

Proximity

Three of the stylistic variables whose occurrence we have charted served to promote proximity in communication: direct addresses to the reader, code-switching, and hyperbole. That appeals (exclamatives, vocatives, imperatives, and questions) reduce the distance between the writer and the recipient needs no further explanation here. That code-switching might do the same is not as obvious; we, however, argue that it *can*. Its occurrence can depend on the writer in that particular context spontaneously expressing herself in a different language to the main language of the letter. When someone writes a letter in a second language (sub-projects 1 and 3) and then unexpectedly switches to their mother tongue, then it must be viewed as an expression of spontaneity. The writer has quite simply written the first words that sprang to mind. That is not to say that all code-switching arises because the writer experiences or wishes to convey proximity to the recipient. It can also be determined by convention, the genre's demands of both writer and reader, or other considerations for the writer. Similarly, we would argue that the use of hyperbole can also be an expression of spontaneity, and to support this view we refer to the fact that spoken language in everyday situations is rich in hyperbole. The results in terms of these three stylistic variables across the five subprojects are mixed, for it is the contents and context of each letter that determines whether the proximity evoked in this way is reassuring or threatening.

Considered by language

Within the individual languages we have also made some interesting observations. In the Latin letters written by Hildegard of Bingen, the use of tropes increases dramatically when the addressee is a man. It is a striking feature of Hildegard's style that the frequency of tropes is notably high: 'sixty-six tropes per hundred macrosyntagms in the FF [female–female] and eighty-eight in the FM [female–male] corpora'.

In her letters to women, she uses noticeably fewer rhetorical figures than in her letters to men; the same is true of the number of words, for she uses far fewer words per macrosyntagm in her letters to women. The explanation that first presents itself is that Hildegard learned her Latin from the Bible.

In the Swedish letters, appeals to the reader are considerably more frequent in those between women than in those from men to women. This can be interpreted as the women's attempt to create a sense that an actual conversation is underway, face to face. There is a greater number of subordinate clauses on a deeper level when the women write to men than when they write to women, the same being true when either letter-writers or recipients were men—in other words, the syntactic depth is markedly greater in letters where men are involved. When women write to men rather than other women, the frequency with which they use metaphor clearly increases. This could be thought a form of recipient adaptation: the women may have thought the use of metaphor to be a masculine habit. When women write to men, there is far more code-switching than is the case in letters between women; again, this is perceptible in the corpus where men are involved, either as recipients or as letter-writers.

In the French letters, appeals to the reader are far more frequent in the letters between women than in those from women to men. A closer look at the detail of the analysis, moreover, reveals interesting linguistic characteristics that seem to reflect the power relations between writers and recipients. These need not have anything to do with differences in age, social position, or gender, for they could also stem from an emotional imbalance between the correspondents, such as infatuation or guilt—and they could be temporary. From a close reading of the women's letters, it can be inferred that when the writers felt inferior to their correspondents, there is a tendency to use longer macrosyntagms and more subordinate elements, as well as longer bases. The term 'base' denotes everything that precedes the finite verb form in the main clause of a sentence (see p. 33). When, on the other hand, there are signals in the text that suggest that the writers felt at ease with their correspondents, they seem also to have allowed themselves to use more irregular macrosyntagms, engage in more frequent code-switching, and use more hyperbole.

In the English letters, it is evident that letters between women contain fewer metaphors than do letters where men figure as either recipients or writers.

In the German letters, the number of appeals shows a distinct increase when men are involved; in other words, when women write to women there are fewer appeals than in all the other types of letter. When women write to men, they rely far more on metaphor than when they write to other women. The syntactic depth grows considerably when women write to men, as shown both in the number of words per macrosyntagm and in the number of subordinate clauses on a deeper level. This is also clear in the entire corpus in which men are involved. Finally, code-switching tendencies are far less in evidence when women write to men than when they write to women, which is true of the entire corpus of letters that includes men.

Considered by topics

If we consider the topics that the letter-writers address in their correspondence, it is apparent that here too there were no topics that were equally important across all five subprojects. Thus it is not the case that such subjects as the body, dress and textiles, or obstetrics are mentioned more often in women's correspondence compared to correspondence where men were involved. That said, in the individual subprojects it *is* the case that certain topics dominate in the correspondence between women. In the Swedish letters between women, there is far more talk of clothing and textiles, kith and kin, and, yes, obstetrics than in the letters where men are involved. Again, in the German letters between women there is far more about clothing and textiles and the body than in letters where men are involved. The English letters are the exception to this rule: in letters between women, far more is made of their social lives, travels, acquaintances, and Nature than in the letters where men are involved.

Conclusion

The comparison of the results of the five subprojects (see 'Project summary and conclusions', p. 123) shows first and foremost that the results are dissimilar. No statistically significant result concerning a single variable has been produced in any of the five subprojects. When a variable has been found to be of high or medium statistical significance in more than one subproject, the findings are sometimes mutually exclusive. In other words, our results can neither verify nor falsify the hypothesis of a female culture independent of time and place. For a detailed account of the comparisons, we refer the reader to Chapter 8.

Despite the interest of our general observations, we must conclude that the essentialist dimension in the hypothesis has thus not been verified. Similarly, there are no indications in any of the individual subprojects that women had a particular mode of expression or style with which they created a special cultural space, and for this reason the constructivist dimension of the hypothesis cannot be verified either.

Notes

1 Löwendahl, Marie, *Min allrabästa och ömmaste vän! Kvinnors brevskrivning under svenskt 1700-tal* (Lund: Makadam, 2007), 29–33.
2 Elaine Showalter (ed.), *The New Feminist Criticism: Essays on Women, Literature, and Theory* (London: Virago, 1985), 262, 259–60.
3 See Löwendahl 2007, 42–49.

CHAPTER I

Theoretical foundation

Eva Hættner Aurelius

In essence, feminist literary scholarship can be divided into three separate approaches: first, what Elaine Showalter has called 'the feminist critique', which examines lacunae and errors in the history of literature and stereotypical literary images of women; second, gynocriticism, which brings to the fore women's texts and sets out to describe potentially distinctive feminine characteristics in the texts and in culture alike; and thirdly, deconstruction, which questions 'woman' and 'feminine' as analytical concepts, and instead suggests that they are in fact social constructions, produced by dichotomies ('woman'/'feminine' is produced as the opposite to 'man'/'masculine') that always represent 'woman' as a deviation from the norm ('man'). 'Woman' and 'feminine' become problems that not only have to be corrected, but also consolidate the dominant position of 'the masculine'. Dichotomous thinking can, in addition, result in actual, individual women being locked into stereotypical gender roles and/or heterosexual identities. What feminist research should do is question this dichotomy in various ways, and show how the social construction of 'woman' is produced. Simply put, these three main approaches can be fitted into a chronological perspective: the feminist critique belongs to the 1960s and 1970s, gynocriticism to the 1980s, and deconstruction to the end of the 1980s and the 1990s.

Our investigation takes as its point of departure a critical theory that was first presented by Elaine Showalter in the well-known article 'Feminist Criticism in the Wilderness', originally published in 1981 in *Critical Inquiry*.[1] Her main purpose was to formulate a theory of women's writing or women's culture and its special characteristics: Showalter claimed that, until that point, Anglo-American research into women's literature had been theoretically naïve. Influenced by such feminist theorists as Cixous, Kristeva, and Irigaray, among others, Showalter attempted to formulate a comprehensive theory of women's writing. The term 'gynocriticism' is, in fact, Showalter's own, coined to differentiate the feminist critique, which focuses on the reader and the history of literature, from gynocriticism, which focuses on the female author. In 1981, Showalter analysed the state of research about women's literature—Anglo-American feminist research dealing with women's writing, that is—and concluded that while women's texts had begun to be examined, scholars did not have any way of defining what it was they were investigating. Showalter continued: 'It is no longer the ideological dilemma of reconciling revisionary pluralisms but the essential question of difference. How can we constitute women as a distinct literary group? What is *the difference* of women's writing?'[2] One of the reasons for Showalter's theoretical concern was the fact that during the 1970s a number of scholars in the US and the UK had written histories of women's literature without theoretically clarifying the subject of their histories. A similar objection can, incidentally, be made about the multi-volume *Nordisk kvinnolitteraturhistoria* ('History of Nordic Women's Literature', (1993–2000) and the project that preceded it.

Showalter identifies four theoretical models of differentiating 'female/feminine' or 'woman' from 'male/masculine' and 'man': biological, linguistic, psychoanalytical, and cultural. The biological theory bases difference in the uniqueness of the female body and in women's bodily experiences; the linguistic, in the assumption or hypothesis that women and men use language in different ways; the psychoanalytical, in the assumption that there are fundamental differences in the psychology of men and women as described by the psychoanalytical tradition. The differing psychosexual development of women compared to that of men has left women with a different relationship to language, creativity, imagination, and culture. Showalter herself is a proponent of the fourth or cultural theory, which is distinctly anthropological. This is because it is capable of incorporating all of the other theories:

> A theory based on a model of women's culture can provide, I believe, a more complete and satisfying way to talk about the specificity and difference of women's writing than theories based in biology, linguistics, or psychoanalysis. Indeed, a theory of culture incorporates ideas about women's body, language, and psyche but interprets them in relation to the social contexts in which they occur. The ways in which women conceptualize their bodies and their sexual

and reproductive functions are intricately linked to their cultural environments. The female psyche can be studied as the product or construction of cultural forces. Language, too, comes back into the picture, as we consider the social dimensions and determinants of language use, the shaping of linguistic behaviour by cultural ideals. A cultural theory acknowledges that there are important differences between women as writers: class, race, nationality, and history are literary determinants as significant as gender. Nonetheless, women's culture forms a collective experience within the cultural whole, an experience that binds women writers to each other over time and space.[3]

It is clear that Showalter on the one hand perceives 'woman' and 'feminine' as cultural products, or 'constructions', but that on the other hand she also sees 'woman' and 'feminine' as universals. Because women in different cultures and in different periods share the same experiences, it is reasonable to use concepts like 'woman' and 'feminine'. The question is whether or not this constitutes essentialism (in other words, whether it is a purely ideological concept, produced by the man/woman dichotomy). Strictly speaking, it does not. Referring to anthropological theories and research, Showalter points out that the important thing is to empirically test the theory of a separate women's culture.

Showalter's concept of culture is an anthropological one: culture equals values, norms, actions, roles, behaviour, and social institutions. When investigating whether or not the concept of a separate female culture is a meaningful one, it is important to point out that such a culture must be one that is defined and maintained by women themselves, not one that society (in other words, men) has prescribed for women. Referring to the anthropologists Gerda Lerner and Shirley and Edwin Ardener, Showalter argues that this hypothetical female culture is not a subculture in the sense that women form a completely separate cultural sphere; on the contrary, they are part of a general culture, one in which both men and women participate. However, because women, being powerless, have generally been a muted group, meaning that their special experiences and perspectives have not been made visible or audible other than as deviations from the norm, their views on reality and themselves have not been made visible either. The Ardeners' model of the culture of the silenced women requires that women always have to 'mediate their beliefs through the allowable

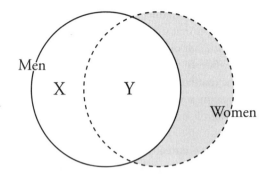

Figure 1. The
relationship between
male and female in
Western culture,
according to
Showalter.[6]

forms of dominant structures',[4] and Showalter follows suit with her argument that 'all language is the language of the dominant order, and women, if they speak at all, must speak through it'.[5] The relationship between the dominant and the muted culture as represented by the Ardeners is given in Figure 1.

The Ardeners call the silenced culture 'the wild zone'. Their definition of this wild zone makes it impossible, by its very nature, to empirically confirm the presence of a female culture in language. Showalter adopts the Ardeners' view on this matter:

> We can think of the 'wild zone' of women's culture spatially, experientially, or metaphysically. Spatially it stands for an area which is literally no-man's-land, a place forbidden to men, which corresponds to the zone in X which is off limits to women. Experientially it stands for the aspects of the female life-style which are outside of and unlike those of men; again, there is a corresponding zone of male experience alien to women. But if we think of the wild zone metaphysically, or in terms of consciousness, it has no corresponding male space since all of male consciousness is within the circle of the dominant structure and thus accessible to or structured by language.[7]

What can be found in this metaphysical wild zone is the subconscious, the unspoken, that which feminism will bring into the light by means of a new language. On the whole, Showalter is sceptical of the idea of attempting to base a theory about the uniqueness of women's writing on analyses of linguistic phenomena.

English and American linguists agree that 'there is absolutely no evidence that would suggest the sexes are preprogrammed to develop structurally different linguistic systems.' Furthermore, the many specific differences in male and female speech, intonation, and language use that have been identified cannot be explained in terms of 'two separate sex-specific languages' but need to be considered instead in terms of styles, strategies, and contexts of linguistic performance.[8]

Showalter emphatically rejects any attempt to describe the potential difference between men's and women's language in terms of linguistic structures:

> dominant groups control the forms or structures in which consciousness can be articulated. Thus muted groups must mediate their beliefs through the allowable forms of dominant structures. Another way of putting this would be to say that all language is the language of the dominant order, and women, if they speak at all, must speak through it.[9]

This leads Showalter to argue that women's writing, women's literature, can be positioned within two traditions: 'Women writing are not, then, *inside* and *outside* of the male tradition; they are inside two traditions simultaneously, "undercurrents", in Ellen Moers's metaphor, of the mainstream.'[10] That is to say that women speak in two voices, and the point of empirical research would be to somehow make audible the second voice. Showalter believes that this second voice, this second language, must be studied within its cultural context: 'Language too, comes back into the picture, as we consider the social dimensions and determinants of language use, the shaping of linguistic behaviour by cultural ideals.'[11]

The researchers in the current project agree with Showalter that any potential difference between the languages of men and women cannot be formulated in terms of *different* languages, and that if differences are found, they are tied to a particular culture. We have taken as our starting-point Showalter's idea that this potential difference between men's and women's languages needs 'to be considered instead in terms of styles, strategies, and contexts of linguistic performance',[12] and we have therefore chosen to study various aspects of linguistic style. Style, in our definition, is the individual stamp given to human language by the conscious or unconscious choice of linguistic features in any given situation. In this way, we modify Showalter's manner of determining how the potential differences between men's and women's language can be identified: for practical reasons, we cannot study the strategies and context of every text we analyse. If Showalter's and the Ardeners' theoretical model is to be tested in this way, it will be necessary to look for linguistic features when women write to women (FF), and compare these with linguistic features, first, when women write to men (FM) and vice versa (MF), and, second, when men write to men (MM). According to our modified theory, the language (style) of the FF category should differ in a significant manner from the language (style) of the three other categories. This linguistic material must be of a kind that any potential differences between these two groups (FF versus FM, MF, and MM) should preferably not be possible to attribute to any other factor than sex/gender. We would like to emphasize that the hypothesis we are testing is not identical to the hypothesis about a women's culture proposed by Showalter: we have, for practical reasons, been unable to study the entire cultural context surrounding each of the texts we have analysed.

Most investigations of the relationship between gender and language attempting to discover potential differences between men's and women's language—an active field of research since the late 1970s—have been conducted on contemporary spoken language. Because we wanted to test the idea of a female literary culture, we have chosen to study written language, and we have chosen a type of text (discourse or genre, if you will) where scholars, irrespective of their field of study, generally agree that women as writers are, or have been, especially prominent and even considered superior to men: the familiar letter. We believe that this genre, where women have played an important role in the history of European culture, provides eminently suitable material on which to test the hypothesis of a separate female culture. One of the premises of the project has been the assumed connection between letter-writing on the one hand and women and womanliness on the other.[13] In terms of literary history, it is true that the relationship between womanliness and letter-writing is seen as both a historical reality (women wrote letters) and a cultural notion (women wrote better letters than men; in letters, it was possible to express womanliness). What then of the relationship between gender (as a social, cultural, and historical construction) and genre? This is a question often addressed in research on women's literature in general, especially when it comes to genres such as autobiography, diaries, and letters; genres that to a greater degree than the usual literary genres have historically been ascribed the ability to be a more immediate expression of the writer's ego and its experiences. In our material, the first category (FF) is compared to the other three (FM, MF, MM) in order to test the hypothesis about the existence of a female culture. The letters are written in five languages: Swedish, English, German, French, and Latin. The letters written in the modern languages date back to the long eighteenth century (*c.*1660–1830), whereas the letters written in Latin date back to the twelfth century. In each language group, the material consists of approximately 250 letters written by women and around 50 letters written by men. The letters in Latin number about 150. These two groups of letters (FF versus FM/MF/MM) are subject to a linguistic analysis focusing on style and content, and the results of this analysis are then compared within each language group. Next, the results of these intra-lingual comparisons are compared to one another in order to chart any differences between the FF corpus and the FM/MF/MM corpus that can be attributed to cultural variables. We would like to emphasize that in our method we have attempted to analyse phenomena relating to language and content that can be applied to all of the languages included in the study. However, we are aware that there are such differences between these languages that such an inter-lingual comparison suffers from a significant number of methodological problems. In order to eliminate (if possible) the alternate hypothesis that the potential similarities or differences between the letters may derive from the fact that they were written in the same historical period, we have included letters from the twelfth century. Also, as will be apparent from the discussion that follows about the relationship of our investigation to linguistic research on potential differences between men's and women's (spoken) language, we have, through our choice of material (letters to and from members of the same social class) attempted to eliminate the alternate hypothesis that any potential differences in the texts are due to an unequal relationship between correspondents, and not to gender differences.

Socio-linguistic research on women's language

Even if our investigation, as far as we can tell, is unique in the sense that it deals with women's written language in medieval, early modern, and modern times, thereby complementing the existing wide-ranging research about men's and women's contemporary spoken language, something should be said about the relationship between our research and the latter. It should be borne in mind that our survey of this extensive field of research is by no means comprehensive. The comparison that follows below is merely a broad outline focusing on general issues and on investigations that have important features in common with our own (for example, studies of women's conversations with women).

The linguistic literature on the relationship between gender and language can, very broadly, be divided into two large fields: firstly, research on stereotypes and norms regarding women in language (which basically amounts to studies of how men have designated the world, including women); and secondly, research on how men and women actually speak. The latter field can, in turn, be divided into research on interaction between the sexes and interaction among members of either sex, and research on women's and men's (and boys' and girls') linguistic behaviour in different institutional circumstances, be they political and legal or socio-cultural (play, gossip). The issues that have been dealt with regarding this spoken material have primarily been the potential differences between the sexes and the possible causes of such difference. Theories about the underlying reasons for gender differences—according to Alice Freed in her 2003 article 'Epilogue: Reflections on Language and Gender Research'—are primarily based on three theoretical traditions: first, the theory that women's language is deficient (the deficit theory) postulates that women's language is inefficient compared to men's, in that it mirrors women's insecurity and powerlessness; second, the domination theory suggests that linguistic differences depend on differences in power and in access to the language; and third, the difference theory stipulates that linguistic differences originate in the fact that 'women and men used specific and distinct verbal strategies and communicative styles which were developed in same-sex childhood peer groups'.[14] This last theory found its most well-known proponent in the American linguist Deborah Tannen, who in 1990 published *You Just Don't Understand: Women and Men in Conversation*.[15] One controversy about perceived gender differences thus centres on whether the reason for such differences should be sought in power structures in general or in cultural differences that, in principle, should be independent of these power structures. Our investigation leans towards the latter theory, and our material—letters between people from the same social classes or groups, to wit the upper classes (in the Swedish and French letters), the middle classes (in the German letters), and the cultural elite (in the English letters)—does not actualize or mirror power relations to any significant degree, in that there are few, and only marginal, class-linked differences or class-related power differences to be found in these letters. Such power differences as can be detected between writer and recipient (and vice versa) have to do either with women's general subordination in the culture being studied or with specific interpersonal relations, such as between mother-in-law and daughter-in-law, or between lender and borrower.[16] Thus, our material may be expected to give an indication of whether there are cultural differences between language that is specific to women and language that is common to both men and women.

Our investigation is also based on the notion that there is a 'silent' or 'silenced' female culture, in the sense that it has not been thoroughly voiced in the public domain, or indeed investigated by scholars. Included in this silenced women's culture are, according to the Scottish linguist Deborah Cameron, linguistic activities that have traditionally been held in contempt: '"gossip", storytelling, private letters and diaries ... But this list of "female" genres gives a valuable clue to the constitution of "women's silence". For none of these genres are especially prestigious, and some, like gossip, are actually disparaged.'[17] Most investigations of women's spoken language have been conducted using material that included both male and female speakers. The English linguist Jennifer Coates, who in 1996 published *Women-Talk: Conversation between Women Friends*,[18] writes about this field of research in the 1998 anthology *Language and Gender: A Reader*:

> The topic of all-female talk, however, was not explicitly addressed until Deborah Jones's paper 'Gossip: Notes on Women's Oral Culture' was published in 1980. Since then, a great deal of research has been carried out on same-sex talk, though nearly all of it has had a comparative focus. For example, Deborah Tannen (1990) compared the talk of same-sex pairs of friends at different ages; Jenny Cheshire ... compared the language used by adolescent single-sex groups in adventure playgrounds in Reading, England; and Marjorie Goodwin ... compared the language used by pre-adolescent single-sex peer groups in a Philadelphia street. All these papers focus on children or adolescents, and all investigate both female and male speakers. It is still rare to find research being carried out

which has as its aim the description of women's conversational practices for their own sake.[19]

Many of these studies are confined to investigating spoken language, in that they attempt to discover different conversational strategies, for example 'topic development'; minimal responses; simultaneous speech; epistemic modality (or hedging); and 'tag questions' or 'overlapping turns, co-constructed talk and positive feedback' and the purposes and goals of the speakers.[20] Regarding women's gossip, Coates found that 'women's friendly talk has as its chief goal the establishment and maintenance of good social relations'.[21] These results have subsequently been confirmed by other researchers. It is self-evident that these analyses of spoken language are quite different from our analysis of written language—we could not possibly investigate these types of oral linguistic strategies, and in our linguistic analysis we have not analysed the function of each and every letter in detail.

In sociolinguistic research on women's and men's spoken language, variations in pronunciation and grammar are often analysed using William Labov's method.[22] The most common finding in such investigations is that women tend to use a more standardized pronunciation and grammar than men do. Cheshire shows, among other things, that 'non-standard grammatical forms were used less often by the girls than by the boys ... a finding which has been widely replicated in variationist studies.'[23] We have avoided this type of study, mainly because spelling and grammar in written texts tend to display much less variation than spoken language.

The English linguist Suzanne Romaine has summarized the research in this area, claiming that 'There are also strong correlations between patterns of social stratification and gender, with a number of now classic findings emerging repeatedly. One of these sociolinguistic patterns is that women, regardless of other social characteristics such as class, age etc., tended to use more standard forms than men.'[24] However, she cautions against relying on results deriving from simple quantitative investigations of women's and men's spoken language: the same linguistic phenomenon can mean a number of different things depending on the context: 'On closer examination, there are few, if any, context-independent gender differences in language'.[25] Freed is even more dismissive in her survey of the entire field of gender-related linguistics:

Sociolinguists, linguistic anthropologists, and other scholars have now analyzed vast quantities of naturally occurring speech samples from a wide range of contexts. These data demonstrate in vivid detail that the amount of talk, the structure of narratives, the use of questions, the availability of cooperative and competitive speech styles, the employment of prestige speech forms, the use of intimate friendly talk, the occurrence of various phonological and prosodic patterns sometimes representative of linguistic change, the occurrence of vernacular speech forms, lexical choices, the use of silence, interruption, aggravated forms of address, and forms of politeness—these do not correlate in any consistent pattern with either sex or gender.[26]

The aim, according to Freed, is to discover how culture (taken to include language and language use) creates and constructs gender—in other words, to explain why notions about men's and women's separate language use have arisen, and how they are expressed and communicated: 'Despite our knowledge base, the stereotypes, the ideas that we might call folklinguistic beliefs, remain strong. As Mary Talbot reminds us … "Stereotyping as a representational practice is at the center of the notion of folklinguistics".'[27] Freed's and other scholars' criticism of research that in various ways has attempted to answer the question of the differences between men's (including boys') and women's (including girls') linguistic behaviour has its theoretical basis in the previously mentioned deconstructionist critique of the dichotomous use of the concepts 'woman' and 'feminine'—in the fact that these concepts have been defined as the opposite of 'man' and 'masculine', which means that what women have said (and done) has, in academic practice, been seen as a deviation from the norm. According to this critique, feminist research on differences between men and women both adopts (and, in so doing, constructs) and reinforces the image of women as deviations from the norm. As pointed out by the British Germanic philologist and linguist Sally Johnson, language does not reflect gender, 'it helps constitute it'.[28] The ultimate goal would be to discover how the linguistic constructions of gender are effected: 'what we really need is to know more about the complex role played by "difference" *in the construction of* "dominance"'.[29]

This kind of conceptual criticism began to make itself felt among linguistic researchers mainly in the late 1990s. Showalter's theory of a female culture was criticized early on in the field of comparative literature,[30] but not until now has the theory been tested empirically on literary written material. Given how matters stand in the field of comparative literature, this theory is therefore of great interest. Moreover, because of its pervasiveness and, in a gender political perspective, its problematic character, it should also be tested empirically.

However, our investigation is also interesting from a linguistic perspective, especially because it tests the theory of the existence of a female culture on older written material. Concerning the criticism regarding the essentialism underlying the concepts of 'woman' and 'feminine' in the fields of linguistics and comparative literature alike, we agree that these concepts can, at bottom, be considered to be empirically empty, and thus too comprehensive to explain any potential differences between men's and women's utterances. These differences may depend on other factors in the context of the utterances. In response to this aspect of theoretical criticism, it may be said that our investigation has attempted to weed out, as far as is possible, culturally dependent power differences in the material (excepting, of course, the gendered power dynamics of the historical culture in question), and, in addition, the utterances' significant dependency on context, in that they are written texts and thus bound by certain generic conventions. The underlying meanings of oral utterances are more dependent on context than those of written ones. In any generically bound written utterance—a letter, for example—the writer, especially in the periods in which our material was written, must not only submit to generic and social conventions, but also shape his or her written statements according to the fact that written language demands a greater linguistic clarity than do spoken utterances, which means that the degree of dependency on context is smaller in our material than would be the case for oral utterances from the same period.

Naturally, this does not mean that we assume that any potential differences between women's language (the FF category) and general language (the FM/MF/MM category) have to originate in some form of universal femininity. Indeed, it can never be assumed that such differences are not the result of one or more factors that we have not been able to discern in particular contexts. However, even if the differences should prove to be independent of their contexts, it does not mean that we believe that we have managed to identify a 'female' essence: such results may just as well be explained as manifestations of femininity, or, to put it more simply, as the result of women being socialized into the female gender role, which, in turn, is an aspect of the desire of the dominant culture to subordinate women. In fact, this interpretation of potential differences does not contradict Showalter's theory, given that she assumes 'woman' to be a social (or cultural) construction:

> Indeed, a theory of culture incorporates ideas about women's body, language, and psyche but interprets them in relation to the social contexts in which they occur. The ways in which women conceptualize their bodies and their sexual and reproductive functions are intricately linked to their cultural environments. The female psyche can be studied as the product or construction of cultural forces. Language, too, comes back into the picture, as we consider the social dimensions and determinants of language use, the shaping of linguistic behaviour by cultural ideals. A cultural theory acknowledges that there are important differences between women as writers: class, race, nationality, and history are literary determinants as significant as gender.[31]

However, because it is possible that there are experiences that are specific to women and, we would add, because women in most societies and in most historical periods have been subordinated to men, and as a consequence of this have been constructed as the opposite of men, it is warranted to test this theory empirically.

Finally, we would like to point out that our purpose in testing this theory empirically does not mean that—if we were to detect significant differences between the two categories in all of the languages under investigation—we would have proven the validity of the theory. In such cases, the hypothesis would merely have been strengthened.

Notes

1 The article 'Feminist Criticism in the Wilderness', *Critical Inquiry*, 8/2 (1981), 179–205 has been anthologized repeatedly over the years; the version cited in the present volume is Showalter 1985, 243–70.
2 Ibid. 248.
3 Ibid. 259–60.
4 Ibid. 262.
5 Ibid.
6 Ibid.
7 Ibid.

8 Ibid. 255, quoting Sally McConnell-Ginet, 'Linguistics and the Feminist Challenge', *Women and Language in Literature and Society*, ed. Sally McConnell-Ginet, Ruth Barker and Nelly Furman (New York: Praeger, 1980), 14.

9 Ibid. 262.

10 Ibid. 264.

11 Ibid. 259–60.

12 Ibid. 255.

13 Marie Löwendahl, *Min allrabästa och ömmaste vän! Kvinnors brevskrivning under svenskt 1700-tal* (Lund: Makadam, 2007), 29–33.

14 Alice F. Freed, 'Epilogue: Reflections on Language and Gender Research', in Janet Holmes and Miriam Meyerhoff (eds.), *The Handbook of Language and Gender* (Oxford: Blackwell, 2003), 701.

15 Deborah Tannen, *You Just Don't Understand: Women and Men in Conversation* (New York: Morrow, 1990).

16 Naturally, there are exceptions. For example, the English material contains a few isolated instances of gentlemanly employers writing to their servants, and writers from the middling classes discussing patronage with members of the nobility.

17 Deborah Cameron, 'Introduction: Why is Language a Feminist Issue?', in ead. (ed.), *The Feminist Critique of Language: A Reader* (London: Routledge, 1990), 4.

18 Jennifer Coates, *Women-Talk: Conversation between Women Friends* (Cambridge, Mass.: Blackwell, 1996).

19 Jennifer Coates (ed.), *Language and Gender: A Reader* (Oxford: Blackwell, 1998), 211 in introducing the section on 'Same-Sex Talk'.

20 Ibid. 212.

21 Ibid. and Jennifer Coates, 'Gossip Revisited: Language in All-Female Groups', in Coates 1998, 226–53, originally published in Jennifer Coates and Deborah Cameron (eds.), *Women in Their Speech Communities* (London: Longman, 1989).

22 Labov, William, *Sociolinguistic Patterns* (Philadelphia: University of Pennsylvania Press, 1972).

23 Cheshire 1998, summarized in Coates 1998, 8 in introducing the section on 'Gender Differences in Pronunciation and Grammar'.

24 Suzanne Romaine, 'Variation in Language and Gender', in Holmes and Meyerhoff 2003, 101.

25 Ibid. 111.

26 Freed 2003, 705.

27 Ibid., quoting Mary Talbot, 'Gender Stereotypes: Reproduction and Challenge', in Holmes and Meyerhoff 2003, 472, under the heading 'Stereotyping'.

28 Sally Johnson, 'Theorizing Language and Masculinity', in Sally Johnson and Ulrike Hanna Meinhof (eds.), *Language and Masculinity* (Oxford: Blackwell, 1997), 23.

29 Ibid. 25; italics in original.

30 For example, Toril Moi, *Sexual/Textual Politics: Feminist Literary Theory* (London: Methuen, 1985); and Alice Jardine, *Gynesis: Configurations of Woman and Modernity* (Ithaca: Cornell University Press, 1985).

31 Showalter 1985, 259–60.

Bibliography

Cameron, Deborah, *The Feminist Critique of Language: A Reader* (London: Routledge, 1990)

— (ed.), 'Introduction: Why is Language a Feminist Issue', in Cameron 1990, 1–28.

Cheshire, Jenny, 'Linguistic Variation and Social Function', in Coates 1998, 29–41.

Coates, Jennifer, *Women-Talk: Conversation between Women Friends* (Cambridge, Mass.: Blackwell, 1996).

— (ed.), *Language and Gender: A Reader* (Oxford: Blackwell, 1998).

— 'Gossip Revisited: Language in All-Female Groups', in Coates 1998, 226–53, originally published in Jennifer Coates and Deborah Cameron (eds.), *Women in Their Speech Communities* (London: Longman, 1989).

Freed, Alice F., 'Epilogue: Reflections on Language and Gender Research', in Holmes and Meyerhoff 2003, 699–721.

Holmes, Janet and Miriam Meyerhoff (eds.), *The Handbook of Language and Gender* (Oxford: Blackwell, 2003).

Jardine, Alice A., *Gynesis: Configurations of Woman and Modernity* (Ithaca: Cornell University Press, 1985).

Johnson, Sally, 'Theorizing Language and Masculinity', in Johnson and Meinhof 1997, 8–26.

— and Ulrike Hanna Meinhof (eds.), *Language and Masculinity* (Oxford: Blackwell, 1997).

Labov, William, *Sociolinguistic Patterns* (Philadelphia: University of Pennsylvania Press, 1972).

Löwendahl, Marie, *Min allrabästa och ömmaste vän! Kvinnors brevskrivning under svenskt 1700-tal* (Lund: Makadam, 2007).

Moi, Toril, *Sexual/Textual Politics: Feminist Literary Theory* (London: Methuen, 1985).

Romaine, Suzanne, 'Variation in Language and Gender', in Holmes and Meyerhoff 2003, 98–119.

Showalter, Elaine (ed.), *The New Feminist Criticism: Essays on Women, Literature and Theory* (London: Virago, 1985).

— 'Feminist Criticism in the Wilderness', in ead. 1985, 243–70, originally published in *Critical Inquiry*, 8/2 (1981), 179–205.

Tannen, Deborah, *You Just Don't Understand: Women and Men in Conversation* (New York: Morrow, 1990).

CHAPTER 2

Linguistic stylistics— methodological considerations

Hedda Gunneng & Börje Westlund

Terminology

This study is based on a quantitative mapping of a number of select stylistic variables in five text corpora written in five different European languages. Among the stylistic variables that have been mapped, some can be found on the lexical level, some on the syntactic level, and some on the textual level. Prior to the mapping, all the variables have been defined. It is not self-evident that a stylistic variable defined in a certain way can be found in several different languages; however, we have found that our definitions have made it possible to identify almost all variables within each text corpus.

The definitions are informed by contemporary Swedish stylistic research, which means that we have used the common concepts from this field, with respect to both the lexical and the syntactic levels. We have, however, chosen to publish the results in English in order to make them available to a greater number of readers. In this transfer from Swedish to English we have encountered certain problems in translating the concepts used. There have been no difficulties on the lexical level. The two languages have the concept of word classes (in English usually called parts of speech) and word class definitions in common. English-language stylistics also use a division of nouns, adjectives, and verbs into certain semantic categories that are similar to the Swedish. On the syntactic level, however, there are discrepancies in the formation of concepts. In the field of English grammar, it is traditional to use certain central concepts for syntactic analysis that differ from the ones used in the Scandinavian languages. This has made the translation problematic, and has in some instances given the English terms a meaning that diverges from what is commonly accepted within English language studies.

The concept of the *mening* (Eng. *sentence*) is uncontroversial. The concept of the *macrosyntagm*, which we have used in the hypotaxis analysis, exists within the field of English grammar as well, although it is not as common as in Swedish grammatical analysis. When dividing the sentence into its largest constituent parts, on the other hand, different concepts are used in Swedish and English grammar. The largest constituent part is, according to Swedish grammar, the *sats*,[1] defined as a string of words containing a subject and a predicate, which together form a nexus construction.[2] The subject and the predicate are constitutive—essential—components of a *sats*. A sentence may consist of one *sats* alone, when it is termed simple; it may also be complex, containing several *satser*, one of which is superordinate to the others and is called a *huvudsats* (main *sats*). The other *satser* are subordinate to the main *sats* and are called *bisatser* (subordinate *satser*). In addition to the subordinate *satser*, the main *sats* may have subordinate phrases, which are incomplete *satser*, but nevertheless contain a nexus relationship which while only implied is nonetheless clear to the reader. The definition of these phrases, which are commonly called *satsförkortningar* (contracted *satser*), may vary somewhat among different grammatical models. Our definition is presented on p. 47. We have chosen to call these phrases *satsvärdiga fraser*, which we translate as *clause equivalents*.

In English grammar the largest constituent of the sentence is called a *clause*. Clauses are divided into three types: the finite clause, 'a clause whose verb element is finite'; the non-finite clause, 'a clause whose verb element is nonfinite'; and the verbless clause, 'a clause that does not have a verb element'.[3] In other words, in the definition of a clause there is no requirement that there should be a predicate. The fact that all three types of phrases are considered to be clauses is motivated in the following manner by Sidney Greenbaum and Randolph Quirk: 'We recognize nonfinite and verbless structures as clauses because we can analyse their internal structure into the same functional elements that we distinguish in finite clauses'.[4] The examples provided show that it is the implicit nexus relationship that Greenbaum and Quirk are referring to here. There is, for the reader, a clear nexus relationship in such phrases, despite the fact that the verb element is missing or has a non-finite form.

When considering clauses as the main components of a sentence, it is clear that the existence of a finite verb form in the clause is a requirement for the clause to be called the main or superordinate clause in the sentence.[5] Furthermore, a main clause can have one or more subordinate or dependent clauses. The sentence is then said to be complex. All three types of clause mentioned above can be subordinate clauses. The clauses that lack a finite verb are in some grammatical models called *reduced clauses*. The translation problem may be formulated as follows:

- Swedish and English grammar share the concept that in Swedish is called *huvudsats* and in English main clause.
- What in Swedish is called a *bisats* has the same functional, but not the same formal, definition as the English subordinate clause.
- The Swedish definition of a *satsvärdig fras* (phrase equivalent to a sats) varies according to the grammatical model. There is less need to distinguish something that would be comparable to a *satsvärdig fras* in English grammar.

Another concept that lacks an equivalent in English is the so-called *fundament*, which we translate here as 'base'. The concept was introduced in 1962 by Paul Diderichsen,[6] and since then it has been frequently used in Scandinavian, especially Swedish, grammatical analysis. The term denotes everything that precedes the finite verb form in the main clause of a sentence—something without a direct equivalent in English grammatical terminology.[7] As we see it, that which constitutes the base can coincide with the string of words that in English grammar books is called the 'topic' or 'theme' in a sentence. However, grammarians discuss these concepts within the framework of theme–rheme (topic–comment, topic–focus), 'the end-weight principle', 'the information principle', and so on.[8]

The problems of translation may be illustrated by the variation in methods applied in English grammar books for Swedish university students, written in a contrastive perspective. A classic Swedish-language university grammar of English is the one written by Jan Svartvik and Olof Sager.[9] Where a reader conversant with English grammar expects to find a term for the concept clause, he or she will find the Swedish word *sats*. As a consequence, *satser* are said to be finite, non-finite, or verbless in Svartvik and Sager.[10] A different strategy has been chosen by Maria Estling Vannestål, who has written her university grammar in English.[11] The two most important components in a clause are said to be 'the subject and the verb', which normally means the subject and the predicate. Clauses are thereafter divided into two categories: main

33

clauses and dependent clauses. A main clause is said to always have a finite verb form as a predicate, while dependent clauses may have a finite verb form, a non-finite verb form, or no verb at all.[12]

Based on the terminology used by Estling Vannestål, we have chosen to use the following terms in the English translation:

Makrosyntagm	Macrosyntagm
Mening	Sentence
Sats	Clause
Överordnad sats	Superordinate clause
Huvudsats	Main clause
Underordnad sats	Subordinate clause
Bisats	Dependent clause
Satsvärdig fras	Clause equivalent

In the present text, these English terms are used as definitional equivalents to the Swedish terms given here.

Abbreviations used in the text

CP0 main clause(s) or expanded interjectional or vocative macro-syntagm(s) on the 0 level

FF corpus of letters from female writers to female recipients

FM corpus of letters from female writers to male recipients

MF corpus of letters from male writers to female recipients

MM corpus of letters from male writers to male recipients

M composite corpus of the corpora FM, MF and MM

Variables of style

The quantitative method used in this project is that of linguistic stylistics. The underlying assumption is that human language acquires its individual stamp through conscious or subconscious choices of linguistic expressions in any given situation. Such choices are primarily made on two linguistic levels: the lexical level (words and expressions), and the syntactic level (sentence structure).

The variables under investigation are mainly those that have been in use for a considerable length of time in the linguistic analysis of style in Swedish texts, as described in modern handbooks.[13] They also correspond almost exactly to the variables used by Geoffrey Leech and Mick Short in *Style in Fiction*.[14] This work, first published in 1981, marked a turning-point in English stylistics. The authors argue forcefully for a combination of literary and linguistic methods in stylistic analyses of English-language fictional texts.[15] *Style in Fiction* demonstrates how a quantitative mapping of different stylistic variables can be used to support or correct an intuitive description of the style found in a text.[16]

Our investigation differs from *Style in Fiction* in that our aim is not to describe the individual styles of the various letter-writers. Instead, our aim is to investigate whether there were differences in the way women used stylistic variables that were dependent on the sex of the letter recipient. *Style in Fiction* was not the starting-point for our categorization of stylistic variables, but it should be noted that Leech and Short, despite the differences between their approach and ours, arrived at the same categorization. Just as we do, Leech and Short see the result of the quantitative analysis as a sort of stylistic 'thumbprint' of the writer in question.[17] They discuss the use of this thumbprint for characterizing an individual writer's style, while we have investigated whether the thumbprint changes depending on the sex of the letter recipient. This method has, to our knowledge, been less used in French, German, and Latin stylistics, but we have judged it to be, in all essentials, equally useful when analysing texts in these languages as when analysing texts in Swedish.

On the lexical level, the language user can choose between various expressions made up of one or more words. A language's repository of available synonyms provides ample opportunities for choice, and a text can be distinguished by a rich or limited vocabulary. The vocabulary can, in addition, exhibit various general traits. It can be distinguished by a preference for nouns, adjectives, or verbal expressions. In a text there may also be a preponderance of nouns, adjectives, and verbs *of differing semantic types*. Thus, among other things, the nouns can be either concrete or abstract, the adjectives emotive or neutral, the verbs dynamic or stative. Some writers distinguish themselves by their use of an abundance of *foreign words*, others by a predominantly vernacular vocabulary. When examining a sufficiently large number of texts by the same writer it is not uncommon to find that one of the writer's characteristics is a fondness for, or avoidance of, *polysyllabic words*.

Language contains a large number of *rhetorical figures*, also called *figures of speech*. These sometimes consist of only one word, but more often they contain several words and may appear on the lexical as well as the syntactic levels. A text with a wealth of rhetorical figures differs markedly from a text with a dearth of such figures. There are even more possibilities for variation on the syntactic level than on the lexical level. Phrases, clauses, and sentences can, where the individual components are concerned, be structured in a multiplicity of ways. The most conspicuous feature can, for example, be the *length of the sentence*—the number of words it contains. We would like to point out here that the concept of *the sentence* is inexact, and in the field of linguistics has been replaced by other concepts: in the current investigation we therefore use the concept of the *macrosyntagm* to denote a major unit of speech, of whatever length, that is syntactically independent of other units in the text and whose components have a syntactic relationship to one another (see p. 32). A macrosyntagm can be *regular* (containing a subject and a predicate) and it can be, in different ways, *irregular*. If the number of irregular macrosyntagms in a text is large, this contributes to its distinctive character. Macrosyntagms can be *syntactically simple* (made up of a main clause with no subordinate clauses or at most only one subordinate clause) or they can be *complex* (consisting of one or more superordinate clauses, to which are added a number of different kinds of subordinate clauses). Other features contributing to the syntactic complexity of a macrosyntagm are the presence of *clause equivalents* and *embedded macrosyntagms* (see pp. 47 and 50).[18] Regarding syndeton on the syntactic level, see p. 51.

An important concept that has long been used in Scandinavian linguistics is that of the *base*. By base is meant everything that is placed in the base position of the main clause—that is, everything preceding the predicate of the main clause. With respect to the content of an utterance, this verb can be said to be the most significant unit, in that the more the listener or reader must process before the predicate appears, the higher the demands on his or her attention and memory in order to understand the utterance. There is good reason to claim that the length of the base is one of the features that contribute most to giving a text its distinctive character.

This, then, is the basis for the selection of the linguistic variables that we have considered useful to register in each letter, and which have then been processed statistically. Here follows a table of these variables, with definitions.

Variable	Definition
(1) Variables on the lexical level	
(*a*) word classes (parts of speech)	
nouns: concrete | abstract	Abstract nouns are those that, taken out of context, can clearly be identified as abstract. Other nouns are considered to be concrete.
adjectives: emotive | neutral	Emotive adjectives are those that, taken out of context, can clearly be said to express an emotion, for example *terrible, vile, wonderful, lovely*. Other adjectives are considered to be neutral.
verbs: dynamic | stative	Dynamic verbs are those that express *an actual movement in space,* for example *walk, travel, hurry*. Other verbs have been classed as stative.
(*b*) word length	The length of a word in its written form, measured in the number of letters.
(*c*) rhetorical figures	See below, p. 38.
(2) Variables on the syntactic level	
(*a*) number of words in the macro-syntagm	See below, p. 41.
(*b*) irregular clauses	Elliptical clauses and anacolutha.
(*c*) number of main clauses and of sub-ordinate clauses and clause equivalents	See below, p. 44.
(*d*) number of clause equivalents	See below, p. 47.
(*e*) number of embedded macro-syntagms	The number of macrosyntagms embedded between the first and last words of another macrosyntagm.
(*f*) base	Anything preceding (in written text, positioned to the left of) the finite verb in a main clause (see p. 33).
(*g*) asyndeton | polysyndeton	Deviations from the conventional manner of coordinating elements within a macrosyntagm using fewer or more coordinating conjunctions than convention suggests.
(*h*) rhetorical figures	See below, p. 38.
(3) Variables on the textual level	
(*a*) addressing the reader	Directly addressing the reader by means of *exclamatives, vocatives, imperatives,* or *questions.*
(4) Code-switching	
(*a*) mother-tongue words, phrases, or textual passages	Relevant only for letters in French written by Swedish writers and for Hildegard of Bingen's letters.
(*b*) foreign-language phrases or textual passages	The presence of at least two foreign words immediately following one another. May extend over several macro-syntagms.

Rhetorical figures

The rhetorical figures that have been registered have been identified in the usual manner, in accordance with the praxis found in modern Swedish textbooks. As already noted, several of these figures can be found both on the lexical and the syntactic levels. The rhetorical figure of the *parable* can be found on the textual level. The occurrence of individual rhetorical figures varies greatly among the subprojects. Here follows a list of the rhetorical figures that have been registered at least once in the material under investigation:[19]

Alliteration	two or more words in sequence beginning with the same phoneme
Allusion	a reference to events, people, or places in literature
Anaphora	the repetition of the same initial word or phrase in several successive clauses
Animation	collective term for animistic and humanizing metaphors[20]
Antithesis	an opposition or contrast of ideas (see chiasmus)
Aposiopesis	an interruption of speech followed by a direct appeal to the listener
Assonance	internal rhyme, or the repetition of the same vowel in subsequent words
Binomial pairs	words or phrases grouped in pairs
Chiasmus	the order of words in the first of two parallel phrases inverted in the second phrase; often combined with antithesis
Climax	'arrangement of words, phrases, or clauses in an order of increasing importance'[21]
Epizeuxis	asyndetic coordination of at least three words or phrases in order to provide emphasis
Euphemism	'a less distasteful word or phrase used as a substitute for something harsher or more offensive'[22]
Figura etymologica	alliteration created by using words that have the same etymological derivation, in the same phrase or clause
Hendiadys	coordination of two semantically almost equivalent words
Hyperbole	exaggeration
Irony	'the intended meaning is the opposite of that expressed by the words used'[23]
Litotes	understatement

Metaphor	a comparison without using words such as 'like' or 'as' (see simile, metonym)[24]
Metonym	comparing a thing to something to which it is intimately connected (see metaphor). A common kind of metonymy is the synecdoche, where a part of something refers to the whole (*pars pro toto*) or the whole refers to a part of itself (*totum pro parte*)
Oxymoron	combination of two contradictory expressions (a contradiction in terms)
Parable	an allegorical or metaphorical narrative, often biblical
Paradox	(apparently) contradictory statement
Parallelism	'correspondence, in sense or construction, of successive clauses or passages'[25]
Pun	
Repetition	repetition of the same word or expression (see anaphora)
Rhetorical question	a statement framed as a question for greater rhetorical effect; a question not meant to be answered
Rhyme	
Simile	an overt comparison that includes the words 'like' or 'as' (see metaphor)
Synaesthesia	'terms relating to one kind of sense-impression are used to describe sense-impressions of other kinds'[26]
Trope	figurative use of words or expressions
Zeugma	'A figure of speech in which the same word (verb or preposition) is applied to two others in different senses'[27]

The total number of rhetorical figures, as well as the number of tropes, metaphors, and the variable 'other rhetorical figures', are all presented per hundred macrosyntagms.

Application on the lexical level
Word classes

Concordances have been compiled for each constituent corpus—FF, FM, MF, MM, and M (= FM + MF + MM)—in each subproject. These concordances have been designed so that the words are arranged according to the frequency with which they appear in the text, beginning with the most frequent words. The hundred most frequent nouns, adjectives, and verbs have been classified according to the distinctions presented above. All word forms have been included, not just lexemes. This means that all the forms of the lexeme GO, for example (*go*, *goes*, *went*, and *gone*) have been treated as separate verbs. Homographs occur to a varying degree in the five languages under investigation, and in order to determine the word classes of particular homographs that occur in the concordance, we have consulted the context. Because of the large number of homographs in English, no analysis of the word classes has been conducted in the English subproject.

In the Latin, Swedish, German, and French texts the following special problems have occurred:

- *Verbs.* Compound verbs, consisting of an auxiliary verb and a past or present participle, usually denote an action in the past. Examples: 'jag *har gått*', 'ich *bin gegangen*'. The participles *gått* and *gegangen* have not been classed as adjectives. Here they do not function syntactically as attributes, but as parts of a predicate. Thus, *har gått* and *bin gegangen* should be classed as verbs. This principle has been applied to the analysis of the Swedish and German texts, but because of the large number of compound verbs in Latin and French, no analysis of the most frequent verbs has been conducted for these two languages.
- *Adjectives.* In the French texts, all present and past participles have been excluded, even when they occur in an attributive position.
- *Nouns.* For adjectival nouns, instead of applying a traditional method of identifying word classes, we have elected to be guided by how the words function syntactically, and have classified them as nouns. In the French material all titles and terms of address have been excluded.

Regarding word classes, only the results for the corpora FF and M, in percentages, are presented.

Length of words

In Swedish stylistics, a word is considered to be long if, in its written form, it has more than six letters. The length of words in the Swedish correspondence analysed here can thus be compared to the length of words in modern Swedish prose, just as the length of words can be compared among the five constituent corpora of the two Swedish subprojects

(Subprojects 2 and 4). There are no established definitions of long words in English, German, and Latin, and thus no comparison can be made with other prose within each of these languages. However, the length of words within the different constituent corpora can be compared. German and Latin are, to a greater extent than the other languages under investigation, characterized by a synthetic, non-analytic mode of expression. Thus, they have an inherent tendency to long words, whether the writer has a penchant for long words or not. This, however, as can be seen from the word-length tables, has not diminished the value of the comparisons that have been made within these subprojects.

Word length analysis has not been done in the French subproject.

Application on the syntactic level
Length of macrosyntagms

As the starting-point for our quantitative analyses of syntactic phenomena we have used the *macrosyntagm* as the basic unit. This means that we have not based our analyses on the written sentence.[28] The macrosyntagm is the largest syntactically coherent unit of a text. It is generally made up of a *superordinate clause*, also known as a *main clause*, together with any coordinated clauses or clause equivalent constructions in a subordinate position—usually subordinate clauses or clause equivalents. One main clause or several main clauses connected by a coordinating conjunction, with or without subordinate clauses or phrases, together make up a *macrosyntagm* (which is considered to be a syntactic, not a graphic, unit).

Typology of the macrosyntagm

Most macrosyntagms in a normal text are sentences; however, there are macrosyntagms that do not form regular sentences. Phrases that function as vocatives sometimes hold a syntactically independent position, and when they do, they count as macrosyntagms, but they are not constructed as clauses. In the example 'Darling, come here!', 'Darling' is self-contained: it is syntactically independent from whatever word immediately precedes it and ends the previous macrosyntagm, and from the following word, which begins a new macrosyntagm. The same applies to interjections. Such phrases are called interjectional and vocative macrosyntagms.

The purpose of these macrosyntagms is to direct the reader's or listener's attention to what follows immediately afterwards, and they may be said to begin an utterance.[29] Despite this, they are considered to be macrosyntagms in their own right.

An initial vocative phrase is thus considered to be a macrosyntagm:[30]

⟨Dear Sir,⟩ ⟨It makes me extremely happy to find it in my power…⟩[31]

⟨Ma trés chêre et très aimable sœur,⟩ ⟨voici une lettre de Calling…⟩[32]

⟨Werthester Herr!⟩ ⟨Was werden Sie sagen, daß ich einmal einen ordentlichen Geschäftsbrief an Sie schreibe?⟩[33]

⟨Certissime et mitissime pater,⟩ ⟨audi me in tua bonitate…⟩[34]

⟨Min bästa vän!⟩ ⟨Vet du att jag darrar ännu för den olyckan som kunnat hänt oss…⟩[35]

An initial interjection is also considered to be a macrosyntagm:

⟨for Heaven's sake⟩ ⟨let ye poor Manager have some respite from his many labours⟩[36]

⟨Hélas,⟩ ⟨quand et comment la tirerons-nous de cette compagnie sotte et bête?⟩[37]

⟨Ach,⟩ ⟨was war das eine süße Zeit!⟩[38]

⟨Ack!⟩ ⟨Vad jag länge dröjt med att avlägga min tacksamhet för så många gracieusa och sköna brev!⟩[39]

An initial interjectional phrase and an accompanying initial vocative phrase are considered to be two macrosyntagms.

⟨Damn it,⟩ ⟨*John!*⟩

⟨Adieu,⟩ ⟨mon plus que chèr cœur⟩[40]

⟨Nein,⟩ ⟨Du Gute Seele…⟩[41]

⟨Heu me⟩ ⟨mater⟩[42]

⟨Åh,⟩ ⟨ditt tok!⟩[43]

Greetings such as *hello* and *good-bye* are considered to be elliptical clauses (in other words, clause equivalents), which is why a greeting of this kind, followed by a vocative phrase, is considered to be one macrosyntagm.

⟨Good morning, my dear child!⟩
⟨Adieu meine Liebe⟩[44]
⟨Adieu min lilla impertinenta gubbe!⟩[45]

In the Latin texts, phrases such as *O, filia Dei* ('O daughter of God') have been treated as a single macrosyntagm (a vocative macrosyntagm). In our analysis we consider *O* to be an intensifier of the vocative case in the word *filia*.[46] This is in opposition to phrases of the kind *O quam mirabilis* ('Oh, how wondrous '), where *O* is considered to be an interjectional macrosyntagm on its own.

A string of words of the type *Alas, alas, alas* has been treated as *one* interjectional macrosyntagm.

The length of the macrosyntagms in a text has been indicated both in terms of the number of words per hundred macrosyntagms, and in terms of the most commonly occurring length of macrosyntagms measured in number of words.

Irregular clauses

A clause normally contains both a subject and a predicate. By *irregular* clauses we mean *elliptical clauses* and *anacolutha*. The majority of clauses are *complete*; in other words they include all the requisite syntactic units and/or structures. A clause can also be *incomplete*: the regular syntactic clause structure has been interrupted or has not been completed in the normal fashion.

⟨Still complaining, my dear Madam, of my Injustice?⟩ ⟨Still seeking redress by producing a Catalogue of Grievances?⟩[47] [Subject and predicate have been omitted.]

⟨Und warum?⟩[48] [Subject and predicate have been omitted.]

⟨Quomodo?⟩ ⟨Faciendi⟩ ⟨creandi⟩ ⟨perficiendi⟩[49] [Subject and predicate have been omitted.]

⟨Skada att det senare kanske blir skämt innan det hinner fram.⟩[50] [Subject and predicate have been omitted.]

In many typical examples such as these, the incomplete clause will be considered normal and in accordance with convention. In other cases the reader will feel that a necessary part of the clause is missing, and the text then becomes difficult to comprehend. In order to differentiate the

43

former cases from the latter, we have only registered incomplete clauses that have more than nine words. This distinction is intuitively based. An *anacoluthon* is a clause that is grammatically absurd. For example:

⟨Our party to Ashe to-morrow night will consist of Edward Cooper, James (for a Ball is nothing without *him*), Buller, who is now staying with us, and I— I look forward with great impatience to it, as I rather expect to receive an offer from my friend in the course of the evening.⟩[51]

⟨Reichtum besticht die Anbeter der Natur daß sie ihre Freuden die allenthalben blühen wo sie wirkt und wo man Gutes tun kann für den nachgemachten Glanz ihres kleinsten Werkes verlassen.⟩[52]

⟨Den vänskap Hans Excellens ger mig så autentiqua bevis på gör mig (till det få människor kan säga sig) fullkomligt lycklig, ja så säll att quand même jag hade reella olyckor, som ofelbart annars skulle snart med min ringa dosis philosophie nedslå mig, men ägarinna av ett gott samvete, i anseende till mina närvarande plikters uppfyllande och Hans Excellens dyrbara vänskap, vågar jag nästan försäkra mig i stånd att bravera starka stormar, om försynen skulle vilja försöka min undergivenhet för hans heliga vilja och skickelse.⟩[53]

The number of irregular clauses has been indicated per hundred macrosyntagms.

Syntactic complexity

The aim of the hypotaxis analysis is to demonstrate a certain type of syntactic complexity, or what is normally referred to as *syntactic depth*. The analysis involves demonstrating the relationship between superordinate and subordinate clauses. An additional, less sophisticated measure of syntactic depth is the number of words per macrosyntagm. It follows logically that the more numerous the clauses and phrases that are subordinated to the main clause(s), the more words there are in a macrosyntagm. Indicating the number of words per macrosyntagm can thus be seen as a complement to indicating the number of subordinate clauses and phrases.

The elements that have been classified with respect to hypotaxis are those that contain a nexus relationship that is clear or implied (see p. 32); or, expressed in terms of clauses, main clauses, subordinate clauses, and subordinate clause equivalents. The superordinate clause of the macrosyntagm, or a clause that functions as an equivalent to the superordinate clause, has been given the level number 0. Moreover, the distribution of subordinate clauses at different levels of subordination is presented. Subordinate clauses and clause equivalents have been given the level numbers 1, 2, 3, and so on.

A macrosyntagm may contain one or more coordinated main clauses. Coordination by a coordinating conjunction enables them to be syntactically linked, and thus they do not make up two separate macrosyntagms. At the same time, the main clauses are independent in nature, and therefore none of them have been classed as subordinate. However, a macrosyntagm can be subordinate to another macrosyntagm if it has been embedded in, or follows immediately after, the macrosyntagm to which it is linked. The latter case usually refers to direct quotes that function as the object to a reporting verb. The former case may also refer to embedded complete macrosyntagms:

⟨Mrs Allen begs her love to you, and that you will be so kind as to acquaint Mr Allen with the good News of my mother's being, ⟨we hope⟩ much better.⟩[54]

⟨Ne le laissez jamais plus échapper, ⟨je vous le conseille,⟩ puisque vous l'avez heureusement près de vous.⟩

⟨Fühlt nur eine jede Euren Werth ⟨Ihr habt Ursache dazu⟩ und denkt dann, was Klopstock ist.⟩[55]

⟨Et hoc faciat in uerbo illo quod dominator terre dixit: ⟨Quod Deus coniunxit, homo non separet⟩ in irrisione diaboli.⟩[56]

⟨Han darrade och tog vinglaset och sade: ⟨Gud välsigne dem!⟩⟩[57]

Normally, a string of words that occupies the 0 level constitutes a main clause. In addition, because of its special characteristics, the letter genre contains numerous vocative phrases, and sometimes also interjections, that make up their own macrosyntagms and are found on level 0. It is reasonable to assume that these are numerous enough to distort the results of the hypotaxis analysis by significantly increasing the number of elements on level 0. In order to avoid this potential source of error we have divided the interjections and vocative phrases on the 0 level into two subcategories. The first subcategory consists of interjectional and vocative macrosyntagms that have been expanded by adding subordinate relative clauses:

⟨My dearest sister, who is so kind to me!⟩

⟨Mon tout ce, que j'ai de plus cher au monde.⟩[58]

⟨Tu que magistra es in fulgore salientis fontis, quod est in uice Christi ...⟩[59]

⟨Adieu, adieu nu,⟩ ⟨din lilla stygga, som har så roligt!⟩[60]

In this case, the vocative macrosyntagm is part of a hypotactic structure and may be seen as equivalent to a main clause. In the presentation, this type of interjectional and vocative macrosyntagm has therefore been put on an equal footing with main clauses on the 0 level (in the tables, this group in its entirety is called 'clauses and phrases on the 0 level', or CP0). In the second category we have interjectional and vocative macrosyntagms to which a subordinate phrase has not been added. These interjectional and vocative macrosyntagms have been included in the total number of clauses and phrases (called 'elements' in the tables) on the 0 level.

The syntactic analysis of each subproject thus includes a presentation of:

- the number of macrosyntagms
- the number of elements on the 0 level
- the number of main clauses and expanded interjectional and vocative phrases on the 0 level
- the number of unexpanded interjectional and vocative phrases on the 0 level

The definition of subordinate clauses in Latin, Swedish, French, and German is relatively uncomplicated in this context. There are, however, phrases that traditionally have been considered as incomplete subordinate clauses, or subordinate clauses where one element has been omitted. The missing part may be the subordinator, the predicate, or something else. Here are a few examples:

(*a*) ... while I walk and Jane rides a bike [the subordinator has been omitted]

(*b*) ... while I walk fast and Jane slowly [the predicate has been omitted]

(*c*) ... while I walk faster than Jane [the predicate has been omitted]

We have not treated these phrases as incomplete subordinate clauses whose level of subordination requires separate indication. Instead, we regard the first two cases as coordination phrases (*Jane rides a bike* and *Jane slowly*) that are coordinated with whatever precedes them by a coordinator (*and*). Both (*a*) and (*b*) are thus considered to be examples of a single subordinate clause.[61]

The third example, (*c*), is a little more complicated. According to traditional Swedish and German grammatical analysis, the predicate, *walks*, is implicit following *than Jane*. We, on the other hand, have chosen to treat the phrase *than Jane* as the equivalent of a prepositional phrase. According to this view, *than* here functions as a preposition, which is in accordance with French written and English oral usage. Example (*c*) is thus also considered to be one single subordinate clause.[62]

Regarding *embedded* vocative and interjectional macrosyntagms, that are considered to be subordinate, see p. 50.

Clause equivalents

In the hypotaxis analysis, certain phrases are regarded as clause equivalents and therefore equivalent to subordinate clauses. They constitute their own level of subordination. In every subproject, clause equivalents have been defined by the individual scholar on the basis of the traditional grammatical analysis of the language in question. An analysis of the syntactic depth in the English letters has not been performed.[63]

In the Latin letters, the following structures are considered to be clause equivalents:

- the accusative and infinitive
    ... qui aurea zona precinctus demonstrat *se esse Deum et hominem*[64]
- the nominative and infinitive (no example of the nominative and infinitive has been found in the material under investigation)
- the participium coniunctum
    ... et uenatores *uenientes* ciuitatem illam inspiciebant *uolentes* dispergere recta instituta eius[65]
- the ablative absolute
    Ab infantia autem mea *ossibus et neruis et uenis meis nondum confortatis* uisionis huius munere in anima mea usque ad presens tempus semper fruor.[66]

The gerund has been excluded because of its typically nominal character; it can, for example, be governed by a preposition. The gerundive has also been excluded because of its nominal character, which is made clear by the fact that the gerundive can only occur as a modifier of a noun.

Regarding the definition of clause equivalents in Swedish, we have followed Erik Andersson, *Grammatik från grunden*:[67]

- 'objekt med infinitiv' (object and infinitive construction)
  Stierneld bad *mig cedera* åt Charlotte en 3 eller 4 av mina rum för henne och hennes pojke.[68]
- 'subjekt med infinitiv' (subject and infinitive construction)
  Han sågs *komma*.
- 'predikativ satsmotsvarighet' (predicative clause equivalent)
  Men jag beklagar mig själv, baron Bork och flera, dom uti henne mist en redlig vän, som hon alltid var, *oaktat sin vivacité uti små lappri saker*.[69]
- 'fristående satsmotsvarighet' (independent clause equivalent)
  Väl hemkommen tog han av sig skorna.

The following structures are considered to be clause equivalents in the French letters:[70]

- 'propositions participe absolu' (absolute participle clauses): Dieu *aidant*, nous vaincrons, etc.[71]
- 'propositions infinitive complément d'objet' (object complement realized by an infinitive clause): Je lui commande, je le prie *d'obéir*, etc.[72]
- 'propositions relatives' (relative clauses): Il indique l'endroit *où pratiquer la plaie*, etc.[73]
- 'propositions non introduites par une conjonction' (clauses not introduced by a conjunction):

  J'irai le voir *avant de partir*. (temporelles)[74]
  A force de bavarder, Gorju se fit un nom. *Honteux de son échec*, il n'osait se montrer; etc. (causales)[75]
  Il fut assez hardi *pour y aller*; etc. (consecutives)[76]
  J'accomplissais ma besogne avec ponctualité, *sinon avec enthousiasme*; etc. (concessives)[77]

Au lieu d'étudier, il ne fait que se divertir. (d'opposition)[78]
A les entendre, ils ne sont pas coupables. (conditionnelles)[79]
A raconter ses maux souvent on les soulage. (comparatives et autres propositions circonstancielles)[80]

In the German texts only two kinds of structures have been regarded as clause equivalents:

- 'der absolute Akkusativ' (the accusative absolute)
  Frau F. kam zurück, *einen Brief in der Hand*.[81]
- 'Objekt im ackusativ mit prädikativen Attribut' (an object in the accusative with a predicative attribute)
  Sie traf *ihren Mann krank*.[82]

Thus, the hypotaxis analyses in each subproject (the English subproject excepted) have also presented:

- the number of subordinate clauses and clause equivalents
- the number of subordinate clauses
- the number of clause equivalents
- the number of subordinate clauses and clause equivalents on subordination level 1
- the number of subordinate clauses and clause equivalents on subordination level 2, etc.

Every stylistic variable on the syntactic level has been presented both per hundred macrosyntagms and per CP0 (main clauses or expanded interjectional or vocative phrases on the 0 level).

A selection of variables can be found in the appendix, namely:

- the most commonly occurring length measured in number of words,
- the number of subordinate clauses and clause equivalents per main clause or expanded interjectional and/or vocative macrosyntagm on the 0 level (CP0),
- the number of subordinate clauses and clause equivalents on the first, second, etc. levels per hundred macrosyntagms and per CP0.

Embedded macrosyntagms

Embedded macrosyntagms are macrosyntagms that are placed somewhere between the first and last word of another macrosyntagm. An embedded macrosyntagm is always regarded as being subordinate to the macrosyntagm in which it is embedded (see p. 42).

⟨Mrs Allen begs her love to you, and that you will be so kind as to acquaint Mr Allen with the good News of my mother's being, ⟨*we hope*⟩ much better.⟩[83]

⟨I'm sure I like her method much better, which has ⟨*I think*⟩ exactly hit that difficult path between the gay and the severe, and is neither too loose nor affectedly Prude.⟩

⟨Ne le laissez jamais plus échapper, ⟨*je vous le conseille,*⟩ puisque vous l'avez heureusement près de vous.⟩

⟨Comme tout ce qui vous touche, ⟨*mon aimable Ulla,*⟩ m'intéresse comme à moi-même…⟩

⟨Er hat sie mir gelassen, ⟨*sein Name sei gelobt,*⟩ u er hat sie mir so gelassen, dass sie sich noch immer vermehrt.⟩[84]

⟨Fühlt nur eine jede Euren Werth ⟨*Ihr habt Ursache dazu*⟩ und denkt dann, was Klopstock ist.⟩[85]

⟨Et hoc faciat in uerbo illo quod dominator terre dixit: ⟨*Quod Deus coniunxit, homo non separet*⟩ in irrisione diaboli.⟩[86]

⟨Gud välsigna och bevara i många många år vår ömt älskade, vördade och ⟨*jag kan säga*⟩ tillbedna Carl Sparre!⟩[87]

The length of the base

An analysis of the length of the base has not been conducted for the Latin texts. This is because word order in Latin, though relatively free, is limited in the sense that the predicate in the main clause of the sentence in many cases has to follow the subject and any objects and adverbials if the sentence is to be unambiguous. There are, in other words, inherent rules that make long bases necessary, and for this reason the length of the base is considered uninteresting.

In the French texts certain words have not been counted as being part of the base, to wit subject and object forms of personal pronouns and the first part of a negation (*ne*). This is because these words must precede the finite verb according to the rules of French syntax.

The number of bases that are longer than eight words are indicated per hundred macrosyntagms.

Syndeton on the syntactic level

We define *polysyndeton* and *asyndeton* as deviations from the conventional rule of coordination, which states that a coordinator should be inserted only between the two final elements in an enumeration of words or phrases. By coordination in this context we mean *only* coordination using the coordinator 'and'. The presence of a coordinator between every element is known as polysyndeton; the complete absence of a coordinator between the elements is known as asyndeton. There is yet another prerequisite for polysyndeton: the number of enumerated elements must exceed two.

The elements of interest in this context are superordinate clauses and subordinate clauses. According to our method of analysis, coordination is not possible on the level of macrosyntagms, in that the coordination of macrosyntagms is not possible. From this it follows automatically that asyndeton and polysyndeton are not applicable concepts on this level.

The linking of the elements in the graphic sentence 'I came, I saw, I conquered' is not a case of asyndeton. Instead, the sentence consists of three separate, independent macrosyntagms.[88] Enumerations of the type 'I came, saw, and conquered', which include a coordinator only between the two final elements, constitute the norm in modern written language and are not considered to be examples of either asyndeton or polysyndeton. Polysyndeton means that there is a coordinator between *every* element, not merely between the two final ones. 'I came and I saw and I conquered' is a case of polysyndetic coordination of three main clauses. This is true in Swedish, French, German, and English. It is also true of medieval Latin, in which the syndetic coordination rules of classical Latin had been abandoned.

In the material under investigation there are also cases of polysyndetic and asyndetic coordination of subordinate clauses. All cases of asyndeton and polysyndeton on the syntactic level are presented per hundred macrosyntagms.

Addressing the reader

We have limited the registration of various ways of addressing the reader to include only instances of address in the form of *exclamatives* of three main types, *vocatives, imperatives,* and *questions.*

- interjections[89]
  Fie! Huzza!
  Hélas!
  Kors! Nå, nå![90]
- exclamations in the form of a statement[91]
  Shame on you!
  Vad här är ont om karlar![92]
- more or less formulaic utterances such as the optative subjunctive[93]
  God forbid!
  Dank, Dank sei unserm Gott![94]
- vocatives—the recipient's name or other vocative phrases—used in order to attract her or his attention
  Most honourable lady
  Ma très chère et très aimable sœur[95]
  Meine, meine Schmidten…[96]
  Min allra nådigaste pappa![97]
- imperatives in Latin, Swedish, German, French, and English, and hortative subjunctives in Latin
  Let the poor Manager have some respite from his many labours[98]
  Sois assuré[99]
  Stille also, Carl Spener![100]
  Glöm ej din trogna pumpa![101]
- questions
  ⟨What?⟩ ⟨Still complaining, my dear Madam, of my Injustice?⟩[102]
  Habt ihr euch auch alle recht darüber gefreut?[103]
  Vet du väl att Pumpan är ett nöt?[104]

These four ways of addressing the reader are presented per hundred macro-syntagms.

Code-switching

The presence of foreign words in a text is a stylistic variable commonly studied in the field of Swedish stylistics. By foreign words we mean words of different origin than the language of the main text. It has proven impossible to find clear and firm criteria for the identification of foreign words in our texts. The most important reason is the lack of orthographic norms in the period in question. For example, words originating in the French language can be spelled in several different ways in Swedish texts from the seventeenth to the nineteenth centuries, even in one and the same text. Another reason is the difficulty of determining where the words in question were *perceived* as foreign by the correspondents. Accordingly, we have limited ourselves to registering the following:

- words and phrases in the mother tongue of the writer if the letter as a whole is written in a foreign language
  Postea posuit Deus sapientiam in aurora. *Ach, ach, ach!*

- the occurrence of at least two words in sequence whose foreign character is clear from the syntactic relation between them
  You are impatient, my dearest *cousine*, to know *de quoi il s'agit.*[105]
  Kann sie sie ihm nicht ohne Lärm und *sans façon* geben?[106]
  Min gud! Vad du min vän tager *au tragique* lilla C[harles] L[ouis] idé om att gå in i cadettecorpsen![107]
  Om jag ändå hade en karl med mig, *c'est a dire* en karl *dens toute l'entendue du terme!*[108]

According to this method of analysis, the sentence 'Var försäkrad om min *tendresse!*' ('Be assured of my *tendresse!*') does not contain any foreign words. However, the sentence 'Var försäkrad om *ma tendresse!*' ('Be assured of *ma tendresse!*') does.

Both features have been registered under the generic term of *code-switching*, with its occurrence presented per hundred macro-syntagms.

Topics

A number of topics have been registered. The list of possible topics was determined by a close scrutiny of the letters constituting the individual corpora and is hence in itself a reflection of the culture of letters of the 18th Century.

Each letter has been read through, and an indication has been made as soon as one of the nineteen topics has been touched upon by the letter-writer. A topic has only been counted once in each letter, even if it is touched upon several times.

The analysis of the topics of the letters has not been conducted in Subproject 1, due to the fact that all letters in the Latin corpus delve on official and/or religious matters.

In Subprojects 2 & 4, 5 and 6, three main topics per letter were registered. In Subproject 3, a (theoretical) maximum of nineteen topics were registered.

Below is a list of topics that have been registered at least once in the material under investigation.

1 House and home
2 Fabrics and clothes
3 Children and their upbringing
4 Family and relatives
5 Obstetrics
6 The body
7 Sensory impressions
8 The emotional life of the self and others
9 Economy
10 Social life
11 Travelling
12 Nature
13 Politics and war
14 Education, wit, learning
15 Opinions about people
16 The relationship between letter-writer and recipient
17 Metacomments
18 Fictionalization
19 Accidents, sensational events

Summary of the registration of variables and the statistical processing of data

Variable	Action taken
1. Variables on the lexical level	
(*a*) word classes	Counted manually in lists created by a concordance programme
nouns (concrete | abstract)	
adjectives (emotive | neutral)	
verbs (dynamic | stative)	
(*b*) word length	Counted automatically by a concordance programme
c) rhetorical figures (figures of speech)	Tagged
2. Variables on the syntactic level	
(*a*) the number of words in the macrosyntagm	The macrosyntagms have been tagged, and the number of words in each macrosyntagm have been counted automatically
(*b*) irregular clauses	Tagged
(*c*) the number of main clauses and the number of subordinate clauses and clause equivalents	Counted manually during the hypotaxis analysis
(*d*) the number of clause equivalents	Counted manually during the hypotaxis analysis
(*e*) the number of embedded macrosyntagms	Tagged
(*f*) bases	Tagged
(*g*) syndeton (asyndeton | polysyndeton)	Tagged
(*h*) rhetorical figures	Tagged
3. Variable on the textual level	
instances of addressing the reader	Counted manually
4. Code-switching	
(*a*) mother-tongue words, phrases, or text passages	Tagged
(*b*) foreign-language phrases and text passages	Tagged
4. Topics	
occurences of letter topics	Counted manually

Notes

1 Singular *sats*, plural *satser*.

2 See Ulf Teleman, Staffan Hellberg, Erik Andersson, and Lisa Christensen, *Svenska Akademiens grammatik* (Stockholm: Nordstedts, 1999), i. 201, s.v. 'nexusrelation'.

3 Here we have used the account given by Sidney Greenbaum and Randolph Quirk, *A Student's Grammar of the English Language* (Harlow 1990) in order to illustrate the differences between Swedish and English grammar.

4 Greenbaum and Quirk 1990, 285.

5 Ibid. 205.

6 Paul Diderichsen, *Elementær dansk Grammatik* (3rd edn., [Copenhagen]: Gyldendal, 1966), 185.

7 The term 'base' was used by Ulf Teleman ('What Swedish Is Like: A Mini-Grammar for Those Who Need It', *NordLund: Småskrifter från institutionen för nordiska språk i Lund*, 1:1983. The word is used in the section on basic constituent order (ibid. 3), albeit without any definition or discussion of alternative translations of the Swedish term *fundament*. Diderichsen used the English term 'front position' in a similar way to denote the 'fundament' in his brief work, *Essentials of Danish Grammar* (Copenhagen: Akademisk Forlag, 1964).

8 See, for example, Greenbaum and Quirk 1990, 397; and Maria Estling Vannestål, *A University Grammar of English: With a Swedish Perspective* (Stockholm: Studentlitteratur, 2007), 404. Note that Geoffrey Leech and Mick Short, *Style in Fiction: A Linguistic Introduction to English Fictional Prose* (2nd edn., Harlow: Longman, 2007), 62 & 182–4 discuss the phenomenon of a 'delaying of the main information point by anticipatory or parenthetic structure', and use the expression 'major anticipatory constituent' for everything that precedes the main clause.

9 Jan Svartvik and Olof Sager, *Engelsk universitetsgrammatik* (2nd edn., Stockholm: Almqvist & Wiksell, 1996).

10 Ibid. 322–3. No definition of this concept is provided.

11 Estling Vannestål 2007.

12 Ibid. 74–5.

13 For example, Peter Cassirer, *Stilistik och stilanalys* (2nd edn., Stockholm: Natur & Kultur, 1993); Ulf Teleman and Anne-Marie Wieselgren, *ABC i stilistik* (Lund: Liber Läromedel, 1990); and Birger Liljestrand, *Språk i text: handbok i stilistik* (Lund: Studentlitteratur, 1993).

14 Geoffrey Leech and Mick Short, *Style in Fiction: A Linguistic Introduction to English Fictional Prose* (2nd edn., Harlow: Longman, 2007).

15 The first edition of Leech and Short 2007 was preceded by Geoffrey Leech, *A Linguistic Guide to English Poetry* (London: Longman, 1969).

16 On the importance of *Style in Fiction* and Mick Short's contributions to stylistics, see McIntyre and Busse 2010, 3–5. For a survey of development within the field since the first edition of *Style in Fiction*, see Leech and Short 2007, 282–304; see also Carter, Ronald, 'Methodologies for Stylistic Analysis: Practices and Pedagogies', in McIntyre and Busse 2010, 55–68.

17 Leech and Short 2007, 10.

18 The use of the macrosyntagm as a syntactic unit of analysis and its typologization was codified by Bengt Loman and Nils Jörgensen, *Manual för analys och beskrivning av makrosyntagmer* (Lundastudier i nordisk språkvetenskap, series C,

Studier i tillämpad nordisk språkvetenskap, 1; Lund: Studentlitteratur, 1971). The concept of the macrosyntagm has been successfully used when analysing medieval Latin, Old Swedish, and modern texts in Swedish and in other languages (see Lars Wollin, *Svensk latinöversättning*, ii: *Förlagan och produkten* (Uppsala: Svenska fornskriftsällskapet, 1983), 11–12).

19 For a different categorization of rhetorical figures, see Leech 1969.

20 Leech gives the following definitions: 'The animistic metaphor ... attributes animate characteristics to the inanimate. ... The humanizing metaphor ... attributes characteristics of humanity to what is not human' (ibid. 158).

21 Edward P. J. Corbett and Robert J. Connors, *Classical Rhetoric for the Modern Student* (4th edn., New York: Oxford University Press, 1999), 393.

22 OED, s.v. 'euphemism', n. 2.

23 OED, s.v. 'irony', n. 1*a*.

24 See Leech, 156. For a formal linguistic definition, see Andrew Goatly, The Language of Metaphors (London: Routledge, 1997), 8; for the metaphor as a cognitive concept, see George Lakoff and Mark Turner, *More than Cool Reason: A Field Guide to Poetic Metaphor* (Chicago: University of Chicago Press, 1989).

25 OED, s.v. 'parallelism', n. *3*.

26 OED, s.v. 'synaesthesia', n. 2.

27 J. A. Cuddon (ed.), *A Dictionary of Literary Terms and Literary Theory* (Harmondsworth: Penguin, 1976).

28 Leech and Short 2007, 175 point out that the syntactic sentence and the written sentence are not necessarily 'co-extensive'. In their analysis they take as their starting-point the syntactic sentence, although they do not use the term 'macrosyntagm'.

29 This kind of syntagm is called '*initialställd*' (initial) in Wollin 1983, ii. 14.

30 Chevrons are used to indicate the beginnings and ends of macrosyntagms.

31 Fanny Burney to Stephen Allen, 13 November [1773], in *The Early Journals and Letters of Fanny Burney*, ed. Lars E. Troide et al., 4 vols. (Oxford: Clarendon, 1987–2003), iv. 317.

32 Augusta Törnflycht to Brita Stina Sparre, 1 March 1740 (Riksarkivet (Swedish National Archives), Stockholm (RA), Börstorpssaml. E 3100).

33 Therese Huber to Carl Spener, 22 May 1788, in *Therese Huber: Briefe*, i: *1774–1803*, ed. Magdalene Hauser & Corina Bergmann-Törner (Tübingen: Niemeyer, 1999), letter 123. Please note that the spelling in the German examples has, in some instances, been normalized.

34 *Hildegardis Bingensis epistolarium*, ed. L. Van Acker, 3 vols. (Corpus christianorum, Continuatio medievalis; Turnhout: Brepols, 1999–2001), part 3, Anhang, letter IV R, 184.

35 Julie Ekerman to Carl Sparre 11 May 1784 (RA, Börstorpssaml. E 3052).

36 David Garrick to Frances Abington, 18 June [1774], in *The Letters of David Garrick*, ed. David M. Little and George M. Kahrl, 3 vols. (London: Oxford University Press, 1963), iii. 942.

37 Ulrika Lovisa Sparre to Carl Gustaf Tessin, 5 January 1731 (RA, Ericsbergsarkivet, C.G. Tessins saml. vol. 5–6).

38 Meta Klopstock to Friedrich Gottlieb Klopstock, 15 October 1752, in Meta Klopstock, *Es sind wunderliche Dinger, meine Briefe: Meta Klopstocks Briefwechsel mit Friedrich Gottlieb Klopstock und mit ihren Freunden 1751–1758*, ed. Franziska & Hermann Tiemann (Munich: Beck, 1980), letter 134.

39 Gustafva Eleonora Gjörwell to Carl Christoffer Gjörwell, 12 February 1792 (Kungliga Biblioteket (National Library of Sweden), Stockholm (KB), C.C. Gjörwell, Brevväxling, Familjebrev Supp. II, EpG 12:1–7).

40 Ulrika Lovisa Sparre to Carl Gustaf Tessin, 5 January 1731 (RA, Ericsbergsarkivet, C.G. Tessins saml. vol. 5–6).

41 Therese Huber to Regula Hottinger, 10 April 1794, in Huber, *Briefe*, letter 167.

42 *Hildegardis Bingensis epistolarium*, part 1, letter 64, 147.

43 Julie Ekerman to Carl Sparre, 2 November 1789 (RA, Börstorpssaml. E 3052).

44 Therese Huber to Luise Mejer, 19 September 1782, in Huber, *Briefe*, letter 16.

45 Hedvig Ulrika de la Gardie to Gustaf Mauritz Armfelt, 10 November 1792 (RA, Armfeltska saml. E 3135).

46 As opposed to Wollin, *Svensk latinöversättning*, i: *Processen* (Lund: Ekstrand, 1981), 18, example 1. He considers *O* to be an interjectional macrosyntagm and *filia Dei* a vocative macrosyntagm, i.e., two macrosyntagms in total.

47 David Garrick to Frances Abington, June 18 [1774] in *Letters of David Garrick*, iii. 942.

48 Meta Klopstock to Friedrich Gottlieb Klopstock, 13 April 1751, in Klopstock, *Es sind wunderliche Dinger, meine Briefe*, letter 8.

49 *Hildegardis Bingensis epistolarium*, part 1, letter 40 R, 104.

50 Julie Ekerman to Carl Sparre, 20 September 1789 (RA, Börstorpssaml. E 3052).

51 Jane Austen to Cassandra Austen, 14–15 January 1796, in *Jane Austen's Letters*, ed. R. W. Campbell (3rd rev. edn., rev. Deirdre Le Faye, Oxford: OUP, 1995), 3.

52 Therese Huber to Carl Spener, 31 October 1785, in Huber, *Briefe*, letter 96.

53 Julie Ekerman to Carl Sparre, 20 September 1789 (RA, Börstorpssaml. E 3052).

54 Fanny Burney to Stephen Allen, 13 November [1773], in *Early Journals and Letters of Fanny Burney*, iv. 317.

55 Meta Klopstock to Margaretha Moller-Dimpfel, 5 August 1755, in Klopstock, *Es sind wunderliche Dinger, meine Briefe*, letter 225.

56 *Hildegardis Bingensis epistolarium*, part 1, letter 52 R, 128.

57 Gustafva Eleonora Gjörwell to Carl Christoffer Gjörwell, 26 December 1791 (KB, C.C. Gjörwell, Brevväxling, Familjebrev Supp. II, EpG 12:1–7).

58 Ulrika Lovisa Sparre to Carl Gustaf Tessin, 5 January 1731 (RA, Ericsbergsarkivet, C.G. Tessins saml. vol. 5-6).

59 *Hildegardis Bingensis epistolarium*, part 1, letter 49 R, 121.

60 Gustafva Eleonora Gjörwell till Johan Niklas Lindahl, 2 February 1797 (KB, C.C. Gjörwell, Brevväxling, Familjebrev Supp. II, EpG 12:1–7).

61 See Wollin, *Svensk latinöversättning*, i. 16.

62 See *Svenska Akademiens Grammatik*, iii. 672 ('Subjunktionsfraser' §6); see also Greenbaum and Quirk 1990, 331 on 'ellipsis in comparative clauses'.

63 See Estling Vannestål 2007, 75 on 'reduced clauses'; Svartvik and Sager 1996, 347 on 'ellipsis'; and Greenbaum and Quirk 1990, 285 on 'finite, nonfinite and verbless clauses'.

64 *Hildegardis Bingensis epistolarium*, part 1, letter VI, 16.

65 Ibid., 14.

66 *Hildegardis Bingensis epistolarium*, part 2, letter 103 R, 261.

67 Erik Andersson, *Grammatik från grunden: en koncentrerad svensk satslära* (Uppsala: Hallgren och Fallgren, 1993), ch. 36, 99–102. Andersson uses the term '*satsmotsvarigheter*' instead of '*satsvärdiga fraser*'. See *Svenska Akademiens grammatik*, i. 222, s.v. *satsekvivalent*.

68 Hedvig Ulrika de la Gardie to Gustaf Mauritz Armfelt, 19 February 1793 (RA, Armfeltska saml. E 3135).

69 Julie Ekerman till Carl Sparre 25 January 1790 (RA, Börstorpssaml. E 3052).

70 The definition of clause equivalents in French follows that of Maurice Grevisse, *Le bon usage: grammaire française avec des remarques sur la langue française d'aujourd'hui* (9th edn., Gembloux: Duculot, 1969), sections 803, 1006, 1007, 1013, 1019, 1024, 1030, 1031, 1034, 1041, 1044, 1045.

71 Ibid. section 803.

72 Ibid. section 1007.

73 Ibid. section 1013.

74 Ibid. section 1019.

75 Ibid. section 1024.

76 Ibid. section 1030.

77 Ibid. section 1031.

78 Ibid. section 1034.

79 Ibid. section 1041.

80 Ibid. section 1045.

81 Folke Freund & Birger Sundqvist, *Tysk grammatik* (Stockholm: Natur & Kultur, 1995), section 1285. See also section 1287.

82 Sven-Gunnar Andersson, *Tysk syntax för universitetsnivå* (Lund: Studentlitteratur, 2002), 326. See also Freund & Sundqvist 1995, sections 1627–30, and Inger Rosengren, Ingemar Persson & Margareta Brandt, *Tysk syntax för högskolebruk plus* (Malmö: Liber, 1990), sections 280–86.

83 Fanny Burney to Stephen Allen, 13 November [1773], in *Early Journals and Letters of Fanny Burney*, iv. 317.

84 Meta Klopstock to Elisabeth Schmidt, 24 August 1754, in Klopstock, *Es sind wunderliche Dinger, meine Briefe*, letter 203.

85 Meta Klopstock to Margaretha Moller-Dimpfel, 5 August 1755, in Klopstock, *Es sind wunderliche Dinger, meine Briefe*, letter 225.

86 *Hildegardis Bingensis epistolarium*, Part 1, Letter 52 R, 128.

87 Julie Ekerman till Carl Sparre 28 January 1790 (RA, Börstorpssaml. E 3052).

88 Cf. Toolan, Michael, 'The Intrinsic Importance of Sentence Type and Clause Type to Narrative Effect: Or, How Alice Munro's 'Circle of Prayer' Gets Started', in McIntyre and Busse 2010, 324.

89 Regarding expanded interjectional phrases, see Andersson 2002, 51.

90 Gustafva Eleonora Gjörwell to Carl Christoffer Gjörwell the younger, 8 June 1797 (KB, C.C. Gjörwell, Brevväxling, Familjebrev Supp. II, EpG 12:1–7).

91 Andersson 2002, 130.

92 Hedvig Ulrika de la Gardie to Gustaf Mauritz Armfelt, 1 July 1788 (RA, Armfeltska saml. E 3135).

93 Andersson 2002, 129.

94 Meta Klopstock to Friedrich Gottlieb Klopstock, 24 November 1752, in Klopstock, *Es sind wunderliche Dinger, meine Briefe*, letter 145.

95 Augusta Törnflycht to Brita Stina Sparre, 1 March 1740 (RA, Börstorpssaml. E 3100).

96 Meta Klopstock to Elisabeth Schmidt, 30 December 1754, in Klopstock, *Es sind wunderliche Dinger, meine Briefe*, letter 213.

97 Julie Ekerman to Carl Sparre, 28 January 1790 (RA, Börstorpssaml. E 3052).

98 David Garrick to Frances Abington, June 18 [1774], in *Letters of David Garrick*, iii. 942.

99 Ulrika Lovisa Sparre to Carl Gustaf Tessin, 5 January 1731 (RA, Ericsbergsarkivet, C.G. Tessins saml. vol. 5-6).

100 Therese Huber to Carl Spener, 21 January 1787, in Huber, *Briefe*, letter 116.

101 Hedvig Ulrika de la Gardie to Gustaf Mauritz Armfelt, 25 October 1792 (RA, Armfeltska saml. E 3135).

102 David Garrick to Frances Abington, June 18 [1774], in *Letters of David Garrick*, iii. 942.

103 Meta Klopstock to Elisabeth Schmidt, 1 September 1754, in Klopstock, *Es sind wunderliche Dinger, meine Briefe*, letter 204.

104 Hedvig Ulrika de la Gardie to Gustaf Mauritz Armfelt, 20 March 1793 (RA, Armfeltska saml. E 3135).

105 Frances Boscawen to Julia Evelyn, 10 August 1737, in Cecil Aspinall-Oglander, *Admiral's Wife: Being the Life and Letters of the Hon. Mrs Edward Boscawen from 1719 to 1761* (London: Hogarth Press, 1942), 5–6.

106 Rahel Varnhagen to David Veit, 15 November 1794, in Rahel Varnhagen, *Rahel Varnhagen: Briefe und Aufzeichnungen*, ed. Dieter Bähtz (Leipzig: Gustav Kiepenheuer, 1985), 15.

107 Hedvig Ulrika de la Gardie to Gustaf Mauritz Armfelt, 4 March 1793 (RA, Armfeltska saml. E 3135)

108 Hedvig Ulrika de la Gardie to Gustaf Mauritz Armfelt, 24 March 1793 (RA, Armfeltska saml. E 3135).

Bibliography

Andersson, Erik, *Grammatik från grunden: en koncentrerad svensk satslära* (Uppsala: Hallgren och Fallgren, 1993).

Andersson, Sven-Gunnar, *Tysk syntax för universitetsnivå* (Lund: Studentlitteratur, 2002).

Carter, Ronald, 'Methodologies for Stylistic Analysis: Practices and Pedagogies', in McIntyre and Busse 2010, 55-68.

Cassirer, Peter, *Stilistik och stilanalys* (2nd edn., Stockholm: Natur & Kultur, 1993).

Cuddon, J. A., *A Dictionary of Literary Terms and Literary Theory* (Harmondsworth: Penguin, 1976).

Diderichsen, Paul, *Essentials of Danish Grammar* (Copenhagen: Akademisk Forlag, 1964).

— *Elementær dansk grammatik* (3rd edn., [Copenhagen]: Gyldendal, 1966).

Estling Vannestål, Maria, *A University Grammar of English: With a Swedish Perspective* (Stockholm: Studentlitteratur, 2007).

Freund, Folke, and Birger Sundqvist, *Tysk Grammatik* (3rd edn., Stockholm: Natur & Kultur, 1995).

Goatly, Andrew, *The Language of Metaphors* (London: Routledge, 1997).

Greenbaum, Sidney, and Randolph Quirk, *A Student's Grammar of the English Language* (Harlow: Longman, 1990).

Grevisse, Maurice, *Le bon usage: grammaire française avec des remarques sur la langue française d'aujourd'hui* (9th edn., Gembloux: Duculot, 1969).

Lakoff, George, and Mark Turner, *More Than Cool Reason: A Field Guide to Poetic Metaphor* (Chicago: University of Chicago Press, 1989).

Leech, Geoffrey N., *A Linguistic Guide to English Poetry* (London: Longman, 1969).
— and Mick Short, *Style in Fiction: A Linguistic Introduction to English Fictional Prose* (2nd edn., Harlow: Longman, 2007).
Liljestrand, Birger, *Språk i text: en handbok i stilistik* (Umeå: Institutionen för nordiska språk, 1987).
— *Språk i text: handbok i stilistik* (Lund: Studentlitteratur, 1993).
Loman, Bengt and Nils Jörgensen, *Manual för analys och beskrivning av makrosyntagmer* (Lundastudier i nordisk språkvetenskap, serie C, Studier i tillämpad nordisk språkvetenskap, 1; Lund: Studentlitteratur, 1971).
McIntyre, Dan and Beatrix Busse (eds.), *Language and Style: In Honour of Mick Short* (Palgrave: Macmillan, 2010).
McIntyre, Dan and Beatrix Busse, 'Language, Literature and Stylistics', in McIntyre and Busse 2010, 3-5.
Quirk, Randolph, Sidney Greenbaum, Geoffrey Leech, and Jan Svartvik, *A Comprehensive Grammar of the English Language* (Harlow: Longman, 1985).
Rosengren, Inger, Ingemar Persson, and Margareta Brandt, *Tysk syntax för högskolebruk plus* (2nd edn., Malmö: Liber, 1990).
Svartvik, Jan, and Olof Sager, *Engelsk universitetsgrammatik* (2nd edn., Stockholm: Almqvist & Wiksell, 1996).
Teleman, Ulf, *Manual för grammatisk beskrivning av talad och skriven svenska* (Lundastudier i nordisk språkvetenskap, serie C, 6; Lund: Studentlitteratur, 1974).
— 'What Swedish Is Like: A Mini-Grammar for Those Who Need It', *NordLund: Småskrifter från institutionen för nordiska språk i Lund* (1:1983).
— and Anne-Marie Wieselgren, *ABC i stilistik* (Lund: Liber Läromedel, 1990).
— Staffan Hellberg, Erik Andersson, and Lisa Christensen, *Svenska Akademiens grammatik*, 4 vols. (Stockholm: Svenska Akademien, 1999).
Toolan, Michael, 'The Intrinsic Importance of Sentence Type and Clause Type to Narrative Effect: Or, How Alice Munro's 'Circle of Prayer' Gets Started', in McIntyre and Busse 2010.
Wollin, Lars, *Svensk latinöversättning*, i: *Processen* (Lund: Ekstrand, 1981) .
— *Svensk latinöversättning*, ii: *Förlagan och produkten* (Uppsala: Svenska fornskriftsällskapet, 1983).

CHAPTER 3

Medieval letters in Latin

Hedda Gunneng

The material

The purpose and method of the project as a whole have determined the selection of the letter material. The following criteria were used when selecting the material for Subproject 1:

- the letters should be available in modern scholarly editions;
- all the letters in the subproject, from both male and female correspondents, should have been written in the same historical period;
- all the letters should have been written in Latin and preserved in the original language;
- all the letters should be *bona fide* letters—in other words, they should have been written with the aim of bridging 'the epistolary gap' between the writer and one or more persons who are not in the writer's presence;[1]
- the letters should be taken from large letter collections;
- each writer should have written to both men and women.

The only extant collection of letters by a female writer in the medieval period that fulfils all these criteria is the correspondence of Hildegard of Bingen.

Hildegard is revered as a saint, although she was never canonized. She was born in 1098 as the tenth and youngest child of a noble family residing in the present-day German federal state of Rhineland-Palatinate. She was to spend her entire life in this area, except for four preaching tours that she undertook during the last twenty years of her life, three along the Rhine and one in Swabia. When she was eight years old, her continued upbringing was entrusted to the nun Jutta of Spanheim, an anchoress in a cell belonging to the Benedictine monastery of

Disibodenberg. At some time between the ages of fourteen and seventeen she took her vows and entered the convent that had developed out of Jutta's anchorhold. The abbess of this convent was Hildegard's teacher Jutta, whom Hildegard succeeded as abbess at Jutta's death in 1136. Hildegard was then thirty-eight years old and had already received a number of revelations over a period of several years. In 1147 Pope Eugene III appointed a commission to review her visions, which were found to be authentic. Her extensive correspondence with people outside the convent began soon after her revelations had received papal approval, and continued until her death.

Following a divine command, Hildegard left Disibodenberg in 1150 together with eighteen or twenty nuns in order to found a new convent just to the north, on the crag of Rupertsberg close to Bingen on the Rhine. In this new convent Hildegard authored a unique body of texts, whose originality has always been beyond dispute. At her death, she left a large number of works about God, Creation, Man, and the proper way to live. Her perspectives were those of theology, natural history, psychology, and medicine. She also wrote liturgical music and poetry. She died in 1179.

In the twelfth century, people were aware of the value of preserving collections of letters. The correspondence of prolific letter-writers was systematically collected in letter collections and preserved by having them copied into large manuscript tomes.[2] There are 390 of Hildegard's letters still in existence, 70 of which are addressed to women. These letters are available in a modern edition.[3] Earlier scholars determined that the letters were, in all essentials, composed by Hildegard herself in Latin.[4] It is likely that she had access to secretaries and other scribes throughout the period when she was an active writer. Many of them are known by name. In various parts of her works, she herself described the extent and limitations of the tasks of the secretaries: if necessary, they were supposed to correct her morphology and her syntax, but they were not allowed to change the content or her choice of words.[5] From this it is possible to infer that she herself composed her visions in Latin and that she relied on her own vocabulary.

A large number of Hildegard's letters were written in response to letters of inquiry she had received from other people. Other letters urge reform of the Church and the nobility. Among Hildegard's correspondents were popes, bishops, abbots and abbesses, nuns and monks, royalty, and laymen and -women of the nobility and burghers. The letters she received were frequently preserved, and her correspondence was often included in the letter collections compiled during her lifetime and soon after her death. Rumour of her visionary abilities spread across Northern and Central Europe, and many people, both clergy and laity, wrote to her for comfort and advice about their religious doubts and acedia, among them the heads of religious houses who, faced with difficult tasks, were wrestling with their consciences.

It has proved difficult to find a similarly extensive collection of letters by men who corresponded with both women and men. Many collections of letters written in Latin have been preserved and published in modern editions, but female recipients are conspicuous by their absence. The male letter-writers in this subproject are Petrus Damiani (Peter Damian) (c. 1006–1072), saint, poet, and Cardinal Bishop of Ostia; John of Salisbury (c. 1120–1180), who was clerk to Theobald, Archbishop of Canterbury, and a supporter of Thomas Becket; Bernard of Clairvaux (1090–1153); Bernard's friend and correspondent Petrus Venerabilis (Peter the Venerable) (c. 1092–1156), abbot of Cluny; and Hildegard's last secretary, Guibert of Gembloux (c. 1124–1213). Of Petrus Damiani's letters, only those to male correspondents have been preserved. Of John of Salisbury's letters, only one to a female correspondent has been preserved. Among the letters of Petrus Venerabilis there are two letters to nuns, one of them Abelard's beloved Héloïse. Among the letters of Bernard of Clairvaux, however, there are a number addressed to women, of which I have analysed five, one of them addressed to Hildegard. Guibert of Gembloux, finally, left several letters addressed to Hildegard, and five of these have been included in this subproject.

In Subproject 1, all the female-authored letters have thus been written by a single person, Hildegard of Bingen. This means that a comparison between the FF and FM constituent corpora becomes a comparison between letters written by *one* woman to other women and to men. The letters in the MF and MM constituent corpora, however, have five different authors. The size and composition of the various corpora are given in Table 1.1.

Table 1.1 Size and composition of the various Subproject 1 corpora.

Constituent corpus	FF	FM	MF	MM	M
Number of letters	70	68	13	22	103
Number of words	15,739	16,448	5,999	10,434	32,881

The stylistics analysis has uncovered a number of statistically significant differences between FF and the other constituent corpora, and between FF and the M corpus. A survey of these is provided in Table 1.2. All results are based upon a comparison with the FF corpus. The inequality signs indicate a greater (>) or lesser (<) occurrence of the variable. The statistical significance is graded, with * signifying low statistical significance, ** medium significance, and *** high significance.

Survey of statistically significant differences in Subproject 1

Table 1.2 Survey of the statistically significant differences in Subproject 1

Variable	FF < / >	Degree of significance
Textual level		
Addressing the reader	FF > MF	***
Syntactic level		
Number of words per macrosyntagm	FF < FM	*
	FF < MF	**
	FF < MM	*
	FF < M	***
Irregular macrosyntagms	FF < FM	*
Embedded macrosyntagms	FF < MF	***
	FF < MM	***
Polysyndeton/asyndeton	FF < MF	**
	FF < MM	*
	FF < M	*
Lexical level		
Total number of tropes	FF < FM	***
	FF > MF	***
	FF > MM	***
	FF < M	***
Metaphor	FF < FM	***
	FF > MF	***
	FF > MM	***
	FF < M	***
Simile	FF > MF	**
	FF > MM	***

Personification	FF > MF	*
	FF > MM	**
Other rhetorical figures	FF < FM	***
	FF < MF	***
	FF < MM	***
	FF < M	***
Alliteration	FF > MM	**
Parallelism	FF < MF	***
Pun	FF < MF	*
Polysyndeton on the phrasal level	FF < FM	*
	FF > MF	***
	FF < M	*
Code-switching	FF > FM	**
	FF > M	***

Variables on the textual level

By addressing the recipient of the letter by means of questions, exclamatives, imperatives, and, above all, vocatives, the letter-writer gives the reader a sense of being addressed in person. These stylistic variables can be used by the writer to create a feeling of familiarity and intimacy. In a negatively charged context they can be used to create a strong sense of criticism and even hostility. It is therefore interesting to find that Hildegard's letters, which are often responses to appeals for good advice, contain as many instances of address when written to men as when written to women. By contrast, letters from men to women contain fewer instances of address, and the difference is of high statistical significance. Letters from men to other men contain somewhat fewer examples of address than do Hildegard's letters, though this is not statistically significant.

Another variable that can be tied to this observation is the most common length of macrosyntagms in the various constituent corpora—in other words, the length of the macrosyntagm, measured in number of words, which occurs most frequently in each constituent corpus. The most common length in the FF corpus is three words, in the M corpus eighteen words. This fact is reflected in the most common macrosyntagm lengths in the FM corpus (three and two words) on the one hand, and in the MM and MF corpora on the other: the most common length in the MF corpus is nineteen words, and the two most common lengths in the MM corpus are twelve and eighteen words, respectively. This difference between Hildegard's and the male writers' letters may well be explained by the fact that a significant number of these short macrosyntagms would seem to consist of interjections and vocatives, phrases that for natural reasons consist of only one, two, or three words. If this assumption is correct, it further strengthens the assertion that Hildegard's letters contain many instances of direct address.

Variables on the syntactic level

The syntactic rules of classical Latin make it possible to construct macrosyntagms with a high degree of syntactic complexity. The use of clause equivalents is a variable that further contributes to this complexity. Another variable is the option of allowing clauses to be embedded within superordinate clauses, which in their turn are embedded within other superordinate clauses. Because classical Latin is a synthetic language, many semantic categories are conveyed by means of inflectional endings. These semantic categories can thus be found on the morphological level, while in analytic languages, such as contemporary Swedish and English, they are represented on the syntactic level. This, too, is a factor that for the modern reader lessens the readability of texts written in classical Latin. Contributing to this complexity is also a certain degree of free word order within the sentence.

In many texts written in medieval Latin this classical syntax is in a state of disintegration. The syntax is beginning to approach that of modern analytic languages. Word order is not as free, prepositions replace inflectional endings in nouns, and subordinate clauses follow complete superordinate clauses. If the sentence structure of texts written in classical Latin can be likened to Chinese boxes, the typical sentence structure of texts written in medieval Latin can be said to be more linear, as in modern Swedish and English. However, the option of following the syntactic rules of classical Latin remained valid throughout the Middle Ages, and was used primarily by writers who were greatly affected by the Latin literature of antiquity. This freedom to choose between styles makes the syntactic complexity of the FF corpus especially interesting to study and compare to that of the FM, MF, and MM corpora.

Syntactic complexity is without doubt an important variable affecting the readability of a text. The *number of words in the macrosyntagm* has been mentioned as a possible measure of syntactic depth, and thus also of syntactic complexity. The greater the number of subordinate clauses and clause equivalents within each macrosyntagm, the more words it will contain. A possible objection to this line of reasoning is the fact that a clause—be it main or subordinate—can have several subordinate clauses on the same level. Such a construction does not increase the syntactic depth and does not necessarily make reading more difficult. Another possible objection is the fact that certain types of subordinate clauses—specifically, relative subordinate clauses and subordinate noun clauses—allow themselves to be added to one another without lessening readability. The macrosyntagm does grow in length, but the reader does not have to reconstruct a temporal, causal, or conditional course of events.[6] Nevertheless, macrosyntagmatic prolixity can diminish readability, provided the inflectional endings of nouns have not yet been replaced by prepositional phrases. Nouns in different *casus obliqui* provide the reader with several alternative interpretations until the correct combination of interpretations is found—the one that gives each word in the clause a correct syntactic function and the clause a logical content. The more words in the macrosyntagm, the more things for the reader to remember before the sentence arrives at its definitive interpretation.

All the letter-writers considered in this subproject only rarely let prepositional phrases replace inflected nouns. Moreover, unlike Hildegard, the male writers display a preference for classical syntax. However, the *hypotactic structure of the macrosyntagms* in the FM, MF, MM, and M corpora does not differ from that of the FF corpus to a significant extent, either in the number of subordination levels, the number of subordinate clauses and clause equivalents per macrosyntagm, or the number of clauses and clause equivalents per element on the 0 level.

Irregular clauses can reduce readability. Irregular clauses are rare in Hildegard's letters. The FM corpus has more irregular clauses than the FF corpus, a difference of low statistical significance. No explanation for this can be given. The absolute value for the MF corpus is lower than that for the FF, while the value for the MM corpus is greater than the value for the FF.

Embedded macrosyntagms include vocative phrases, interjectional phrases, and parenthetically embedded utterances, which according to classical rhetoric contribute to the liveliness and spontaneity of a text. The number of *embedded macrosyntagms* in letters written by men is greater than the number of embedded macrosyntagms in Hildegard's letters, a fact of high statistical significance. It is interesting to note that this stylistic device is so rare in Hildegard's texts, in the FF corpus as well as in the FM corpus, that it can be taken as evidence of the fact that her schooling as a writer had not followed the classical pattern, a conclusion that is supported by the few facts that are known about her life.

The presence of *clauses coordinated by means of polysyndeton* can be seen as a colloquial feature, that is to say a lesser degree of linguistic planning. However, in a text that is carefully composed, polysyndeton can provide increased impact, and contribute to emphasizing certain aspects of the content of the text. In both cases, polysyndeton in letters contributes to bridging 'the epistolary gap', the temporal or geographical gap between the sender and the recipient of the letter. *Clauses coordinated by means of asyndeton,* on the other hand, can, at least in Latin texts, delay the resolution of the clauses into their constituents and thus reduce readability. Where asyndeton does not make the syntactic analysis more difficult for the reader, it can, however, also increase the impact of the text. Both stylistic devices are deviations from convention and, as such, they always attract the reader's attention.

Variables on the lexical level

The *word class analysis* of nouns and adjectives in the FF and M corpora does not point to any significant differences in regard to the number of abstract versus concrete nouns, or in the number of emotive versus neutral adjectives.

The diagrams showing the *length of words* in the FF and FM corpora illustrate that the differences in word length distribute themselves in almost exactly the same way in these two corpora. This is true of the distribution of the length of words in the MF and the MM corpora as well. The proportion of two-letter words is slightly higher in the FF and FM than in the MF and MM corpora (a difference mirrored in the M corpus). The differences are counterbalanced by the proportion of three-letter words. Apart from these minor, statistically insignificant differences, all constituent corpora show a very similar distribution of different word lengths. Words with only one letter make up a very small proportion, and words with two letters—conjunctions, prepositions, and pronouns—make up the main proportion. For words longer than two letters, the percentages are reasonably evenly distributed. The longest words in Hildegard's letters have seventeen letters (one occurrence in the

FF corpus and two in FM). The longest words in MF have sixteen letters (two occurrences), and in MM twenty-one. In total, the MM corpus has five words with more than seventeen letters. These small differences do not carry as much weight as the fact that the diagrams of word length for the FF, FM, MF, and MM corpora have almost identical profiles.

Rhetorical figures

It is a well-known fact in the field of literary research that Hildegard of Bingen used a great many tropes. The number of tropes in her texts is astoundingly high: sixty-six tropes per hundred macrosyntagms in the FF and eighty-eight in the FM corpora, a number far exceeding the MF and MM corpora, and a difference that is of high statistical significance. The most important difference here is that between Hildegard's texts on the one hand and the other texts on the other, but there are two further points of interest. The first is the verified increase of tropes in the FM in comparison to the FF corpus—a highly significant increase that demands explanation. The second is the fact that Hildegard's use of metonyms does not show a significant difference vis-à-vis the other constituent corpora, while her use of other tropes—metaphors, similes, and animation—is more frequent, a difference that again is of high statistical significance.

Hildegard's use of *other rhetorical figures* (those whose function is purely for embellishment) is least frequent in the FF and most frequent in the FM corpus, the latter having high statistical significance. In both of the constituent corpora written by men (MF and MM), 'other rhetorical figures' are used to a greater extent than in the FF corpus. This is of high statistical significance. The reason for these 'other rhetorical figures' being more frequent in Hildegard's letters to men than in those to women may be that she adapted her style to the recipients of her letters. Alliteration is the purely embellishing rhetorical figure that occurs most frequently in Hildegard's letters, followed by polysyndeton on the phrasal level.

Notes

1   Giles Constable, *Typologie de sources du moyen âge occidental*, xvii : *Letters and Letter Collections* (Turnhout: Brepols, 1976), 13–15.

2   Ibid. 56.

3   *Hildegardis Bingensis epistolarium I–III*, ed. Lieven van Acker & Monika Klaes-Hachmüller (Corpus christianorum, Continuatio Mediaeualis, vol. XCI–XCI B;

Turnhout: Brepols, 1991–2001). An English translation is available in *The Letters of Hildegard of Bingen,* trans. Joseph L. Baird and Radd K. Ehrman, 3 vols. (Oxford: OUP, 1994–2004).

4 Hildephonse Herwegen, 'Les collaborateurs de Sainte Hildegarde', *Revue Bénédictine,* 21 (1904), 192–203, 302–315, 381–403; Marianna Schrader and Adelgundis Führkötter, *Die Echtheit des Schrifttums der Heiligen Hildegard von Bingen: quellenkritische Untersuchungen* (Cologne: n.p., 1956); Peter Dronke, *Women Writers of the Middle Ages* (Cambridge: CUP, 1984), 148.

5 Herwegen 1904.

6 For a similar analysis see Toolan, Michael, 'The Intrinsic Importance of Sentence Type and Clause Type to Narrative Effect: Or, How Alice Munro's "Circle of Prayer" Gets Started', in McIntyre, Dan and Beatrix Busse (eds.), *Language and Style: In Honour of Mick Short* (Palgrave: Macmillan, 2010), 324.

Bibliography

Constable, Giles, *Typologie de sources du moyen âge occidental,* xvii: *Letters and Letter Collections* (Turnhout: Brepols, 1976).

Dronke, Peter, *Women Writers of the Middle Ages* (Cambridge: CUP, 1984).

Herwegen, Hildephonse, 'Les collaborateurs de Sainte Hildegarde', *Revue Bénédictine,* 21 (1904).

Hildegardis Bingensis epistolarium I–III, ed. Lieven van Acker & Monika Klaes-Hachmüller, (Corpus christianorum, Continuatio Mediaeualis, vol. XCI–XCI B; Turnhout: Brepols, 1991–2001). An English translation is available in *The Letters of Hildegard of Bingen,* trans. Joseph L. Baird and Radd K. Ehrman, 3 vols. (Oxford: OUP, 1994–2004).

Schrader, Marianna & Adelgundis Führkötter, *Die Echtheit des Schrifttums der Heiligen Hildegard von Bingen: quellenkritische Untersuchungen* (Cologne: n.p., 1956)

Toolan, Michael, 'The Intrinsic Importance of Sentence Type and Clause Type to Narrative Effect: Or, How Alice Munro's "Circle of Prayer" Gets Started', in McIntyre, Dan and Beatrix Busse (eds.), *Language and Style: In Honour of Mick Short* (Palgrave: Macmillan, 2010).

CHAPTER 4

Swedish letters
c.1700–1740 and c.1740–1800

Marie Löwendahl & Börje Westlund

The material

The results for Subprojects 2 and 4 will be presented jointly in this chapter. Subproject 2 (Börje Westlund) is an analysis of material from the period *c.*1700–1740, and Subproject 4 (Marie Löwendahl) deals with material from the period *c.*1740–1800. The reasons for presenting the results of the projects jointly stem partly from the fact that the material analysed was written in the same language, partly from the difficulty involved in finding enough letters in each constituent corpus from the earlier period. The material for the analyses shares some features with the letters of Subproject 3 (Swedish letters in French in the eighteenth century), and in some cases there has been an overlap—that is, some writers have written letters in both Swedish and French.

The composition of the various constituent corpora regarding the number of letters and words per corpus is presented in Table 2.1.

Table 2.1 Size and composition of the various corpora in Subprojects 2 & 4.

Corpus	FF	FM	MF	MM	M
Number of letters	107	173	12	19	204
Number of words	44,899	83,982	5,942	10,466	100,390

The majority of the texts are transcriptions of manuscript letters. Printed editions have been used when available (for example, the letters of poets and prose writers Hedvig Charlotta Nordenflycht, Anna Maria Lenngren, Johan Henrik Kellgren, Thomas Thorild, and Carl Christoffer Gjörwell).

For the period between the end of the seventeenth century to *c.*1740 the following letter-writers have been selected: Hedvig Ulrika Posse (m. Törnflycht), Ulrika Maria Tessin (m. Sparre), Augusta Törnflycht (m. Wrede-Sparre), Agneta Wrede (m. Lillie), Brita Christina Sparre (m. Törnflycht), Eva Stenbock (m. Barnekow), Beata Stenbock (m. Sparre), and Regina Westerskiöld (m. Estenberg). For the later period the following writers have been selected in addition to the poets and authors from the earlier period: Hedvig Ulrika De la Gardie (m. Armfelt), Julie Ekerman (m. Björckegren), Brite Louise Gjörwell (m. Almqvist), Gustafva Eleonora Gjörwell (m. Lindahl), Brita Christina Sparre (m. Törnflycht), Magdalena Christina Stenbock (m. De la Gardie), and Beata Christina Strömfelt. Most of the letter-writers belonged to the upper class, and, in some cases, to the upper middle class. They can thus be said to represent the Swedish social elite of the time.

Survey of statistically significant differences in Subprojects 2 & 4

Table 2.2 shows the statistically significant differences between the FF constituent corpus and the other constituent corpora. In each comparison, the inequality signs signify whether the frequency of the variables in the FF corpus is greater (>) or lesser (<) than in the corpus to which it is compared. The strength of the statistical significance of these differences has been indicated using asterisks, from low (*) to high (***).

Table 2.2 Survey of the statistically significant differences in Subprojects 2 & 4

Variable	FF < / >	Degree of significance
Textual level		
Instances of address	FF > MF	***
Topics		
Fabrics and clothes	FF > FM	***
	FF > MM	*
	FF > M	***
Family and relatives	FF > MM	***
	FF > M	*
Obstetrics	FF > FM	***
	FF > M	***
The emotional life of the self and others	FF > FM	*
	FF > M	*
Nature	FF < MF	*

Education, wit, learning	FF < MF	***
	FF < MM	***
The relationship between letter-writer and recipient	FF < FM	*
	FF < MM	***
	FF < M	*
Metacomments	FF < FM	***
	FF < M	***

Syntactic level

Words per macrosyntagm	FF < MF	*
	FF > MM	**
Irregular macrosyntagms	FF < MM	*
Hypotaxis:		
SCC/macrosyntagm	FF < FM	*
	FF > MM	*
	FF < M	*
SCC1/macrosyntagm	FF > MM	**
SCC2/macrosyntagm	FF < FM	***
	FF > MM	*
	FF < M	***
SCC/CP0	FF < FM	**
	FF < M	**
SCC2/CP0	FF < FM	**
	FF < M	**

Lexical level

Total number of rhetorical figures	FF > FM	*
	FF < MF	***
	FF > M	*
Total number of tropes	FF < MF	*
Metaphor	FF < FM	***
Hyperbole	FF > MF	*
Rhetorical figures except for tropes	FF > FM	*
	FF < MF	*
	FF > M	*
Code-switching	FF < FM	***
	FF < MF	*
	FF < MM	*
	FF < M	***

Variables on the textual level
Addressing the reader

The frequency of this variable is higher in the FF corpus than in the MF corpus; the statistical significance is high.

Topics

(1) *Fabrics and clothes.* Statistically significant differences can be found when comparing the FF corpus to the FM, MM, and M corpora. The FF corpus exhibits the higher values, and the statistical significance is high when comparing it to the FM and M corpora, low when comparing it to the MM corpus.

(2) *Family and relatives.* The FF corpus has a higher value than MM, for which the statistical significance is high, and M, for which the statistical significance is low.

(3) *Obstetrics.* The FF corpus has a higher value than the FM and M corpora; the statistical significance is high in both cases.

(4) *The emotional life of the self and others.* The value for the FF corpus is higher than those for the FM and M corpora; the statistical significance is low.

These four topics exhibit the same pattern in the letters under investigation: they occur more frequently in women's letters to other women than in the other constituent corpora.

(5) *Nature.* The FF corpus has a lower value than the MF corpus; the statistical significance is high.

(6) *Education, wit, and learning.* The value for the FF corpus is lower than those for the MF and the MM corpora; in both cases the statistical significance is high.

(7) *The relationship between letter-writer and recipient.* The value for the FF corpus is lower than those for the FM, MM, and M corpora. When FF is compared to FM and M the statistical significance is low, when FF is compared to MM the statistical significance is high.

(8) *Metacomments.* The value for the FF corpus is lower than those for the MF and the M corpora; in both cases the statistical significance is high.

The pattern seen in these four topics is the opposite of that in topics (1)–(4): when one of the correspondents is a man, subjects (5)–(8) occur more frequently than when both correspondents are women.

Just over half, or ten, of the total nineteen topics investigated in the present project exhibit a statistically significant difference in frequency when comparing the FF corpus to the other constituent corpora. No such differences have been found in relation to the other nine topics: *The body, Sensory impressions, Money and economy, Social life, Travelling, Politics and warfare, Opinions about people, Fictionalization* (does not occur at all in the present subprojects), and *Accidents and sensational events*.

Variables on the syntactic level
Words per macrosyntagm

The value for the FF corpus is lower than that for the MF corpus. The statistical significance is low. However, the value for the FF corpus is higher than that for the MM corpus, and here the statistical significance is moderate. The female letter-writers thus seem to use longer macrosyntagms on average than do the male writers.

Irregular macrosyntagms

A statistically significant difference appears only when comparing the FF and MM corpora, with the latter exhibiting a higher frequency of this variable. The statistical significance is low.

Hypotaxis

Total number of subordinate clauses and phrases per macrosyntagm (SCC per macrosyntagm). The value for FF is lower than those for the FM and M corpora, but higher than that for the MM corpus; in all cases the statistical significance is low.

Number of subordinate clauses and phrases on level 1 per macrosyntagm (SCC1 per macrosyntagm). The value for the FF corpus is higher than that for the MM corpus; the statistical significance is moderate.

Number of subordinate clauses and phrases on level 2 per macrosyntagm (SCC2 per macrosyntagm). It is reasonable to assume that the quantity of this variable is dependent on the quantity of SCC per macrosyntagm, and that the relationship between the constituent corpora should be similar to that indicated for the SCC1 per macrosyntagm, above. This assumption turns out to be correct: the value for the FF corpus is higher than that for the MM corpus, although the statistical significance is only low. In addition, differences also emerge when comparing the FF corpus to the FM and M corpora, a comparison that shows that the value for the FF corpus is the lower one. In both cases the statistical significance is high. The number of subordinate clauses on level 2 thus increases when the women write to men compared to when they write to other women. This happens to such a high degree that the value for the M corpus is higher than that for the FF corpus, despite the fact that this particular use of subordinate clauses occurs more frequently in women's letter to women than in men's letters to men.

Total number of subordinate clauses and clause equivalents per clause or phrase on the 0 level (SCC per CP0). The values for the FF corpus are lower than those for the FM and M corpora; in both cases the statistical significance is moderate. Also in this case an increase in frequency can be found when women write to men compared to when they write to other women.

Number of subordinate clauses and phrases on level 2 per clause or phrase on the 0 level (SCC2 per CP0). The FF corpus exhibits lower values than do the FM and M corpora. The statistical significance is high in both cases. Also, an increase in the use of subordinate clauses on level 2 can be detected in letters written by women when they write to men compared to when they write to women.

In sum, the female letter-writers tend to use more subordinate clauses when writing to men than when writing to women.

Variables on the lexical level
Rhetorical figures

Total number of rhetorical figures. The FF corpus exhibits a higher value than do the FM and M corpora. In both cases the statistical significance is low. However, the FF corpus exhibits a higher value than the MF corpus, a statistically highly significant circumstance.

Total number of tropes. The FF corpus has a lower value than the MF corpus; the statistical significance is low.

Metaphors. The FF corpus has a lower value than the FM corpus; the statistical significance is high.

Hyperbole. The FF corpus has a higher value than the MF corpus; the statistical significance is low.

The tropes for which no statistically significant differences occur in the material are *similes* and *irony*.

Other rhetorical figures. The FF corpus has a higher value than the

FM and M corpora, but a lower value than the MF corpus. In all cases the statistical significance is low.

Specific 'other rhetorical figures' for which no statistically significant differences can be found in the material are *rhetorical question* and *climax*.

All told, the use of rhetorical figures as a whole is more prominent in letters written by men than in letters written by women. This is true even in the specific cases of the *total number of tropes* and 'other rhetorical figures'. With respect to the use of metaphors, the statistically significant difference is that women use more metaphors when writing to men than when writing to women. Only when it comes to hyperbole do the female writers use a figure of speech more often than do the male writers.

Code-switching

The FF corpus has a lower value than the FM and M corpora (the statistical significance for this is high) and the MF and MM corpora (the statistical significance for this is low). It would seem that the men in general are more prone to code-switching than are the women.

Summary
The textual level—variables of content

Addressing the reader occurs more frequently in the FF constituent corpus than in the M corpus. Most likely this is the result of a stylistic tendency that is typical of the female letter-writers in these subprojects. This is in accordance with the eighteenth-century understanding of the letter-writing genre. Since classical antiquity, the genre of the familiar letter has been considered a type of text in which spontaneity and intimacy should prevail. The letter should, both on stylistic and contentual levels, resemble a conversation between friends rather than a rhetorical treatise. Eventually (primarily during the seventeenth century in France), this view of the letter genre became linked to the concept of the feminine, in the sense that the ideas relating to the nature of women were matched, so to speak, with the ideas regarding the letter genre (for example in concepts such as '*négligence*', '*bagatelle*', '*spontanité*', and so on). During the eighteenth century, the generally accepted notion was that women, perhaps because of their lack of formal education, were better suited to writing (supposedly) 'natural' letters than men. Writing spontaneously is of course also an art, but the artistry was meant to be concealed. The close relationship between the letter-writer and the recipient is central to the genre of the familiar letter, something manifested in the use of instances of address. By directly addressing the reader using vocatives, questions, and directives, the writer attempts to include the recipient in what is written, so that an illusion of real dialogue, face to face, is created. From this perspective, the finding that the female letter-writers use instances of address to a greater extent than the male writers is not surprising.[1]

Where *topics* are concerned we find a division between topics that are more common in the FF corpus and those more common in the FM, MF, and MM constituent corpora. The former are topics (1)–(4): *Fabrics and clothes, Obstetrics, The emotional life of the self and others,* and *Family and relatives.* In the letters between women these are more frequent than when one of the correspondents is a man. The latter are topics (5)–(8): *Nature, Education, wit, and learning, The relationship between letter-writer and recipient,* and *Metacomments.* These topics are more frequent when the writer or recipient is a man—in other words, they are more common in the FM, MM, MF, and M corpora.

The distribution of topics in the letters is not particularly surprising considering the eighteenth-century notion of what was typically 'male' and 'female', as well as the social spheres associated with men and women during this period. The differences that can be discerned regarding education and day-to-day existence are mirrored in the letters.[2] It is only to be expected that the female writers to a great extent comment on things that concerned home and family, because even elite women were largely confined to this sphere. Similarly, one might expect male letter-writers (and women who write to men) to tend to deal with, for example, education and wit. Somewhat surprising, however, is the topic *Nature,* which could have been expected to occur in the FF corpus to a greater extent than in the other corpora. This is because there was, at least towards the end of the eighteenth century—following Rousseau—an association between the idea of Nature and the idea of the feminine.

Metacomments appear more often in the FM and the M corpora than the FF corpus. It is clear that this topic is advantageously affected by the fact that one of the parties in the correspondence is a man; this is true also where the topic *The relationship between letter-writer and recipient* is concerned. *Metacomments* and *The relationship between letter-writer and recipient* give the text a reflexive character and increase the distance to the topic about which the writer is writing. This stylistic tendency seems to be associated with the fact that the letter-writer or the recipient is male. An example of metacomments can be found in a letter from Hedvig Ulrika De la Gardie to her husband, Gustaf Mauritz Armfelt; here the writer comments on both the letter's length and its contents:

Du får nu en faslig epistel, men som 6 blad voro skrivna med mycket onödigt sladder redan, så får du tråka igenom det om du vill; annars så bränn upp det, det är ej bättre värt.[3]

This also displays another of the common features of the familiar letter—its informal, 'gossipy' nature.

Formal variables—the lexical and the syntactic levels

The macrosyntagms are on average longer in the FF than in the MM constituent corpus. This could be because the male use of subordinate clauses is more limited than the female use of this linguistic variable. However, at the same time, the value for FF is lower than that for MF. The results are in this case rather difficult to interpret. It was not expected that the length of the macrosyntagm would be greater in FF than in MM, and this may conflict with current ideas concerning women's letters. Another difference between male and female writers can also be found on the syntactic level: the value for FF is higher than that for MM. At the same time, same line of reasoning is valid, for if one compares the FF corpus with the FM and with the entire category in which either the recipient or the writer is male (M), it becomes apparent that the value for the FF category is lower than the values for the two latter categories (FM, M).

Longer hypotactic sequences result in comparatively long macrosyntagms and subordinate clauses on level 2 and higher. This type of sentence structure suggests that the writer has attempted to syntactically tie together the different links of a chain of thought rather than finish the macrosyntagm and begin the next one with a connecting word.

It is interesting to note that there are fewer subordinate clauses in women's letter to women than in women's letters to men, and, as a consequence, the macrosyntagms are on average shorter in the former group. This lends support to the idea of a 'feminine' style of writing. It is possible to argue that shorter macrosyntagms and fewer subordinate

clauses chime with the colloquial stylistic ideal—based on the idea of
the letter as a substitute for conversation—that was associated with the
familiar letter, and with female letter-writers in particular. If so, this
ideal should be manifested more strongly in letters between women
and should give a spontaneous and natural impression. Note, however,
that the stylistic ideal is not colloquial spoken language in a true sense,
only a kind of imitation of it.

One possible explanation for the difference between FF and FM
regarding the length of the macrosyntagms and syntactic depth is that
the female writers may have sought to achieve a 'higher' style when
writing to men; this in spite of the ideal of the 'natural' feminine letter-writing style. This rhetorical tension is less obvious when women
write to women. In the material studied here this can be seen in letters written by Hedvig De la Gardie and Julie Ekerman for example.
In Ekerman's letters—addressed to her former lover, the Governor of
Stockholm Carl Sparre—there are a number of examples of enormous
macrosyntagms with several subordination levels. The following constitutes one example, in which the writer praises her virtuous friend:

> Den vänskap hans excellens ger mig så autentiqua bevis på, gör
> mig—till det få människor kan säga sig—fullkomligt lycklig, ja så
> säll, att quand même jag hade reella olyckor som ofelbart annars
> skulle snart med min ringa dosis Philosophie nedslå mig, men
> ägarinna av ett gott samvete i anseende till mina närvarande plikters
> uppfyllande och hans excellens dyrbara vänskap, vågar jag nästan
> försäkra mig i stånd att bravera starka stormar; om försynen skulle
> vilja försöka min undergivenhet för hans heliga vilja och skickelse.[4]

These lengthy structures result in the writer's not being able to keep the
whole sentence in her head, which results in an anacoluton.

There is a difference of low statistical significance regarding the
frequency of *irregular macrosyntagms* between women's letters to
women and men's letters to men. This frequency is somewhat higher
in the men's letters. This may seem unexpected, especially given the
observation that the female letter-writers (when writing to men) tend
to use relatively complicated syntactic structures, which sometimes
break down. However, it should be noted that the kind of irregular
macrosyntagms that dominate in this material are not anacolutha
but elliptical clauses. The latter do not indicate a lack of linguistic

planning; rather the reverse. The fact that the frequency of irregular clauses is higher in the MM group can possibly be explained by this circumstance. There are fewer *Rhetorical figures* in the FF than in the MF corpus. The greater number of rhetorical figures in the MF corpus is due to the variable *Total number of tropes*. The main reason for this is to be found in the *metaphor* variable, where the statistical significance for the greater number found in the MF corpus is high. The opposite is true for the variable *hyperbole*, however, where a predominance of low statistical significance can be found in the FF corpus. Furthermore, when it comes to the frequency of other rhetorical figures than tropes, there is a predominance of low statistical significance in letters written by men.

The greater frequency of rhetorical figures, especially metaphors, in letters written by men indicates a somewhat different stylistic ideal among the male letter-writers than among the female writers. This indicates a style influenced to a greater extent by classical rhetoric; a style that was easily adopted by a more formally educated writer. The exception to this is hyperbole, which is used more often by women than by men. Hyperbole, associated as it is with emotional spontaneity, is a rhetorical figure that can be said to belong to a supposedly 'natural' letter-writing style, and it is therefore not surprising to find that it occurs more often among the female writers (see *Addressing the reader*, p. 76).[5]

Code-switching is more common in the MM than in the FF corpus, but the difference has only a low statistical significance. It is unclear whether any importance should be attached to this difference.

Comparisons and conclusions

Regarding Subprojects 2 & 4 it can be said that there are some differences on the formal level between the FF constituent corpus and the constituent corpora to which it has been compared, but that these differences are mainly to be found on the level of content. The results are therefore not unambiguous, and a pattern does not appear in which the FF category distinguishes itself at all levels. For this reason Showalter's hypothesis about a separate female culture cannot be verified here. However, several interesting differences among the various categories can be noted, for example, between FF and FM. These seem be linked to the development of the letter genre and the fact that the female letter-writers adapted their style to suit their male recipients.

The results of the combined Subprojects 2 & 4 can be compared to the findings of a doctoral thesis on Swedish letter-writing in the nineteenth century by Kristina Persson.[6] While it deals with a later historical period and does not differentiate throughout between female- and male-authored letters, nevertheless Persson offers certain reflections on the potential differences between male and female letter-writing that are of interest in the present context.

Persson's source material is the correspondence of the Swedish priest and MP Axel Eurén (1803–79) and his family. The other writers are his wife, Sophie; his mother, Brita; his sister, Aurore; and his children, Maria, Axel, and Oscar. The letters were written between 1825 and 1860. Persson primarily analyses the structure of the correspondence of the Eurén family from a network perspective, but the letters are also studied as physical objects, and their linguistic usage is examined. This last component is what is interesting here. The linguistic analyses are based on 293 letters (some 160,000 words), distributed among the different writers and written in four distinct periods selected by Persson (1824–25, 1836–37, 1847–48, and 1857–58).[7]

Persson's linguistic analysis operates on several different levels. The first level is that of content, textual disposition, and execution, which implies not only a kind of general characterization of individual letters/letter-writers, but also an investigation of the ways in which paragraph division, editing, and punctuation are used. The second level is that of the letters' syntax, which here means the relationship between the length of the sentences/main clauses, the length of the base, coordination/subordination, and completeness/incompleteness. The third level concerns vocabulary, including the presence of French loan words, together with abbreviations and long and short forms of certain words, such as *hava* versus *ha* ('to have'), *bliva* versus *bli* ('to become'). The fourth level deals with the inflection or conjugation of certain word forms, and the fifth with spelling; for example, the choice between ö and y as in *böxor* or *byxor* ('trousers').[8]

From this it is apparent that the selected linguistic features only partially resemble those in the 'Women's language' project. The analysis of the linguistic features in Persson's study is constructed around the individual letter-writers, which makes a comparison with the results of Subprojects 2 & 4 in the present project difficult. Among other things, Persson concludes that French loan words became less common as the century progressed (which is connected to the general linguistic development of the Swedish language), and that the female letter-writers used a more quotidian vocabulary than the male writers. In addition, she finds that the female writers used a less complicated sentence structure, while the men used a syntax which was more typical of written, as opposed to spoken, language.[9] A problem connected to the methodology used in Persson's thesis is that the analyses of syntax and vocabulary do not take into account her entire corpus of letters. Persson also investigates the custom of addressing the recipient of the letter, which she considers an oral trait in written texts.[10] Address includes both what Persson calls 'clause-integrated address' (which is grammatically necessary) and 'non-clause-integrated (free) address'. In the 'Women's language' project the category *Addressing the reader* includes only the latter type of address. Instances of free address (vocatives) can in Persson's analysis occur before and after the clause, or they can be embedded in it. Persson gives the instances of address per thousand consecutive words for each individual letter-writer, and concludes that the largest group of instances of address (a total of 60 per cent) consists of the syntactically necessary word 'you'. The other significant group is free address with attributes (30 per cent). The most common form of free address is a phrase of the kind 'my beloved Maria'. One interesting conclusion Persson draws is that it is the female letter-writers who address the reader most often, which accords with the findings of Subprojects 2 & 4 of the present project.

Notes

1 See Marie Löwendahl, *Min allrabästa och ömmaste vän! Kvinnors brevskrivning under svenskt 1700-tal* (Gothenburg: Makadam, 2007), ch. 1, in particular 42–8; see also Jon Helgason's essay in the present volume.

2 For the upbringing and education of women during the eighteenth century, see, for example, Jessica Parland-von Essen, *Behagets betydelser: Döttrarnas edukation i det sena 1700-talets adelskultur* (Möklinta: Gidlund, 2005).

3 Hedvig Ulrika De la Gardie to Gustaf Mauritz Armfelt, 10 November 1792 (Riksarkivet (National Archives of Sweden) Stockholm, RA, Armfeltska saml. E 3135). The spelling and punctuation have been standardized. Translation: 'I now send you a terribly long letter, but as I have already covered 6 pages with a good deal of unnecessary gossip, you may bore yourself reading through it as you please; else you may burn it, its worth is not better than that'.

4 Julie Ekerman to Carl Sparre, 20 September 1789 (RA, Börstorpssaml. E 3052). The spelling has been standardized. Translation: 'The friendship of which Your Excellency gives me such authentic proof makes me—what few people can say—perfectly happy, yea so blissful that even if I was struck by real misfortune which

otherwise inevitably would have soon disheartened me, who possesses such an insignificant measure of Philosophy; however, as I am the owner of a good conscience on account of the fulfilment of my present duties and the precious friendship of Your Excellency, I almost dare ensure myself that I am capable of braving fierce storms; if Providence would try my submissiveness to His sacred will and dispensation'.

5 Cf. Löwendahl 2007, 200 & 263.
6 Kristina Persson, *Svensk brevkultur på 1800-talet. Språklig och kommunikations-etnografisk analys av en familjebrevväxling* ['The culture of Swedish letter-writing in the nineteenth century: an analysis of a family correspondence from the perspective of linguistics and ethnography of communication'] (Uppsala universitet, Institutionen för nordiska språk, 2005); subsequently published as *'Äfven i dag några rader': familjebrevskrivning på 1800-talet* (Ord och Stil, 39; Uppsala: Hallgren & Fallgren, 2008).
7 Persson 2005, 53–54; ibid. 59–63 for an explanation of the principles of the reproduction of the handwritten documents.
8 See the survey of selected linguistic features in ibid. 99.
9 See the summary in ibid. 169–80.
10 See ibid. ch. 8.

Bibliography

Löwendahl, Marie, *Min allrabästa och ömmaste vän! Kvinnors brevskrivning under svenskt 1700-tal* (Gothenburg: Makadam, 2007).

Parland-von Essen, Jessica, *Behagets betydelser: Döttrarnas edukation i det sena 1700-talets adelskultur* (Möklinta: Gidlund, 2005).

Persson, Kristina, *Svensk brevkultur på 1800-talet. Språklig och kommunikationsetnografisk analys av en familjebrevväxling* (Uppsala universitet, Institutionen för nordiska språk, 2005), subsequently published as *'Äfven i dag några rader': familjebrevskrivning på 1800-talet* (Ord och Stil, 39; Uppsala: Hallgren & Fallgren, 2008).

CHAPTER 5

Letters in French in the eighteenth century

Elisabet Hammar

The material

The French letters in the 'Women's language' project were all written by bilingual members of the upper class in eighteenth-century Sweden.[1] With two exceptions, they all belonged to the same social networks, often the same noble families: primarily the houses of Tessin, Sparre, and Törnflycht, which were closely associated with the courts of Gustav III and his mother, Louisa Ulrika of Prussia.[2] They wrote to and about one another, and may be said to constitute a closely connected social grouping.[3] The two who did not fit this pattern, Charlotta Oxenstierna at the turn of the eighteenth century and the German-born Princess Hedvig Elisabeth Charlotta at the turn of the following century, moved in the same social environment without having participated in the same social networks as the others.[4]

The advantages of investigating letter-writers who are as homogenous as these are obvious in a project of this kind. As always when working with material from a historical period as distant as the eighteenth century, the writers have had to be chosen primarily on the basis of the survival of the source material. These families had an interest in preserving their documents and letters, and the means to do so, something that enables a researcher to find letter-writers who corresponded on a large scale and, crucially, at length with a wide range of correspondents, both men and women.

In the event, the disadvantages of working with bilingual people who generally wrote letters in a language other than that generally spoken in their country of residence, turned out to be less significant. The French used in these letters is a functional, natural French, learned at an early age from native speakers, and kept up by reading French literature and by the fact that noble families generally used French when communicating with one another.[5] While no scholarly investigation has been conducted in order to determine whether the French used in these letters is comparable to that of native French speakers, analyses have been undertaken in French repositories on a random selection of French letters written by native speakers at the same time and in the same social environment, and no significant differences could be observed. Moreover, it is doubtful whether the possible differences between the language in the Swedish letters and that used in French letters written by native speakers is a variable of importance in this particular project, where the main focus is on the potential differences in language use between people of different sexes in the same language area—which in this case is French used by bilingual people in the comparatively isolated social environment of the Swedish social elite.

Table 3.1 Swedish letters and letter-writers, 1694–1797.

Female letter-writers	Period	To women	To men	Total
Charlotta Oxenstierna	1694–1707	16	5	21
Ulla Sparre (m. Tessin)	1724–1768	24	27	50
Hedvig Elisabeth Sack	1728–1758		7	7
Augusta Törnflycht (m. Wrede-Sparre)	1735–1777	11	23	34
Charlotta Ulrika Lillienstedt (m. Spens)	1736	6		6
Lotta Sparre (m. von Fersen)	1739–1789	17	15	32
Brita Stina Sparre (m. Törnflycht)	1739–1770	14	9	23
Ulla Strömfelt (m. Sparre)	1756–1778	12	26	38
Hedvig Elisabeth Charlotta	1777–1797	8	6	14
Total		**108**	**117**	**225**
Male letter-writers	**Period**	**To women**	**To men**	**Total**
Carl Gustaf Tessin	1739–1768	10	10	20
Carl Sparre	1740–1779	12	5	17
Axel Wrede-Sparre	1741–1771	11	4	15
Fredrik Sparre	1751–1773	11	4	15
Total		**44**	**23**	**67**

The female letter-writers are nine in number, the male writers four, and the distribution of the 292 letters they wrote between them is given in Table 3.1.[6] If the texts are divided into their constituent corpora—letters written by women to women (FF), women to men (FM), men to women (MF), and men to men (MM)—and, in addition, a combined corpus is constructed where a man is involved either as the writer or the recipient of a letter (M), the distribution of the number of letters and the number of words is as indicated in Table 3.2.

Table 3.2 Size and composition of the various Subproject 3 corpora.

Corpus	FF	FM	MF	MM	M
Number of letters	108	117	23	44	184
Number of words	77,795	71,176	31,195	15,055	117,426

The total number of words is thus some 200,000, and individual letters are, for obvious reasons, very different from one another in length. The fact that neither the letters nor the words are evenly distributed among the different letter-writers has not been considered a problem in this project, given the hypothesis it was designed to test. The results of the empirical testing of the hypothesis that there exists a specifically female language should remain unaffected even if a significant portion of the body of texts was written by a particular individual. Furthermore, because the letters and collections of letters have been analysed separately, it was easy to establish whether any one writer significantly deviated from the others, and this could then be taken into account. The selection of letters was governed rather by practical reasons, such as availability and readability. Because this subproject deals almost exclusively with manuscript letters, the readability is, for obvious reasons, of some importance.

When the letters were selected, their contents were transcribed by hand from the manuscript itself or from a photocopy of it. In the case of published letters, the published text was collated with the original letter in order to detect possible deletions in the printed version. Because it was decided early on in the 'Women's language' project that the spelling in the letter texts had to be normalized in order to facilitate searchability, this normalization was effected directly in this subproject, without the creation of an intermediate, literal copy. The strict and early implementation of standardized spelling rules in the French language made this normalization comparatively unproblematic.

The ways in which this body of texts has subsequently been analysed, 'by hand' and using digitalized aids, are explained in the method chapter. However, each language has its distinctive characteristics, which means that there have had to be some departures from the norm in this subproject, both in the manner of conducting the analysis and when determining whether or not a particular analysis was feasible.[7] Thus in presenting the results of each analysis, I begin by outlining the specific difficulties that have arisen and the allowances made for the French language in particular.

Survey of the statistically significant differences in Subproject 3

Table 3.3 Survey of the statistically significant differences in Subproject 3

Variable	FF < / >	Degree of significance
Textual level		
Addressing the reader	FF > FM	***
	FF > M	***
Topics		
Fabrics and clothes	FF > FM	*
	FF > M	*
Obstetrics	FF > FM	*
	FF > M	*
Metacomments	FF < FM	*
	FF < M	*
Syntactic level		
Embedded macrosyntagms	FF < FM	*
Lexical level		
Rhetorical figures		
Hyperbole	FF > M	*
Metaphor	FF < FM	**
Rhetorical question	FF > FM	***
Code-switching	FF < FM	*
	FF < M	*

Variables on the textual level
Addressing the reader

In the French letters it appears to be the recipient who decides whether or not many instances of address are used or not. The most numerous are directed to female recipients (FF, MF), especially by other women (FF). In letters where a man is the recipient (FM, MM) there is a marked difference to the FF and MF constituent corpora, and if comparing the FF corpus with the corpus where a man is either the recipient or the writer (M), there is still an apparent difference. Concerning the number of times a letter-writer directly addresses the recipient, there is in the French letters a statistically significant difference between the FF corpus (more instances of direct address) and the other constituent corpora.

Topics

Each letter in this subproject has been read through, and a note made as soon as one of the nineteen topics selected for the project is touched upon by the letter-writer. A topic is only counted once in each letter, even if it is mentioned several times. In each letter there can thus be, in principle, a maximum of nineteen topics.

A few of the topics can only be found rarely in the French material, if at all, regardless of the constituent corpus: *Sensory impressions, Fictionalization,* and *Accidents and sensational events.* Other topics can be found in more than 50 per cent of the letters, regardless of the constituent corpus: *Metacomments, The emotional life of the self and others, The relationship between letter-writer and recipient, Opinions about people, The body,* and *Family and relatives* (in approximate descending order of frequency of occurrence). Regarding other subjects, the female writers in this subproject tend to mention *Fabrics and clothes, The body,* and *Social life,* while the male writers tend to deal with *Economy* and *Education, wit, and learning.*[8] In a textual material consisting of letters that were largely exchanged between relatives and between man and wife, it is unsurprising to find that men, as well as women, mention *Family and relatives, The emotional life of the self and others,* and even *Obstetrics* equally often.

Variables on the syntactic level

Hypotaxis

The fact that the project analyses are based on the concept of the macro-syntagm instead of the sentence has made the analysis of the French letters easier, as the material consists mainly of manuscript texts. This is because in manuscript letters it is extremely difficult to determine where the writer has paused or finished a sentence. When it comes to clause equivalents, I have had to develop a method partially my own, because French grammars are inexact when dealing with this phenomenon, despite the fact that it is so characteristic of the French language.[9] The result has been a fairly broad definition of clause equivalents, but because this is such a significant stylistic indicator in French, I wanted to make explicit the extent to which each letter-writer has been able to master this stylistic feature. For the main components of the definition applied, see p. 48.

Neither in the case of the number of words in a macrosyntagm, nor the number of subordinate clauses and phrases per macrosyntagm, nor the feature 'main clause/s or expanded interjectional or vocative macrosyntagm/s on the 0 level' (CP0), can any statistically significant differences between the FF and the other constituent corpora be found in the French material.

Regarding the method used to calculate the length of the base, see p. 50.

When considering syntactic elements (embedded and irregular macrosyntagms, long bases, and syndeton), the results are not unambiguous, except those relating to the base, where it appears as if not only the male writers (MF, MM) are prone to using long bases, but that the female writers, too, adapt to this stylistic habit when writing to men (FM). This difference is not statistically significant, however.

Variables on the lexical level
Word classes

In order to be able to conduct the word class analysis, the texts in each individual subproject were analysed by a special computer programme (see pp. 37 and 137), so that it was possible to draw up lists detailing the frequency of words. Once complete, the most frequent words were organized into groups based on word class—nouns, verbs, and adjectives—and these in turn were arranged in terms of binary opposites: abstract versus concrete nouns, stative versus dynamic verbs, and neutral versus emotive adjectives.

When working with the French material, there was a problem from the outset with identifying the correct word class of each word, for the same reasons that make it impossible for this analysis to be conducted for the letters in the English subproject: there are quite simply too many words in these two languages which cannot be identified as belonging to one word class or another without consulting the context in which they appear. Words of uncertain word class were thus identified as belonging to the word class in which I judged the word to appear most often. Wherever there was the least doubt, I excluded the word altogether. Using this principle was a practical necessity due to the large number of texts studied, which made it impossible to look at each word in context.

Concerning the application of the analysis model in Subproject 3, see p. 40.

Rhetorical figures

Only when looking at rhetorical figures is it possible to find what seem to be actual differences in language use between the male and female letter-writers. The male writers use a significantly larger number of rhetorical figures than do the female writers, but where the total number of rhetorical figures is concerned, the female writers do not appear to adapt to this practice when writing to men (FM). If, on the other hand, individual rhetorical figures are considered, a certain adaptation by writers of both sexes to their correspondents can be discerned, in that both male and female writers use other rhetorical figures when writing to men than when writing to women.

In the sample of French texts in this subproject, some rhetorical figures are used more often by the female writers and others are used primarily by the male writers. Hyperbole is more common in female-authored texts, and metaphors in texts written by men. When the female letter-writers write to men (FM) they generally use less hyperbole and increase the amount of metaphor, and when the male writers write to women (MF) they do the opposite. It seems reasonable to assume that metaphor is a figure of speech that can be tied to the reading of classical literature, in this case primarily in Latin, while hyperbole belongs to a more primitive and 'home-made' type of figure of speech.

There are statistically significant differences in the use of stylistic variables in the French letters, for example, in the cases of code-switching, the total number of rhetorical figures, and metaphor (all of which are most common in letters written by men), and hyperbole (which is most commonly used by female writers).

Code-switching

Code-switching is more in evidence when a man is one of the correspondents, whether as a writer or recipient (M), and the difference is statistically significant. My spontaneous reaction to this result is that the female writers continue using the language they have switched into for a longer period of time before reverting to the original language, thus code-switching less often, especially when writing to women (FF).

When considering the French material, it is important to remember that the writers were clearly bilingual, and moreover were generally immersed in an environment where their native language was usually spoken.[10] Code-switching was thus very natural for them.

Summary

In the French subproject it has thus not been possible to detect any statistically significant differences in language use between the letters written by female writers to other women (the FF constituent corpus) and the letters in the other constituent corpora, other than with regard to the number of rhetorical figures, the preferred type of figure of speech, the number of times code-switching is done in a letter, and the number of times the recipient is explicitly addressed. In addition, there are differences concerning the topics discussed in the letters. I believe that these differences can be explained by differences in education, the gendered division of responsibilities, and the daily activities of the sexes.

If the analysis is considered in detail, however, it is possible to discover interesting linguistic characteristics that seem to be based on power relations between the writer and the recipient. These power relations need not had anything to do with differences in age, social position, or gender, but can also have derived from an emotional imbalance between the correspondents, such as infatuation or guilt, and they could be temporary. When, based on a close reading of the text, it is reasonable to infer that the writers felt inferior to their correspondents, there is also a tendency to use longer macrosyntagms and more subordinate elements, as well as longer bases. When, on the other hand, there are signals in the text that suggest that the writers appear to have felt at ease with their correspondents, they also seem to have allowed themselves to use more irregular macrosyntagms, engage in more frequent code-switching, and use more hyperbole. Investigating this more closely would probe deeper into the intricate problem of how we choose to express ourselves in relation to our fellow human beings.

Notes

1   For French letter-writing in the eighteenth century, see Anne Chamayou, *L'esprit de la lettre: XVIIIe siècle* (Perspectives littéraires; Paris: Presses universitaires de France, 1999); Roger Chartier, Alain Boureau, and Cécile Dauphin, *Correspondence: Models of Letter-Writing from the Middle Ages to the Nineteenth Century*, trans. Christopher Woodall (Oxford: Polity Press, 1997); Cécile Dauphin, *Prête-moi ta plume—:les manuels épistolaires au XIXe siècle* (Paris: Kimé, 2000); and Marie-France Silver & Marie-Laure Girou Swiderski, *Femmes en toutes lettres: les épistolières du XVIIIe siècle* (Studies on Voltaire and the eighteenth century 2000:04; Oxford: Voltaire Foundation, 2000).

2   Gustaf Elgenstierna, *Den introducerade svenska adelns ättartavlor*, 9 vols. (Stockholm: Norstedt, 1925–36); Sigrid Leijonhufvud, *Omkring Carl Gustaf Tessin*, 2 vols.

(Stockholm: Norstedt, 1917–18); Elisabeth Mansén, *Ett paradis på jorden: om den svenska kurortskulturen 1680–1880* (Stockholm: Atlantis, 2001); *Tableaux de Paris et de la cour de France 1739–1742: lettres inédites de Carl Gustaf, comte de Tessin*, ed. Gunnar von Proschwitz (Romanica Gothoburgensia 22; Gothenburg: Acta Universitatis Gothoburgensis, 1983); Carl Gustaf Tessin, *Carl Gustaf Tessins Skräplåda: Åkerödagboken, förd året 1757* (Stockholm: Tempera, 1985).

3 See also Philippe Ariès & Georges Duby, *Histoire de la vie privée*, iii: *De la Renaissance aux Lumières* (L'univers historique; Paris: Seuil, 1986); François Bluche, *La Vie quotidienne de la noblesse française au XVIIIᵉ siècle* (Paris: Hachette littérature, 1973); Anne Coudreuse, *Le goût des larmes au XVIIIe siècle* (Écriture; Paris: Presses universitaires de France, 1999); Benedetta Craveri, *L'âge de la conversation* (Paris: Gallimard, 2002).

4 See Hedvig Elisabeth Charlotta, *Hedvig Elisabeth Charlottas dagbok*, trans. Carl Carlson Bonde, 9 vols. (Stockholm: Norstedt, 1902–1942).

5 See Elisabet Hammar, *L'enseignement du français en Suède jusqu'en 1807: méthodes et manuels* (Stockholm: Akademilitt., 1980) and *Franskundervisningen i Sverige fram till 1807: undervisningssituationer och lärare* (Stockholm: Fören. för svensk undervisningshistoria, 1981). See also the French version '*La Française'. Mille et une façons d'apprendre le français en Suède avant 1807* (Acta Universitatis Upsaliensis. Uppsala Studies in Education 41; Uppsala, 1992).

6 The full list of recipients can be found in Appendix 3.

7 Louis-Nicolas Bescherelle, *La grammaire pour tous* (Paris: Hatier, 1997); Maurice Grevisse, *Le bon usage: grammaire française* (9th edn., Gembloux: Duculot, 1969; 12th edn., Paris: Duculot, 1986); Hervé-D. Béchade, *Grammaire française* (Collection Premier cycle; Paris: Presses universitaires de France, 1994); Claire Stolz, *Initiation à la linguistique* (Paris: Ellipses, 1999).

8 For the significance of clothing during this period, see Daniel Roche, *La culture des apparences: une histoire du vêtement, XVIIe–XVIIIe siècle* (Paris: Fayard, 1989).

9 See Bescherelle 1997; Grevisse 1969; Béchade 1994; Stoltz 1999; and see also Annie Boone, 'Subordination, subordonnées et subordonnants', *Documents pour l'Histoire du Français Langue Etrangère ou Seconde*, 29 (2002), 11–25.

10 For deviations in French regarding stylistic variables, see Frédéric Calas and Dominique-Rita Charbonneau, *Méthode du commentaire stylistique* (Paris: Nathan, 2000); Catherine Fromilhague and Anne Sancier-Château, *Introduction à l'analyse stylistique* (Collection Lettres supérieures; Paris: Dunod, 1996); and Joëlle Gardes-Tamine, *La Stylistique* (Paris: Colin 1997)

Bibliography

Ariès, Philippe & Georges Duby, *Histoire de la vie privée*, iii: *De la Renaissance aux Lumières* (L'univers historique; Paris: Seuil, 1986).

Béchade, Hervé-D., *Grammaire française* (Collection Premier cycle; Paris: Presses universitaires de France, 1994).

Bescherelle, Louis-Nicolas, *La grammaire pour tous* (Paris: Hatier, 1997).

Bluche, François, *La Vie quotidienne de la noblesse française au XVIIIe siècle* (Paris: Hachette littérature, 1973).

Boone, Annie, 'Subordination, subordonnées et subordonnants', *Documents pour l'Histoire du Français Langue Etrangère ou Seconde*, 29 (2002), 11–25.

Calas, Frédéric & Dominique-Rita Charbonneau, *Méthode du commentaire stylistique* (Paris: Nathan, 2000).

Chamayou, Anne, *L'esprit de la lettre: XVIIIe siècle* (Perspectives littéraires; Paris: Presses universitaires de France, 1999).

Chartier, Roger, Alain Boureau & Cécile Dauphin, *Correspondence: Models of Letter-Writing from the Middle Ages to the Nineteenth Century*, trans. Christopher Woodall (Oxford: Polity Press, 1997).

Coudreuse, Anne, *Le goût des larmes au XVIIIe siècle* (Écriture; Paris: Presses universitaires de France, 1999).

Craveri, Benedetta, *L'âge de la conversation* (Paris: Gallimard, 2002).

Dauphin, Cécile, *Prête-moi ta plume—les manuels épistolaires au XIXe siècle* (Paris: Kimé, 2000).

Elgenstierna, Gustaf, *Den introducerade svenska adelns ättartavlor*, 9 vols. (Stockholm: Norstedt, 1925–36).

Franskundervisningen i Sverige fram till 1807: undervisningssituationer och lärare (Stockholm: Fören. för svensk undervisningshistoria, Stockholm 1981), also published in French as '*La Française'. Mille et une façons d'apprendre le français en Suède avant 1807* (Acta Universitatis Upsaliensis. Uppsala Studies in Education, 41; Uppsala: Textgruppen, 1992).

Fromilhague, Catherine & Anne Sancier-Château, *Introduction à l'analyse stylistique* (Collection Lettres supérieures; Paris: Dunod, 1996).

Gardes-Tamine, Joëlle, *La Stylistique* (Paris: Colin 1997).

Grevisse, Maurice, *Le bon usage: grammaire française* (9th edn., Gembloux: Duculot, 1969; 12th edn., Paris: Duculot, 1986).

Hammar, Elisabet, *L'enseignement du français en Suède jusqu'en 1807: méthodes et manuels* (Stockholm: Akademilitt., 1980).

Hedvig Elisabeth Charlotta, *Hedvig Elisabeth Charlottas dagbok*, trans. Carl Carlson Bonde, 9 vols. (Stockholm: Norstedt, 1902–1942).

Leijonhufvud, Sigrid, *Omkring Carl Gustaf Tessin*, 2 vols. (Stockholm: Norstedt, 1917–18).

Mansén, Elisabeth, *Ett paradis på jorden: om den svenska kurortskulturen 1680–1880* (Stockholm: Atlantis, 2001).

Roche, Daniel, *La culture des apparences: une histoire du vêtement, XVIIe–XVIIIe siècle* (Paris: Fayard, 1989).

Silver, Marie-France & Marie-Laure Girou Swiderski, *Femmes en toutes lettres: les épistolières du XVIIIe siècle* (Studies on Voltaire and the eighteenth century 2000:04; Oxford: Voltaire Foundation, 2000).

Stolz, Claire, *Initiation à la linguistique* (Paris: Ellipses, 1999).

Tableaux de Paris et de la cour de France 1739–1742: lettres inédites de Carl Gustaf, comte de Tessin, ed. Gunnar von Proschwitz (Romanica Gothoburgensia 22; Gothenburg: Acta Universitatis Gothoburgensis, 1983).

Tessin, Carl Gustaf, *Carl Gustaf Tessins Skräplåda: Åkerödagboken, förd året 1757* (Stockholm: Tempera, 1985).

CHAPTER 6

English letters from the long eighteenth century

Lena Olsson

The material

The English epistolary corpus used in this study is based solely on letters available in published collections and does not include transcribed manuscript letters. The selected writers were primarily representatives of the cultural and artistic, rather than the social, elite, even if most of them also came from privileged backgrounds. A majority were published authors, and it may be argued that their approach to letter-writing was more 'literary', meaning more creative, both linguistically and stylistically, than was that of their contemporaries from similar socio-economic backgrounds. It can therefore be expected that a large number of literary features will be characteristic of the English texts.

In agreement with the general guidelines set out for the 'Women's language' project as a whole, the English corpus is made up of 300 letters written by ten women and five men. The writers came from England, Scotland, and Wales, and were born between 1689 and 1775. All wrote mainly in English, and, even though some corresponded in French and Italian as well, only English-language letters have been included in the corpus. The female letter-writers are Jane Austen, Joanna Baillie, Frances Boscawen, Frances (Fanny) Burney, Sarah Harriet Burney, Elizabeth Lady Melbourne, Hester Lynch Piozzi, Mary Wollstonecraft, Lady Mary Wortley Montagu, and Dorothy Wordsworth; the male writers are James Boswell, David Garrick, Samuel Johnson, Alexander Pope, and Horace Walpole.

Table 5.1 Size and composition of the various Subproject 5 corpora.

Corpus	FF	FM	MF	MM	M
Number of letters	129	121	25	25	171
Number of words	61,563	52,085	12,604	13,129	77,818
Average number of words per letter[1]	477	430	504	525	—

In addition to the basic requirements of the project as a whole, a number of considerations were taken into account when selecting texts to be included in the English study. This is partly due to the socio-cultural background of eighteenth-century Britain, but it also reflects purely practical considerations. The following criteria were applied, listed roughly in order of precedence:

- The letters should be available in published editions.
- The letters should be available in modern critical editions, or in reasonably sound older editions; above all, the letters should not have been shortened or censored.
- It should be possible to select for each correspondent the required number of letters (twenty-five for women, ten for men), of which half should be addressed to men and half to women.
- The letters should have been written in the period 1700–1820.
- The correspondents should, as far as is possible, include people from different backgrounds and geographical locations, and with differing socio-economic status, creeds, and ideologies.
- The letters of each correspondent should be taken from as broad a time frame as possible.
- The recipients of each correspondent's letters should be as diverse as possible, so that no more than three letters to the same person are included.
- Very short and very long letters should be avoided.
- The selection of each correspondent's letters should ideally mirror his or her scope as a letter-writer with respect to emotional involvement, subjects discussed, style, degree of familiarity, and so on.
- The letters should be chosen with their potential for a literary analysis in mind.

Survey of statistically significant differences in Subproject 5

The statistically significant differences that emerged in the present study between the group FF (women writing to women) and M (the composite group of all other letter-writers) are summarized in Table 5.2.

Table 5.2 Survey of the statistically significant differences in Subproject 5.

Variable	FF < / >	Statistical significance
Text variables		
Subject matter		
Social life	FF > M	***
Travelling	FF > M	**
Nature	FF > M	**
Opinions about people	FF > M	***
Sender–receiver	FF < M	*
Stylistic variables		
Tropes	FF < M	*
Metaphors	FF < M	***
Other rhetorical figures	FF > M	*
Allusion	FF > M	**
Code-switching	FF > M	*

Linguistic and rhetorical variables

As can be seen from Table 5.2, a number of features are more commonly found in women's letters to women than in the letters of the composite group. What this might indicate is difficult to judge, however, and it is important to note that any interpretation must needs be very speculative and that more research is necessary before firm theories can be formulated. Many of the results of the analysis appear to lack consistency and in some cases are downright contradictory. The results of this project can neither verify nor falsify the idea that there is a separate female linguistic space in the eighteenth-century familiar letter.

Bearing this in mind, some statistically significant indications can be discerned. On the level of topics, the writers in the M group discussed the relationship between sender and recipient more often than those in the FF group, although the significance of this is only weak. On the other hand, the women in the FF group discuss to a greater extent such topics as social life, travelling, Nature, and opinions about people, the statistical significance of which is strong to medium. Social life and opinions about people are, of course, two topics that feature prominently in traditional ideas about feminine 'gossip', and the incidence of these subjects is statistically strong. This may perhaps indicate that women adhered to socially accepted ideas about what they were supposed to talk about among themselves. However, travelling and Nature do not necessarily carry such cultural baggage, and the reason for the greater incidence of these subjects in the correspondence between women can only be guessed at. On the other hand, there are topics that could be expected to yield statistical differences between the M and FF groups but which do not, for instance that of obstetrics. Because childbirth was such an exclusively female concern in the eighteenth century, despite the growing propensity of especially the higher classes to employ man-midwives,[2] this topic could be expected to show up to a far greater degree in the FF group, but this is not the case. Neither the writers in the M nor those in the FF group mention childbirth particularly often, making it one of the rarest letter topic variables. The reason for this, however, is simple: none of the men had children at the time when they wrote the letters included in the corpus,[3] and many of the women never married, and never had any personal experience of childbirth. Furthermore, several of the women who did marry had very few children—Lady Mary Wortley Montagu had two, Frances (Fanny) Burney one, and Mary Wollstonecraft two—whereas the letters of Hester Piozzi, who had twelve children, were written after she was past childbearing age.[4] It is also possible that women found obstetrics too intimate or immodest a topic to put in a letter (which, in addition, might eventually be published). The exception to this is Mary Wollstonecraft, who was unusually outspoken for someone of her time—a woman in particular. All in all, the results may at best indicate that women to some extent obeyed social dictates about suitable topics when writing their letters, but they also show that individual circumstances, such as the unusually low number of children born to the women in the corpus, may have significantly affected the statistical analysis. A different choice of correspondents might have given a very different outcome.

The results of the analysis also show that the writers in the FF group code-switch more frequently than those in the M group. Because French is the most commonly used foreign language in the corpus, this phenomenon is perhaps explained by the low status of code-switching between English and French, and its connotations of effeminacy and artificiality: French, as has been shown by Michèle Cohen, was commonly believed to 'Debase, not Advance, our Native and Masculine Tongue'.[5] It was in most cases the only foreign language that women were permitted to learn, and thus using French in a letter may have been a way of displaying one of the few intellectual accomplishments permitted to women. However, it is important to note that this variable only has weak statistical significance. The result may be affected by one or two individual authors, for instance Frances Boscawen, who was unusually fond of using French in her letters.

Among the stylistic variables, the writers in the FF group use fewer tropes and metaphors, and more allusions and *Other rhetorical figures*, than those in the M group.[6] In the case of tropes and *Other rhetorical figures* the statistical significance is weak, whereas it is medium for allusions and strong for metaphors. It is difficult to say what this might indicate. Considering the poor educational opportunities for women in the eighteenth century, it would have been unsurprising to find a presumptive female linguistic space that was simpler and less rhetorically refined. This is, indeed, indicated by the high incidence of tropes and, especially, metaphors in the M group, but other rhetorical variables do not show any difference between M and FF, and allusions and *Other rhetorical figures* are in fact used more often by the writers in the FF group. Perhaps the contradictory results stem from the unusually high level of education of the women in the corpus, and from their extremely anomalous linguistic sophistication, which was a result of their positions as authors and cultural personalities. On the other hand, it is also possible that the absence of any unequivocal conclusion simply indicates that no specific discernible female cultural or linguistic space exists in the language of English eighteenth-century letters.

Summary

The present study has resulted in a number of indications that deserve further investigation involving more extensive source material and a larger and more varied corpus. Some of these indications, such as the more frequent use of metaphors by the M group, the higher incidence of discussions about social life in letters among women, and the greater propensity of women to give opinions about other people when writing to other women, are strong enough that it is possible that they may point to general trends in the eighteenth-century familiar letter. If this is the case, then these trends are hardly surprising: they are the effect of men's better educational opportunities, and of the separate spheres that shape the behaviour and actions of both men and women in a patriarchal society. However, there are also results that do not support these conclusions, and the impression is one of ambiguity rather than of clear indications. As trends, the results are far too few and contradictory to support the idea that there was an exclusively female cultural realm which was given voice in the linguistic and rhetorical choices made in the eighteenth-century familiar letter. The premise tested in this project must therefore be considered to be unsupported by the evidence contained in results of the analysis of the English corpus.

Notes

1 The average number of words per letter refers only to the letters included in the current corpus and should in no way be taken as an indication of the average length of English letters in the eighteenth century.

2 This cultural shift has been discussed by numerous historians; see, for example, Angus Wilson, *The Making of Man-Midwifery: Childbirth in England, 1660–1770* (Cambridge, Mass.: Harvard University Press, 1995).

3 James Boswell eventually had children, but the letters chosen from Boswell's correspondence were all written before his marriage to Margaret Montgomerie in November 1769. Elizabeth Porter had had three children when she married Dr Johnson in 1735, but they were already aged between nine and twenty at the time, and they had long since left home by the time Johnson wrote the letters included in this corpus. Alexander Pope, David Garrick, and Horace Walpole were childless.

4 This refers to the letters she wrote after her marriage to Gabriel Piozzi; as Mrs Thrale she also corresponded extensively, but these letters have never been collected in a comprehensive modern edition.

5 Charles Gildon and John Brightland, *A Grammar of the English Tongue* (1711), quoted in Michèle Cohen, *Fashioning Masculinity: National Identity and Language in the Eighteenth Century* (London: Routledge, 1996), 39. At the same time, French was the language of refinement, and the knowledge of it was thought indispensable for a polite gentleman. The problem was to achieve this elegance without risking being emasculated, as French men were believed to be because of their alleged volubility and preference for the company of women; see Cohen 1996, in particular 38–41.

6 Tropes include the rhetorical variables prosopopœia, euphemism, hyperbole, simile, metaphor, and metonymy; *Other rhetorical figures* includes allusions, anaphoras, antitheses, aposiopeses, irony, litoteses, puns, paradoxes, parallelisms, rhetorical questions, climaxes, and symbols.

Bibliography

Cohen, Michèle, *Fashioning Masculinity: National Identity and Language in the Eighteenth Century* (London: Routledge, 1996).

Gildon Charles and John Brightland, *A Grammar of the English Tongue* (1711), in Cohen 1996.

Wilson, Angus, *The Making of Man-Midwifery: Childbirth in England, 1660–1770* (Cambridge, Mass.: Harvard University Press, 1995).

CHAPTER 7

German letters
in the eighteenth century

Jon Helgason

The material

This subproject includes 274 letters distributed among fourteen letter-writers. The female writers are nine in number, the male writers five. A detailed list of letters can be found in the letter list given in the Appendix 3. The size and composition of the various constituent corpora are presented in Table 6.1.

Table 6.1 Size and composition of the various Subproject 6 corpora.

Corpus	FF	FM	MF	MM	M
Number of letters	108	116	25	25	166
Number of words	73,811	61,191	13,510	12,322	87,023

The number of words in the total corpus is, as the table shows, around 160,000. The letters are, mainly for practical reasons, taken from printed letter collections. As far as has been possible, newer, annotated editions have been used. In order to facilitate comparison, the orthography of the letters has been normalized after the letters were transcribed. When collecting the material, the requirements that the writer should have written more than ten letters, and that the recipients should be evenly distributed between the sexes, have been taken into consideration. Efforts have been made to achieve an even distribution of the material over the entire eighteenth century. Despite this, there is a certain predominance of letters from the later half of the century. The reason for this is mainly the rise of letter-writing between 1750–1800, which will be discussed below when considering the development of the letter genre in Germany during the eighteenth century.

The social background of the letter-writers in Subproject 6 was relatively homogenous. Apart from one or two exceptions, the writers represent a group of intellectually and culturally prominent individuals from the upper middle class. In many cases, the letter-writers were part of the same social network. The most evident exception to this is a member of the high nobility, Elizabeth Charlotte, Princess Palatine (Liselotte von der Pfalz) (1652–1722), who as the wife of the Duke of Orléans spent the greater part of her life at the French royal court at Versailles. The educational level among the letter-writers was generally high or very high, in spite of the fact that the female writers did not have access to formal education. The language of the letters and the subjects they address to a certain extent reflect the high educational level of the letter-writers.

In the following commentary on the statistical analysis, I have outlined the most substantial findings from this subproject. To a limited extent, it has been necessary deviate from the common method of the project, and when relevant, an account of these deviations is provided under the appropriate heading. The commentary is followed by an analytical section that offers a brief history of the letter genre in Germany and an outline of linguistic research that may further broaden our understanding of the results of Subproject 6.

Survey of statistically significant differences in Subproject 6

The analysis has identified a number of statistically significant differences between FF and the other constituent corpora, the most prominent of which will be discussed here. All results refer to a comparison with the FF corpus. In each comparison between the FF corpus and another corpus, inequality signs are used to indicate whether the frequency of the FF corpus is greater than (>) or less than (<) the corpus to which it is compared. The strength of the statistical significance has been graded, so that one asterisk (*) signifies a low statistical significance, two (**) signify a medium statistical significance, and three (***) signify a high statistical significance.

Table 6.2 Survey of the statistically significant differences in Subproject 6

Variable	FF < / >	Degree of significance
Textual level		
Addressing the reader	FF < FM	***
	FF < M	***
Topics		
Fabrics and clothes	FF > FM	*
	FF > M	**
The body	FF > FM	**
	FF > M	**
Social life	FF > FM	***
	FF > M	***
Education, wit, learning	FF < FM	*
	FF < M	*
The relationship between letter-writer and recipient	FF < FM	*
Syntactic level		
Number of words per macro-syntagm	FF < FM	***
	FF < M	***
SCC per macrosyntagm	FF < FM	*
	FF < M	**
SCC/CP0	FF < FM	*
	FF < M	**
SCC1 per macrosyntagm	FF < M	*
SCC2 per macrosyntagm	FF < FM	**
	FF < M	***
Embedded macrosyntagms	FF < FM	*
	FF < M	**
Irregular macrosyntagms	FF > FM	*
	FF > M	**
Lexical level		
Total number of tropes	FF < FM	**
	FF < M	**
Metaphors	FF < FM	**
	FF < M	***
Code-switching	FF > FM	**
	FF > M	***

Variables on the textual level
Addressing the reader

Considering the central importance of the conversational metaphor in eighteenth-century letter theory, it was reasonable to expect to find a relatively large number of instances of address in the letters. Many take conventional forms of the type 'dear friend', and these and other ways of addressing the reader, such as exclamations, vocatives, questions, and forms of address are possibly the clearest indications of the inherent dialogic nature of the letter. Instances of address, defined in this way, are clear indications of the rhetorical or stylistic construction of personal address.

The data from Subproject 6 show that there is a difference of high statistical significance between how women use the address function when writing to other women than when writing to men. It is interesting to note that both the FM and the M corpora contain more instances of address per macrosyntagm than does the FF corpus. Intuitively, this result is surprising because the address function, in its guise as an indicator of intimacy, is part of the description of the letter as a typically female genre, yet of the four constituent corpora it is the MM corpus in which the address function appears most often.

One possible explanation for this is that in formal letters, especially to a social superior, the instances of address are more formal, thus making the sheer number of instances of address rather unreliable indicators of intimacy. The result can also be seen as a form of linguistic accommodation to what was perceived as a female literary style. According to this interpretation, male writers tend towards what was perceived as the stylistic ideal at the time—the supposed 'naturalness' of female writing.[1] The fact that the male writers use this stylistic feature to an even greater degree than the female writers can be seen as a form of hypercorrection, in which men reveal themselves as unconfident and self-conscious letter-writers. This, however, highlights another phenomenon that is displayed in the corpus as a whole: the nature and function of address clearly change over the course of the eighteenth century. In the letters of Elizabeth Charlotte, Princess Palatine, there are instances of address that appear to be conventional and rhetorically 'empty'.

Ach, liebe Louise, wie weit bin ich von ma tante selig Tugenden und Verstand! Ach nein, in dieser Welt ist I. L. selig nichts zu vergleichen. Mein Gott, liebe Louise, wie kann ich mich unmöglich von diesem Unglück wieder erholen?[2]

The stylistic devices she uses are exclamatives, vocatives, and questions.

Her letters, written at the beginning of the eighteenth century, can be compared to the letters of the Jewish intellectual Rahel Varnhagen, written around the turn of the nineteenth century:

Haben Sie sich dumm gemacht? Schliefen Sie? brachen Sie? Ich aber, diesen Morgen. Es war mir recht lieb—Muskeln u. Nerven waren so bepackt, daß es bis zu Schmerzen ging; die jedoch keinen Ort hatten. Und nichts entschüttelt so plötzlich u. heilsam, wenn es nicht ausartet. Ich schicke Ihnen ein bißchen vinaigre des 4 volleurs. Er ist mild u. aufweckend, u. hat durchaus nicht das Überreizende der anderen Mittel aus seiner Klasse. Sein Sie nicht zu dankbar.[3]

Varnhagen uses largely the same kind of stylistic devices, but hers, far more than Elizabeth Charlotte's, seem to be tied to the potentially dialogic nature of the letter. Varnhagen thereby achieves a considerably more personal and direct tone in her terms of address.

Topics

In Subproject 6, only three topics per letter have been registered. The relative importance of the topics in a letter was thus gauged in the very process of registering the data. A few of the topics can only be found very rarely or not at all (*Sensory impressions* and *Fictionalization*).

Other topics can be found in up to 50 per cent of the letters. In the FF corpus, *Opinions about people*, can be found in 57 per cent of the letters; the same subject appears in 48 per cent of the letters in the M corpus. In both the FF and the M corpora *The emotional life of the self and others* is popular (42 and 43 per cent respectively). It is well known that one of the functions of the familiar letter is to uphold personal and social relationships. This is evident not least in the topic *The relationship between sender and recipient*, which can be found in 37 per cent of the letters in the FF corpus. This subject is even more common in the M corpus, where it occurs in 46 per cent of the letters.

A stylistically interesting topic, *Metacomments*, is also relatively common both in the FF and the M corpora: 15.5 per cent and 25 per cent, respectively. The topic *Metacomments* refers to those occasions when the letter-writer comments on, in one way or another, the letter-writing situation or letter-writing as an activity.

Of the topics that are most interesting stylistically speaking, there is only one regarding which a statistically significant difference can be found—*The relationship between letter-writer and recipient.* Other statistically significant differences regarding topics concern, *Fabrics and clothes*; *The body*; *Social life*; and *Education, wit, and learning.* *Social life* is the only topic where there is a difference of high statistical significance between the FF and M corpora.

The analysis shows that there seem to be some generally gender-specific topics. The topics that might be expected to be typical of female experience in eighteenth-century Germany, such as *Fabrics and clothes*, *Social life*, and *The body*, live up to their traditional gender categorization by being more common in letters written by women. *Education, wit, and learning* is more common in letters written by and/ or to men, that is to say in the M corpus. It is also interesting to note that the letter-writers of the M corpus display a greater propensity for the topic *The relationship between writer and recipient.* In the four constituent corpora FF, FM, MF, and MM this topic occurs in 51 per cent of the FM letters (37 per cent of FF, 36 per cent of MF, and 32 per cent of MM). The reason for this must be sought not only in the possible existence of romantic undertones in letters between female writers and male recipients in particular, but also in the context of the moral and social codes of the time.[4]

Variables on the syntactic level

Some of the variables on the syntactic level that were found to be statistically significant may be seen as indications of the syntactic complexity in each of the constituent corpora. For example, this is true of the variables *Number of words per macrosyntagm, Number of subordinate clauses and clause equivalents per macrosyntagm, Number of subordinate clauses and phrases per number of clauses and clause equivalents on the 0 level*, and *The number of embedded macrosyntagms.* The values of these variables unambiguously point to a lower degree of syntactic complexity in the FF corpus compared to the other constituent corpora.

Embedded macrosyntagms

Embedded macrosyntagms may be seen as indicators of intimacy. According to classical rhetoric, embedded macrosyntagms help create an impression of liveliness and spontaneity. The variable *Embedded macrosyntagms* thus includes phrases of address, interjectional phrases, and parenthetically inserted utterances. The number of embedded macrosyntagms is fewer in the FF constituent corpus compared to the other constituent corpora; again an unexpected result, because spontaneity and liveliness were qualities commonly attributed to female writers in the eighteenth century. It is possible that the answer lies in the fact that this particular stylistic device originates in classical rhetoric, and for that reason is more commonly used by male writers. This also leads to the tentative inference that the female 'naturalness' of the day was constructed from other linguistic elements, such as a less careful structure of the letters (a form of anacolutha at a syntactical level), shorter and more irregular macrosyntagms, and so on, in order to rhetorically construct a display of excitement, eagerness, and confusion.

Irregular macrosyntagms

The number of irregular macrosyntagms is highest in the FF corpus. When looking at four corpora, the value of the MM corpus is the lowest.

Variables on the lexical level

Tropes/metaphors

The statistical analysis of tropes and metaphors indicates that the gender of the recipient may have been of some importance. Compared to the FF corpus, the total M corpus displays a statistically significant higher frequency of the total number of tropes/metaphors. The results concerning particular tropes in isolation are inconclusive, however, and/or do not display significant statistical differences.

Length of words

No statistical analysis of the length of words in the constituent corpora has been conducted. Within German studies and in German stylistics, no importance is attached to the length of words when analysing texts (see also p. 40).

Code-switching

Code-switching is rare in the total German letter corpus. An overwhelming majority of the examples of code-switching in the total letter corpus are from German into French. Normally, this code-switching is done at phrase level. The position of French as the dominant cultural language in eighteenth-century Europe, not least thanks to the French epistolary tradition, can also be seen in the foreign words that occur in the letters. The vast majority of these foreign words are French. There are also rare occurrences of foreign words in, or code-switching to and from, English, Italian, Latin, and Greek, mostly at phrase level.

The French female epistolary tradition (Madame de Sévigné, Ninon de Lenclos, and Madame de Graffigny) may also have been an important contributing factor in the fact that the writers in the FF corpus—more than those in the M corpus—use foreign words and code-switching as a stylistic device. A writer can of course be both aware and unaware of this kind of influence.

Summary

In the table of statistically significant differences (Table 6.2), several such differences between FF and the other corpora can be seen. These differences between FF and M do not provide an unambiguous answer to the main enquiry of the project—the existence of a specifically female style of writing or a female cultural sphere. Elaine Showalter's hypothesis regarding the existence of an exclusively female culture can thus be neither confirmed nor rejected on the basis of the findings of Subproject 6. On the other hand, it is the case that in the material analysed, specific differences can be discerned between men's letter-writing and women's. In most cases, these differences can be explained by the existence of social and cultural factors in which gender is an important variable.

There is a striking difference of high statistical significance in the use of instances of address, for the results indicate that the letter corpora that include a male writer or recipient contain more instances of address. The results could possibly be strengthened by a qualitative study of the examples of address, analysing them along the axis formal–informal.

However, some cautious conclusions may be drawn. It seems reasonable to explain the differences on the syntactic level by the fact that men and women attained highly divergent levels of education in the eighteenth century. If variables such as the *Number of words per macrosyntagm*, the *Number of subordinate clauses and clause equivalents per macrosyntagm*, *Embedded and irregular macrosyntagms*, and other presumed syntactical complexities are interpreted as illustrating differences in the writers' educational levels, one finds in this material a difference of high statistical significance in the number of words per macrosyntagm. Differences in the number of subordinate clauses and clause equivalents per macrosyntagm, the degrees of subordination, and embedded and irregular macrosyntagms can also be found, with varying statistical significance, between the two large corpora of FF and M.

Women, letters, and linguistic change

One of the difficulties encountered in an investigation such as this is the lack of other, comparable, studies. It is thus only in exceptional cases that the quantitative data that have emerged in the present project can be compared to other studies in order to confirm or reject certain conclusions; most of this data must, for the time being, remain uncontested. Yet this is not to suggest that the conclusions that can be drawn cannot be explained, or that their reliability cannot be verified in other ways.

In Subproject 6, 'German letters in the eighteenth century', some of the data that has been uncovered may well reflect the development of the letter and the letter genre in the German language area during the eighteenth century. I am also of the opinion that the data could be used in a more thorough discussion about the development of the letter genre than can be provided here. It should be possible to relate the results derived from certain stages of the study to the well-documented, generic and stylistic development of the letter during the eighteenth century.[5] For example, there may well be detectable differences between letters written at the beginning of the eighteenth century and letters written at the close of the same century; however, such differences would have to be sufficiently evident that they cannot be interpreted as merely individual anomalies and idiosyncrasies. In addition, as has previously been suggested, it should be possible to tentatively compare the data of the present subproject to some of the other subprojects of 'Women's language', for instance the letters in Swedish (Subprojects 2 & 4), in order to test individual hypotheses.

The German language uses much the same syntactical and grammatical devices as does Swedish: the languages have a number of similarities regarding word endings, word order, function words, and congruency, to name a few.[6] In German, commas are often put between all the constituent clauses of a sentence. Subordinate clauses, such as relative clauses and *that* clauses, are added one after the other in written German sentences. Such comparisons may be justified further because it is possible to surmise that a similar generic and stylistic development took place in Sweden, albeit somewhat later than Germany. It is my impression that the real breakthrough of the so-called familiar letter occurred towards the end of the eighteenth century in Sweden, some decades later than in Germany.

The reasons for the 'rebirth' of the letter genre in eighteenth century Germany were numerous. The breakthrough was of course facilitated by infrastructural developments that made an improved, reliable, and affordable postal service possible. From a linguistic and stylistic standpoint, women played an important part in the renewal of the letter genre, one that before the mid eighteenth century was plagued by the 'Kanzleistil'—the formal, official civil service writing style. That said, the results of Subproject 6 can be further explained by relating them to theories of linguistic change, which would leave them indications of a linguistic and stylistic change in progress. It is my belief that by juxtaposing linguistic theory, in particular theories concerning gender, linguistic change, and the history of the letter genre in eighteenth century, some of the results can be explained and at least partially corroborated.

For instance, the occurrence of the personal pronoun 'I' in the constituent corpora is an example of how the history of the letter genre can be used to explain certain phenomena in the constituent corpora. It is well known that the word 'I'—'ich' in German—occurs very rarely in the 'Kanzleistil' of the seventeenth and early eighteenth centuries. In the concordances compiled for the various constituent corpora in Subproject 6, it is clear that the word 'ich' is the most common word. In the FF corpus, the three most commonly occurring words are 'ich', 'und', and 'die', while in the FM corpus they are 'ich', 'und', and 'sie'. These words recur in the MF and MM corpora, where the most common words are 'ich', 'und', and 'sie', and 'ich', 'und', and 'die', respectively. This development hints at the general historical trend during the eighteenth century towards individualism and the modes of expression available to communicate this individualism.[7]

Letters and linguistic change

In many eighteenth-century German letter manuals, the letter was held up as a genre particularly well suited for a female way of writing. Women were considered better letter-writers because they were unencumbered by the heritage of classical rhetoric;[8] supposedly more natural, more spontaneous in their style of communication, they were thought more successful in mimicking the conversational ideal of the eighteenth-century 'Privatbrief'. The feminine ideal was recognized and encouraged in epistolary theory and in letter manuals of the time. By comparison, in a traditional, historical point of view, the letter in Germany has been seen as a relatively free, non-canonized genre that, because of women's supposedly natural propensity for letter-writing, facilitated female participation in the literary field. The letter genre was the primary field of literary expression available to women in eighteenth-century Germany. This explanation has been severely criticized, however. The German literary historian Silvia Bovenschen, in her classic study *Die imaginierte Weiblichkeit*, sees the letter genre as a mode of literary expression into which women's writing was funnelled, while at the same time the identification of the letter as a female mode of expression became a strait jacket—a way of marginalizing women's writing and keeping women writers out of (or at least delaying their entrance into) the literary canon.[9]

Interestingly, the enforcement and realization of such a 'feminine ideal' correspond to the findings of modern research on linguistic change, where women seem to be more innovative than men with regard to non-stigmatized changes.[10] William Labov's explanation of this so-called 'gender paradox'—that women 'conform more closely than men to sociolinguistic norms that are overtly prescribed, but conform less than men when they are not'—is multicausal.[11] Labov sees women's greater concern for ensuring the social mobility of their children as a key motivating factor for this. And Bovenschen's critique appears, in fact, to be an object lesson in the application of the 'Androcentric Rule', introduced by the gender linguist Jennifer Coates, which states that 'Men will be seen to behave linguistically in a way that fits the writer's view of what is desirable or admirable; women on the other hand will be blamed for any linguistic state or development which is regarded by the writer as negative or reprehensible'.[12] In this view, the letter genre served as a safety valve, being a mode of expression that could do no harm to 'high literature'.

In his research, Labov tried to answer the question, 'Who are the leaders of linguistic change?' and he came to the conclusion that 'The leaders of linguistic change are not individual inventors of some form, but rather those who, by reason of their social histories and patterns of behavior, will advance the ongoing change most strongly'.[13] The 'leaders', according to Labov, are women with a wide social network, who are upwardly mobile, who in their teens display non-standard social and linguistic behaviour, and who develop and retain certain linguistic traits even as they move up the social scale. Based on Labov's and others' research, the Scottish feminist linguist Deborah Cameron has summarized certain principles pertaining to women and linguistic change.

Principle I: For stable sociolinguistic variables (i.e., those not involved in change), men use a higher frequency of nonstandard forms than women.

Principle Ia: In change from above (i.e., where speakers are conscious of the existence and social meaning of competing variants), women favor the incoming prestige form more than men.

Principle II: In change from below (i.e., where speakers are not conscious that change is occurring), women are most often the innovators.[14]

According to Cameron, the use of linguistic variables is arguably the most important way available to women of to assert identity and group membership.[15]

One of the primary explanations of the supposed difference between men's and women's letter-writing in eighteenth-century Germany has been the women writers' lack of formal education. The field of stylistic analysis has proved itself capable of detecting significant linguistic variables that mirror complexity and general levels of education. For instance, Hellspong and Ledin believe that a text can have a 'light' or a 'heavy' style.[16] Important indications of whether a text should be classified as 'light' or 'heavy' are, among other things, the degree of grammatical–syntactical complexity, sentence length, clarity, and how comprehensive or concentrated a text is. Many of these linguistic variables occur on the syntactical level and can help explain some of the statistically significant findings of this subproject.

The development of the letter genre in Germany

In Germany, probably more than in any other European country, it was obvious that the letter genre in all essentials was an expression of the ideas of the Enlightenment, and that it was therefore intimately connected, not just historically, but also ideologically, to the cultural processes of the Enlightenment. The Enlightenment is here primarily regarded as an historical change in 'man's relation to the present, man's historical mode of being, and the constitution of the self as an autonomous subject'.[17] This change affected political and social existence as we know it. In part, the reason for this connection between the letter and the historical process of the Enlightenment is the importance of the letter genre in public life. The letter played the same role in Germany during the Enlightenment as the essay did in France and England in the same period:[18] the letter functioned as a relatively free forum of public cultural debate where opinions on politics, art, and society could be discussed openly. In the same way as the letter genre left its mark on public life, it also had if anything an even greater impact on the private sphere. It is an undisputed fact that in Germany the stylistic ideal of the letter genre towards the mid eighteenth century was shaped by the values of the middle class. 'Good taste' was the guiding principle of the new stylistic ideal. The qualities required of a letter-writer were decency and naturalness. This morality-based aesthetic resulted in a shift from a common, fixed, stylistic ideal to one based on the individual and/or social class. This made the letter a genre which, on the face of it, appeared to have no regulations, but whose implicit rules were clearly derived from middle-class notions of morality, friendship, love, and propriety. In this sense, this new ideal was as normative as the previous one.

The year 1751 is commonly considered the defining moment in German letter culture. No fewer than three separate letter-writing manuals were published that year: Johann Christoph Stockhausen's *Grundsätze wohleingerichtete Briefe*, Johann Wilhelm Schaubert's *Regelmässigen Abfassung Teuscher Briefe*, and Christian Fürchtegott Gellert's *Briefe, nebst einer Praktischen Abhandlung von dem guten Geschmacke in Briefen*. The last of these works had the greatest influence, due to Gellert's considerable popularity among his contemporaries. In the manual, Gellert discusses the letter genre at length, using illustrative examples of what he considers to be worthy of imitation and what he considers objectionable. A few are submitted to proper, close readings. At the heart of his argument is the idea of epistolary correspondence as conversation—a central topos in letter theory since antiquity.[19] In Gellert's words, the letter should be 'eine freye Nachahmung des guten Gesprächs',[20] a choice of wording that simultaneously implies a departure from a normative, rule-based poetics (free imitation) and the introduction of a normative element of a different kind (the good conversation). The letter as such should not imitate to the full the quotidian nature of conversation, but should be modelled stylistically on refined verbal exchange:

> Ein Brief ist kein ordentliches Gespräch; es wird also in einem Briefe nicht alles erlaubt seyn, was im Umgange erlaubt ist. Aber er vertritt doch die Stelle einer mündlichen Rede, und deswegen muß er sich der Art zu denken und zu reden, die in Gesprächen herrscht, mehr nähern, als einer sorgfältigen und geputzten Schreibart.[21]

The so-called 'Kanzleistil', and thus normative, rule-based poetics, were condemned. From the perspective of genre, Gellert saw the letter both as a historical document and a literary prose form that was closely related to the oral tale.[22] The literary potential of letters was a genuine possibility for Gellert: 'Selbst wenn sie [the letter] prosaisch ist, bleibt sie noch allezeit auf gewisse Weise eine Art der Poesie.'[23] The letter, Gellert believed, should be characterized by naturalness, clarity, and simplicity. The first quality in particular, naturalness, was elevated to a governing stylistic principle.

One reason contributing to the success of Gellert's letter doctrine was that it expressed a middle-class, emancipatory aesthetics. This is primarily reflected in Gellert's notion of 'good taste'. In his letter doctrine, this category was expanded to include not just aesthetic but also moral qualities. Thus, the letter-writer's aesthetic sensibility as well as his or her moral qualities are manifested in a well-written letter. For example, Luise Kulmus, the future wife of the author Johann Christoph Gottsched, writes in one of the letters examined in the present project, 'Der ungekünstelte Ton ... ist der Dolmetscher Ihres guten und noch unverdorbenen Herzens'.[24] Evidently, Gellert's letter theory can be regarded as symptomatic of the paradigmatic change in 'the codification of intimacy' and the rhetorical construction of 'true feeling', described by German sociologist Niklas Luhmann.[25]

In the letter manuals published in the mid eighteenth century it was often emphasized that the letter was considered to be a 'female' genre and that women wrote better, more natural letters than did men, whose letters were encumbered by a rhetorical, scholarly heritage. Naturalness, the central concept in the letter genre, was thus connected to women and to what was seen as a typically female manner of expression. In one of Gellert's many letters addressed to female recipients he writes, among other things:

Ich hatte kurz vorher, als ich heute Ihren gütigen Brief erhielt, verschiedne Briefe und Übersetzungen von jungen Herren durchgelesen und verbessert. Ach, rief ich, da ich den Ihrigen gelesen, warum schreiben doch die jungen Herren nicht so, wie dieses Fräulein! so dürftest du nichts tun, als lesen und loben u. dich über ihre Geschicklichkeit erfreuen. Die bösen jungen Herren! und das gute junge Fräulein! Warum hat doch Ihr Geschlecht in Ansehung der Briefe so viel Vorzüge vor dem unsrigen? Vermutlich weil sie das Natürliche weniger durch die Kunst verdrängen.[26]

This again suggests that the supposedly 'natural' quality of women's letters included more or less conscious stylistic devices to represent spontaneity, emotion, and rhetorical 'lack of awareness'. The 'female' letter thus contained stylistic features that did not suggest learning and that were not encouraged in classical rhetoric: logical leaps, prolepses, digressions, anacolutha, and the like, typically used to characterize oral communication rather than written texts. Again, some of these stylistic and linguistic differences were found to be statistically significant in the FF and M corpora, particularly on the textual and lexical levels—as was the case for the high number of irregular macrosyntagms in the FF corpus, for example.

The stylistic ideal in eighteenth-century letter-writing was patterned on contemporary ideas of spoken conversation. It is reasonable to assume that this could be seen in the results of this project's analysis of the letters in a far more substantial way than this short survey permits. The lack of other comparable studies is a disadvantage when it comes to investigations of this kind. However, as hinted at more than demonstrated, the material has made it possible to empirically test several of the truisms of eighteenth-century letter theory (as well as those of German literary history) concerning the letter genre in a way that no other study has done. Further study based on the results of Subproject 6 is required.

Notes

1 For accommodation theory, see Howard Giles and Philip Smith 'Accommodation Theory. Optimal Levels of Convergence', in Howard Giles and Robert N. St. Clair (eds.), *Language and Social Psychology* (Oxford: Blackwell, 1979), 45–65.

2 Elizabeth Charlotte, Princess Palatine, to Louise Degenfeld, 1 July 1714, quoted in *Liselotte von der Pfalz: Elisabeth Charlotte, Duchesse d'Orléans, Madame: Briefe*, ed. Annedore Haberl (Munich: Carl Hanser Verlag, 1996). In the quotation the exclamations are in bold print and the instances of address in italics. Questions have been underlined. Translation: 'Oh, my dear Louise, how far I am from the virtue and wisdom of my blessed aunt [Sophia of Hanover, who had died on 8 June 1714]. Oh no, this world has no comparison to Her Grace. My god, dear Louise, how can I ever recover from this misfortune?'

3 Rahel Varnhagen to Rebecca Friedländer, 15 December 1805, quoted in *Briefe an eine Freundin: Rahel Varnhagen an Rebecca Friedländer*, ed. Deborah Hertz (Cologne: Kiepenheuer & Witsch, 1988). Directives are in bold italics. Translation: 'Have you become stupid? Do you sleep? Do you feel sick? I, however, [do] this morning. I kind of liked it—Muscles and nerves were so tense that it was painful, a pain without a point of origin. And, when overcome, nothing passes so suddenly or gives such relief, when it does not worsen. I send you a small bottle of *vinaigre des 4 volleurs* [a herbal antiseptic]. This mixture is mild and invigorating and does not have overexcitement as a side effect, like this substance tends to have. Do not be too grateful'.

4 Claudia Kaiser, 'Geschmack' als Basis der Verständigung: Chr. F. Gellerts Brieftheorie (Europäische Hochschulschriften, Reihe I, Deutsche Sprache und Literatur 1563; Frankfurt am Main: Lang, 1996), 128. Kaiser writes: 'Die Tugend des "Wohlanständigen" basiert auf Regeln des sozialen Umgangs. Unter diesem Aspekt könnte man Gellerts "Praktische Abhandlung" auch als eine Art Anstandslehre für die bürgerliche Korrespondenz, parallel zu der Tradition aristokratischer Anstandslehren, betrachten.' Translation: 'The virtue of highly decent people is based on the rules of social intercourse. This is also true for Gellert's "Praktische Abhandlung", which can be regarded as a kind of manual of good manners for the correspondences of the bourgeoisie that emulates the aristocratic tradition of manuals of good manners'.

5 See, for example, Rafael Arto-Haumacher, *Gellerts Briefpraxis und Brieflehre: der Anfang einer neuen Briefkultur* (Wiesbaden: DUV, Dt. Univ.-Verl., 1995); Rainer Brockmeyer, *Geschichte des deutschen Briefes von Gottsched bis zum Sturm und Drang* (Diss., Münster: 1961); Jon Helgason, *Hjärtats skrifter: en brevkulturs uttryck i korrespondensen mellan Anna Louisa Karsch och Johann Wilhelm Ludwig Gleim* (Diss., Avdelningen för litteraturvetenskap; Lund: Lunds universitet, 2007); Jon Helgason, *Schriften des Herzens. Briefkultur des 18. Jahrhunderts im Briefwechsel zwischen Anna Louisa Karsch und Johann Ludwig Gleim* (Göttingen: Wallstein, 2012); and Reinhard M. Nickisch, *Die Stilprinzipien in den deutschen Briefstellern des 17. und 18. Jahrhunderts: mit einer Bibliographie zur Briefschreiblehre (1474–1800)* (Diss., Palaestra 254, 1966; Göttingen: 1969).

6 See Folke Freund and Birger Sundqvist, *Tysk Grammatik* (3rd edn., Stockholm: Natur och Kultur, 1995), sections 41–60.

7 See Helgason 2007, 82–3.

8 See Reinhard M. Nickisch, 'Die Frau als Briefschreiberin im Zeitalter der deutschen Aufklärung', *Wolfenbütteler Studien zur Aufklärung*, 3 (1976), 29–65, at 55.

9 Silvia Bovenschen, *Die imaginierte Weiblichkeit: exemplarische Untersuchungen zu kulturgeschichtlichen und literarischen Präsentationsformen des Weiblichen* (Frankfurt am Main: Suhrkamp, 1979), 209–11.

10 Margaret A. Maclagan, Elizabeth Gordon, and Gillian Lewis, 'Women and Sound Change: Conservative and Innovative Behavior by the Same Speakers', *Language Variation and Change*, 11 (1999), 19–41.

11 William Labov, *Principles of Linguistic Change*, ii: *Social factors* (Oxford: Blackwell, 2001), 293.

12 Jennifer Coates, *Women, Men and Language* (3rd edn., London: Longman, 2004), 10.

13 Labov 2001, 33–4.

14 Deborah Cameron, 'Gender Issues and Language Change', *Annual Review of Applied Linguistics* 23 (2003), 187–201, at 190. Cameron's summary of Labov is in part based on Sylvie Dubois and Barbara Horvath, 'When the Music Changes, You Change Too: Gender and Language Change in Cajun English', *Language Variation and Change*, 11 (1999), 287–313.

15 Cameron 2003, 191.

16 Lennart Hellspong and Per Ledin, *Vägar genom texten: handbok i brukstextanalys* (Lund: Studentlitteratur, 1997), 200–202. Hellspong and Ledin list among their influences David Crystal and Derek Davy, *Investigating English Style* (London: Longman, 1969); M. A. K. Halliday and Ruqaiya Hasan, *Cohesion in English* (London: Longman, 1976); and works inspired by Halliday such as Michael J. Toolan (ed.), *Language, Text and Context: Essays in Stylistics* (London: Routledge, 1992); and Mohsen Ghadessy (ed.), *Register Analysis: Theory and Practice* (New York: Pinter Publishers, 1993). Ledin and Hellspong 1997, 288–90 also generally recommend the analytical efforts of the periodical *Discourse and Society*.

17 Michel Foucault, 'What is Enlightenment?', in Paul Rabinow (ed.), *The Foucault Reader* (New York: Pantheon Books, 1984), 32–50, at 42.

18 Herta Schwarz, ' "Brieftheorie" in der Romantik', in Angelika Ebrecht, Regina Nörtemann, and Hertha Schwarz (eds.), *Brieftheorie des 18. Jahrhunderts: Texte, Kommentare, Essays* (Stuttgart: J. B. Metzler, 1990), 225–38, esp. 225–6.

19 Helgason 2007, 48–50 & 57–60.

20 Christian Fürchtegott Gellert, *Briefe, nebst einer Praktischen Abhandlung von dem guten Geschmacke in Briefen* (1751), here quoted in Ebrecht, Nörtemann & Schwarz 1990, 56–98, at 61. Translation: 'a free imitation of good conversation'.

21 Ebrecht, Nörtemann & Schwarz 1990, 61. Translation: 'A letter is no proper conversation. Everything that is allowed in human intercourse is not allowed in a letter. However, the letter replaces conversation and must hence approximate the way of thinking and talking that characterizes conversation rather than that of carefully polished prose'.

22 See Ebrecht, Nörtemann & Schwarz 1990, 64.

23 Ebrecht, Nörtemann & Schwarz 1990, 91. Translation: 'The letter can be regarded as a form of poetry, even though the letter itself is prose'.

24 Luise Kulmus to Caroline Gottsched, 4 June 1759, quoted in *Louise Gottsched — 'mit der Feder in der Hand': Briefe aus den Jahren 1730–1762*, ed. Inka Kording (Darmstadt: Wissenschaftliche Buchgesellschaft, 1999). Translation: 'Your unadorned tone of voice is the interpreter of your kind and still innocent heart'.

25 Niklas Luhmann, *Love as Passion: The Codification of Intimacy* (Stanford: SUP, 1998). Luhmann explores the history of the literary coding of love, beginning in the seventeenth century and spanning four centuries. He sees morality as well as love as symbolic generalizations that are culturally, not least linguistically, codified.

26 Christian Fürchtegott Gellert to Johanna Erdmuth von Schönfeld, 25 January 1759, quoted in *C. F. Gellerts Briefwechsel,* ii: *1756–1759,* ed. John F. Reynolds (Berlin: de Gruyter, 1987). Translation: 'Today, just before I received your kind letter, I was reading through and improving a number of letters and translations written by young gentlemen. Oh, I cried out, when I read your letter, why do not the young gentlemen write like this young lady! Then you need not do anything but read and praise and enjoy their skill. Those bad young gentlemen and this lovely young lady! Why has your sex so many advantages when it comes to writing letters, compared to ours? Most likely by repressing nature less through artifice.'

Bibliography

Arto-Haumacher, Rafael, *Gellerts Briefpraxis und Brieflehre: der Anfang einer neuen Briefkultur* (Wiesbaden: DUV, Dt. Univ.-Verl., 1995).

Bovenschen, Silvia, *Die imaginierte Weiblichkeit: exemplarische Untersuchungen zu kulturgeschichtlichen und literarischen Präsentationsformen des Weiblichen* (Frankfurt am Main: Suhrkamp, 1979).

Brockmeyer, Rainer, *Geschichte des deutschen Briefes von Gottsched bis zum Sturm und Drang* (Diss., Münster, 1961).

Coates, Jennifer, *Women, Men and Language* (3rd edn., London: Longman, 2004).

Cameron, Deborah, 'Gender Issues and Language Change', *Annual Review of Applied Linguistics* 23 (2003).

Ebrecht, Angelika, Regina Nörtemann, and Hertha Schwarz (eds.), *Brieftheorie des 18. Jahrhunderts: Texte, Kommentare, Essays* (Stuttgart: J. B. Metzler, 1990).

Foucault, Michel, 'What is Enlightenment?', in Paul Rabinow (ed.), *The Foucault Reader* (New York: Pantheon Books, 1984).

Freund, Folke and Birger Sundqvist, *Tysk Grammatik* (3rd edn., Stockholm: Natur och Kultur, 1995).

Gellert, Christian Fürchtegott, *Briefe, nebst einer Praktischen Abhandlung von dem guten Geschmacke in Briefen* (1751), in Ebrecht, Nörtemann, and Schwarz 1990.

— *C. F. Gellerts Briefwechsel*, ii: *1756–1759*, ed. John F. Reynolds (Berlin: de Gruyter, 1987).

Giles, Howard and Philip Smith, 'Accommodation Theory. Optimal Levels of Convergence', in Howard Giles and Robert N. St. Clair (eds.), *Language and Social Psychology* (Oxford: Blackwell, 1979).

Gottsched, Luise, *Louise Gottsched — 'mit der Feder in der Hand': Briefe aus den Jahren 1730–1762*, ed. Inka Kording (Darmstadt: Wissenschaftliche Buchgesellschaft, 1999).

Hellspong, Lennart and Per Ledin, *Vägar genom texten: handbok i brukstextanalys* (Lund: Studentlitteratur, 1997).

Liselotte von der Pfalz, *Elisabeth Charlotte, Duchesse d'Orléans, Madame: Briefe*, ed. Annedore Haberl (Munich: Carl Hanser Verlag, 1996).

Helgason Jon, *Hjärtats skrifter: en brevkulturs uttryck i korrespondensen mellan Anna Louisa Karsch och Johann Wilhelm Ludwig Gleim* (Diss., Avdelningen för litteraturvetenskap; Lund: Lunds universitet, 2007).

— *Schriften des Herzens. Briefkultur des 18. Jahrhunderts im Briefwechsel zwischen Anna Louisa Karsch und Johann Ludwig Gleim* (Göttingen: Wallstein, 2012).

Kaiser, Claudia, *'Geschmack' als Basis der Verständigung: Chr. F. Gellerts Brieftheorie* (Europäische Hochschulschriften, Reihe I, Deutsche Sprache und Literatur 1563; Frankfurt am Main: Lang, 1996).

Labov, William, *Principles of Linguistic Change*, ii: *Social factors* (Oxford: Blackwell, 2001).

Luhmann, Niklas, *Love as Passion: The Codification of Intimacy* (Stanford: SUP, 1998).

Maclagan, Margaret A., Elizabeth Gordon, and Gillian Lewis, 'Women and Sound Change: Conservative and Innovative Behavior by the Same Speakers', *Language Variation and Change*, 11 (1999).

Nickisch, Reinhard M., *Die Stilprinzipien in den deutschen Briefstellern des 17. und 18. Jahrhunderts: mit einer Bibliographie zur Briefschreiblehre (1474–1800)* (Diss., Palaestra 254, 1966; Göttingen: 1969).

— 'Die Frau als Briefschreiberin im Zeitalter der deutschen Aufklärung', *Wolfenbütteler Studien zur Aufklärung*, 3 (1976).

Schwartz, Herta, '"Brieftheorie" in der Romantik', in Ebrecht, Nörtemann, and Schwarz 1990.

Varnhagen, Rahel, *Briefe an eine Freundin: Rahel Varnhagen an Rebecca Friedländer*, ed. Deborah Hertz (Cologne: Kiepenheuer & Witsch, 1988).

CHAPTER 8

Project summary and conclusions

Hedda Gunneng

The aim of this project has been to empirically test the hypothesis of the existence of a female culture, according to which there exists a cultural 'sphere' that women share only with other women, as opposed to the sphere that men and women share with one another and that includes the public sphere. Since women must speak through the language of the dominant culture, it can be seen as a 'double-voiced' discourse. We have defined this culture stylistically.

The material for this investigation has been prepared by dividing it into different constituent corpora within the various subprojects, viz.,

1. letters written by women to women: FF
2. letters in which a man has been either the sender or the recipient: M
3. letters written by women to men: FM
4. letters written by men to women: MF
5. letters written by men to men: MM.

Corpus 2 thus consists of corpora 3, 4, and 5.

With respect to linguistic variables and variables of content, the FF corpus has been compared to all the other corpora. The most important comparison in terms of the project's goals is that between the FF and the M corpora. After comparing the FF to the M corpus, the FF corpus has been compared to each of the other four corpora.

When comparing the corpora, any quantitative difference regarding each variable has been noted. However, only the differences that are of *high and medium statistical significance* have been presented in this report. Differences of a low statistical significance have been excluded, as they are potential sources of error in the analysis. The results of the comparisons are presented in Tables A.1, A.2, and A.3 below, with comments following each table.

In the discussion of the tables, some technical expressions have been rephrased in order to improve readability. We have replaced the expression:

- 'of high statistical significance' with the expression 'very often'/'much more often', 'very high'/'much higher', and so on.
- 'of medium statistical significance' with the expression 'often', 'high', and so on.

Differences of high and medium significance

Table A.1. FF compared to M: Differences of high and medium significance.

	Subproject 1	Subprojects 2 & 4	Subproject 3	Subproject 5	Subpro
	12th century	17th–18th centuries	18th century	18th–19th centuries	18th ce
	Latin	**Swedish**	**French**	**English**	**Germa**
(1) Stylistic variable					
Addressing the reader			> M		< M
Number of words per macrosyntagm	< M				< M
Embedded macrosyntagms					< M
Irregular macrosyntagms					> M
Bases > 8					
SCC per macrosyntagm					< M
SCC/CP0		< M			< M
SCC2 per macrosyntagm		< M			< M
SCC2 per CP0		< M			
Total number of tropes	< M				< M
Metaphors	< M			< M	< M
Other rhetorical figures	< M				
Allusion				> M	
Code-switching	> M	< M			> M
(2) Topics					
Fabrics and clothes		> M			> M
The body					> M
Family and relatives		> M			
Obstetrics		> FM > M			
Social life				> M	> M
Metacomments		< M			
Travelling				> M	

124

	Latin	Swedish	French	English	German
Opinions about people				> M	
Nature				> M	
Fictionalization					

The results are disparate. No statistically significant result concerning one single variable has been produced in all of the subprojects (a separate comment on each of the variables is given below). When a variable has been found to be of high or medium statistical significance in more than one subproject, the findings are sometimes mutually exclusive. In other words, our results can not verify the essentialist dimension of the hypothesis of a female culture.

Addressing the reader

Only Subprojects 3 (French) and 6 (German) have found differences of high or medium statistical significance regarding this variable. In the French letters, the variable of address occurs much more often in the FF than in the M corpus, while in the German letters it occurs much more often in the M than in the FF corpus.

Addressing the reader is a rhetorical figure that can be used to create a sense of intimacy. As a rhetorical aid, addressing the reader can also have a persuasive function. If the results had supported the traditional idea of intimacy as being typical of communication between women, there should have been a statistically significant predominance of instances of address in letters between women (FF) far greater than that in all other letters (M)—in other words, the values for FF should be greater than those for M. This relationship can, however, only be found in Subproject 3.

Number of words per macrosyntagm

The number of words per macrosyntagm is often used as a measurement of syntactical complexity. However, only in Subproject 1 (Latin) and Subproject 6 (German) is there a difference between FF and M regarding this variable. In both cases, the number of words per macrosyntagm is much lower in FF than in M.

It is impossible to give an unequivocal description of the effects created by the varying length of the macrosyntagm. If a greater length is achieved by using words that are semantically significant, the result is most likely a text that is closer to a literary, or perhaps a scholarly, style. If, on the other hand, the words are semantically insignificant, the text may perhaps give a more informal impression, but it may at the same time seem unnecessarily verbose. Short macrosyntagms may indicate stylistic planning, but they may also be the result of a writer who is spontaneous rather than calculating.

In order to confirm any notion that women typically use more or fewer words than men when writing, other variables—for instance 'semantic significance'—would have to be taken into account in the investigation.

Subordinate clauses and clause equivalents

The other variables that are considered when measuring syntactic complexity—in other words, the number of subordinate clauses and clause equivalents per macrosyntagm—have been found to be statistically significant only in Subproject 6 (German), where the frequency is higher in M than in FF. A greater degree of syntactic complexity in M than in FF is also indicated by the high number of *subordinate clauses and clause equivalents per clause or phrase on the zero level* and the very high number of *subordinate clauses and clause equivalents on level 2 per macrosyntagm* in this subproject.

Meanwhile, in the combined Subprojects 2 & 4 (Swedish) the frequency is lower in FF than in M for the variables *SCC per CP0* and *SCC2 per macrosyntagm*. This subproject is also the only one in which a highly significant statistical difference regarding *subordinate clauses and clause equivalents on level 2 per clause and phrase on the 0 level* has been found; similarly, the frequency in the FF corpus is lower than in the M corpus: in this subproject, this may indicate a lower degree of syntactic complexity in the letters between women than in the other letters.

Embedded macrosyntagms

Only Subproject 6 (German) shows any statistically significant difference between FF and M when it comes to embedded macrosyntagms. The frequency is higher in M than in FF.

Embedding a macrosyntagm into another usually serves to link two separate thoughts within one graphic sentence. Using this stylistic feature demands a high degree of linguistic planning, and may be said to be primarily a feature of written language. It is usually foreign to an informal stylistic ideal, and, for example, is typical of legal texts. Where a predominance of this stylistic feature might be expected to be found in male letter-writing, it is striking that only one of the subprojects (6) displays the expected relationship in this instance, and then it is only of medium statistical significance.

Irregular macrosyntagms

Irregular macrosyntagms that contain more than nine words have produced statistically significant results only in Subproject 6 (German). In this subproject this variable occurs more often in FF than in M. There are several kinds of macrosyntagms that can be called irregular (see above p. 43). Some, such as subjectless clauses structured as an exclamation or a question, are often typical of a rhetorical style. Anacolutha, however, are indicative of a spontaneous, less planned manner of expression. An assumption about women's letter-writing style was that it was more spontaneous and their letters were worded in a less well-planned manner, something that was a typical feature of, for example, eighteenth-century letter-writing culture, could be confirmed if the irregular macrosyntagms in the material were predominantly of the latter kind (that is, anacolutha). This, however, has not been investigated in the present project, and results concerning this type of stylistic feature are, for now, unavailable for the current discussion about the female cultural sphere.

Tropes

Where the use of tropes is concerned, we have found statistically significant differences only in Subprojects 1 (Latin) and 6 (German). The occurrence of tropes is, in general, greater in M than in FF in both of these subprojects; in Subproject 1 it is even greater. Metaphors occur much more often in M than in FF in both of these subprojects. The occurrence of 'other rhetorical figures' has only been found to be statistically significant in Subproject 1, where the frequency of this variable is higher in M than in FF.

These differences can perhaps be explained as a 'linguistic accommodation', with letter-writers adapting to the predominant stylistic ideal, sometimes even to the point of exaggeration. If this ideal is wholly or partly gender-based, writers of the opposite gender may be expected to 'overcompensate' by overusing stylistic features believed to be typical of the valorized ideal. That being so, it is noticeable that no statistically significant differences regarding metaphors have been found in the other subprojects. In the Swedish, French, and English letters, metaphors are used equally often by women and men. However, it must be borne in mind that the reasons for the differences in Subproject 1 may diverge from those in Subproject 6, and that even if linguistic accommodation is a valid explanation in both subprojects, neither the stylistic ideal nor the purpose of the correspondence were the same during these two historical periods (the twelfth and the eighteenth centuries).

Code-switching

Where code-switching is concerned, differences among the corpora have been found to be statistically significant in Subprojects 1 (Latin) and 6 (German). In these two subprojects, this variable occurs far more often in FF than in M. The difference has been found to be statistically significant in the combined Subprojects 2 & 4 (Swedish) as well, although here the relationship is the opposite: code-switching occurs much more often in M than in FF.

Topics

The topic *Fabrics and clothes* is discussed much more often in FF than in M in the combined Subprojects 2 & 4 (Swedish) and more often in Subproject 6 (German), but not in the other subprojects. *The body* occurs more often in FF in Subproject 6, *Family and relatives* much more often in FF in Subprojects 2 & 4, and *Social life* much more often in FF in Subproject 6. Only the topic *Metacomments* occurs more frequently in M; this is in Subprojects 2 & 4. Here, the variable occurs much more often in M than in FF. No statistically significant differences have been found in the other subprojects concerning *Metacomments*.

The pattern into which the variables of content fall seems to confirm a common idea about what women and men talk about. Subjects of conversation that most commonly occur in letters between women seem to be *Fabrics and clothes*, *The body*, *Family and relatives*, and *Social life*, while the predominance of a topic in the M corpus is only apparent for *Metacomments*. In no case are these differences statistically significant within all the subprojects, however; such differences can only be found in the Swedish and German letters. Thus, no firm conclusions regarding the existence of a female cultural sphere can be drawn on the basis of the content of either.

Gender or context?

The aim of the project has not been to compare every individual aspect of the texts in the six subprojects. Quantitative studies of linguistic phenomena on a systemic level are, by necessity, impossible to compare. It may, however, be interesting to compare the subprojects regarding the *number* of statistically significant differences, and the *patterns* that develop when the statistically significant differences within each subproject are taken into consideration. For this purpose, the differences that are of *high and medium statistical significance* between FF and the other constituent corpora (FM, MF, MM, and M) have been summarized in Table A.2. This table consists of summaries of the tables that can be found in the chapters for each individual subproject.

There is considerable variation among the values in Table A.2. Subproject 1 shows the highest number of differences that are of high and medium statistical significance—twenty-six in total. Then follows Subproject 6 with twenty-three differences, Subprojects 2 & 4 with twenty-one differences, Subproject 5 with eighteen differences, and finally Subproject 3 with four differences. Of five subprojects, one has thus twenty-six, three between twenty-three and eighteen, and the fifth four differences. There is also some variation concerning which differences are statistically significant within each subproject.

One might imagine that these variations are the result of *contextual factors*. The letter corpora of the six subprojects come from five different centuries, and the writers represent different cultural and social groups. In Subproject 1, all of the letter-writers are ecclesiastical functionaries, and the letters were written during the High Middle Ages. In the combined Subprojects 2 & 4 the writers belong to a comparatively homogenous sphere, as do the writers in Subproject 3. The writers in these three subprojects belonged to the top social level in seventeenth- and eighteenth-century Sweden, and they all moved in the same social and cultural circles. The writers of Subproject 5 represent the cultural elite of eighteenth- and early nineteenth-century Britain, but they do not all move in the same social circles (although a number of them do). The writers of Subproject 6 represent the middle-class cultural elite in eighteenth-century Germany and in many cases belong to the same social networks. The various subprojects

Table A.2. FF compared to FM, MF, MM, and M: differences of high and medium statistical significance.

	Subproject 1	Subprojects 2 & 4	Subproject 3	Subproject 5	Subproject
	12th century	17th–18th centuries	18th century	18th–19th centuries	18th centur
	Latin	Swedish	French	English	German
(1) Stylistic variable					
Addressing the reader	> MF	> MF	> FM > M		< FM < M
Number of words per macrosyntagm	< MF < M	> MM			< FM < M
SCC per macrosyntagm					< M
SCC per CP0		< FM < M			< M
SCC1 per macrosyntagm		> MM			
SCC2 per macrosyntagm		< FM < M			< FM < M
SCC2 per CP0		< FM < M			
Embedded macrosyntagms	< MF < MM				< M
Irregular macrosyntagms				> MF	> M
Bases> 8				< MF	
Total number of rhetorical figures		< MF		< MF < MM	
Total number of tropes	< FM > MF > MM < M			< MF	< FM < M
Metaphor	< FM > MF > MM < M	< FM	< FM	< FM < MF < MM	< FM < M
Simile	> MM > MF				
Personification	> MM				
Other rhetorical figures	< FM < MF < MM < M			< MF < MM	

	Latin	Swedish	French	English	German
lliteration	> MM				
llusion				> FM	
arallelism	< MF				
olysyndeton on the phrasal level	> MF				
olysyndeton on the syntactic level	< MF				
hetorical question				> FM	
ode-switching	> FM	< FM			> FM
	> M	< M			> M
) Topics					
abrics and clothes		> FM			> M
		> M			
amily and relatives		> M		> MF	
bstetrics		> FM			
		> M			
ocial life				> FM	> FM
				> MM	> M
avelling				> M	
he body					> FM
					> M
ature				> FM	> FM
ducation, wit, learning		< MF			
		< MM			
pinions about people				> FM	
he relationship between letter-writer and recipient		< MM		< MF	
etacomments		< FM			
		< M			
ctionalization				< MF	< MF

thus represent three different social classes and five different languages. In three subprojects the writers write in their mother tongue, while in two subprojects the writers use a second language.

As was made clear earlier (p. 21), we have in our selection of letter-writers included representatives of different languages (Latin, Swedish, French, English, German), historical periods (twelfth, eighteenth, and nineteenth centuries), and, to some extent, social classes (the nobility and upper middle classes) in order to eliminate potential sources of error when testing the hypothesis that there is a separate female cultural sphere, independent of time, place, and social class. As the analysis has resulted in a wide range of statistically significant linguistic differences, it is fair to conclude that the reason for this can be found in the contextual differences of the letters. This, however, also raises the question whether the letter corpora should not in fact be considered to represent different types of letters.

Comparison of Subprojects 2 & 4 and 3

A comparison of the patterns that form when the statistically significant differences are considered in Subprojects 2 & 4 on the one hand, and Subproject 3 on the other, may shed some light on this issue.

Table A.3. Subprojects 2 & 4 and 3, summary of differences of high and medium statistical significance.

	Subprojects 2 & 4 17th–18th centuries Swedish	Subproject 3 18th century French
(1) Stylistic variable		
Addressing the reader	> MF	> FM
		> M
Number of words per macrosyntagm	> MM	
SCC1 per macrosyntagm	> MM	
SCC2 per macrosyntagm	< FM	
	< M	
SCC per CP0	< FM	
	< M	
SCC2 per CP0	< FM	
	< M	
Total number of rhetorical figures	< MF	
Total number of tropes		
Metaphor	< FM	< FM
Simile		
Other rhetorical figures		
Parallelism		
Polysyndeton on the phrasal level		
Rhetorical question		> FM
Code-switching	< FM	
	< M	

(2) Topics

Fabrics and clothes	> FM
	> M
Family and relatives	> M
Social life	
Obstetrics	> FM
	> M
Education, wit, learning	< MF
	< MM
Opinions about people	
The relationship between letter-writer and recipient	< MM
Metacomments	< FM
	< M

The comparison of the two subprojects shows that the differences between these two letter corpora are distributed in an almost complementary fashion. The only statistically significant difference they have in common is that FF has a smaller number of metaphors than FM. It is also striking that there are so many statistically significant differences in the Swedish letters regarding the selection of topics—differences which are entirely lacking in the French letters. The writers are largely the same in both subprojects, but in the one they write in their mother tongue and in the other in a second language used mainly as a language of refined social intercourse. One may conclude that the Swedish and French letters serve different communicative functions. From this it follows naturally to speak of two different types of letters.

A separate comment for each of the variables in Table A.3 can be found below.

Addressing the reader

In Subprojects 1–4 (Latin, Swedish, French) instances of address occur much more frequently in FF than in the other constituent corpora, including M. In Subproject 6 (German) the reverse is true. In Subproject 5 (English) there are no statistically significant differences in the use of direct address.

The Subprojects 1 (Latin), 2 & 4 (Swedish), and 3 (French) stand out in this context. In letters written by women to women (FF) the instances of address are more numerous than in some of the constituent corpora where one of the correspondents is a man. In Subprojects 1 and 2 & 4 the corpus that deviates from FF is MF, i.e. letters from men to women. In Subproject 3 it is the corpora FM (women to men) and M (all letters with a male correspondent) that deviate from FF. In Subproject 6 (German) the corpora FM and M also deviate from FF, as they do in Subproject 3, but in Subproject 6 the number of instances of address is greater in the FM and M corpora than it is in FF.

In the commentary on Table A.1, it was noted that addressing the reader is a rhetorical device that can be used to create a sense of intimacy, and that thus a traditional idea of intimacy as a typically female communicative trait could be supported by the results attained from the comparison between FF and M. This is also true of the comparison of which we now write. The relationship FF > FM—in other words, the fact that there is a predominance of instances of address in the letters from women to women compared to the letters from women to men—can be found only in Subproject 3. Subprojects 1 and 2 & 4 testify to the fact that the female writers use more instances of direct address than the male writers, but not that they do so when writing to other women. In Subproject 6, the results contradict the traditional idea that addressing the reader is a typical trait in letters that women write to other women. In this subproject, the female writers address the reader more often when writing to men than when writing to other women.

Number of words per macrosyntagm

In Subprojects 1 (Latin) and 6 (German), the letters between women have shorter macrosyntagms than the letters that involve a male correspondent. In Subproject 1 it is MF that deviates by displaying a higher value; in Subproject 6 it is FM. In Subprojects 2 & 4 (Swedish) there is a statistically significant difference only when FF is compared to MM, and then the value found for the latter is lower. In Subprojects 2 & 4 the macrosyntagms are thus shorter on average in the letters between men than in the other corpora. Subprojects 3 (French) and 5 (English) do not display any statistically significant differences where this variable is concerned.

Embedded macrosyntagms

It is primarily the Latin letters (Subproject 1) that display differences in the frequency of embedded macrosyntagms. These are present in

134

greater numbers when men write than when women write to women. However, when women write to men there is no statistically significant difference in comparison to FF. In the Latin letters, embedded macrosyntagms thus appear to be a stylistic feature typical of male letter-writers.

In Subproject 6, the German letters, there is a corresponding difference: there are more embedded macrosyntagms when one of the correspondents is a man than when both are women. The difference is, however, of medium statistical significance. In the commentary on Table A.1 it was emphasized that, in terms of the linguistic function of the embedded macrosyntagm, this linguistic feature is typical of written language, while its use entails a high degree of planning on the writer's part. This holds true for all the modern European languages. In written Latin the situation may be different. Here, syntactic connections are expressed more often by way of inflectional suffixes than by separate words (such as prepositions or adverbs), from which it follows that grammatical embeddings do not interrupt the textual flow in the same way as in the French or German texts, for example. Using an embedded macrosyntagm may thus seem more natural when writing letters in Latin than when doing so in a modern European language. Therefore, one should probably be careful not to see the embedded macrosyntagm as a reliable testimony to male habits of writing in the Latin letters.

Irregular macrosyntagms

Statistically significant differences regarding this variable can be found in Subprojects 5 (English) and 6 (German), in that the frequency of irregular macrosyntagms in the letters between women is greater in Subproject 5 when compared to the MF corpus (FF > MF), and in Subproject 6 when compared to the M corpus (FF > M). In both cases the statistical significance is high. See, in addition, the commentary on Table A.1 (p. 124).

Metaphor

Among the rhetorical figures it is the metaphor that attracts the greatest interest in the project material. This is because differences that have a high statistical significance can be found in all of the subprojects except for Subproject 3 (French), where the statistical significance is only medium. In letters written in the modern languages the tendency is unambiguous: letters between women have fewer metaphors than letters where one of the correspondents is a man. The Latin letters paint a different picture. The letters from Hildegard to other women clearly contain more metaphors than the letters written by men, but they also contain significantly fewer metaphors than Hildegard's letters to men. Concerning the use of metaphors, some of the Latin letters must clearly be evaluated according to completely different criteria than the letters written in the modern languages. This is true of those among Hildegard's letters in which she relates her spiritual visions and divine revelations: in these letters, the frequency of metaphor is considerably higher than in letters that have a different content. This stylistic feature is typical of visionary representation, a genre that can be studied for numerous female and male writers during the European Middle Ages, and they often contain a striking wealth of metaphors (as do the writings of St Bridget of Sweden, for example). It is natural to connect this stylistic tendency to the difficulties the visionaries had in verbally conveying impressions that had been perceived in other ways than by the five senses. Metaphor can here be used in an attempt to express that which cannot really be put into words.

Closing remarks

In this summary I have presented and discussed the statistically most palpable differences between letters between women (the FF corpus) and all letters where a man was at least one of the correspondents (the M corpus). In addition, the FF corpus has been compared to each individual corpus where at least one of the correspondents was a man: letters from women to men (FM); letters from men to women (MF); and letters between men (MM).

As has been made clear, the variables that are lacking in the presentation of the results are those whose differences are not statistically significant to a high or medium degree. These are, above all, the syntactic variables.

Appendix I

Tables and diagrams

The division of the project into subprojects will be adhered to in the following presentation of the results, albeit with some modifications. Subprojects 2 (Swedish letters 1600–1740) and 4 (Swedish letters *c.*1740–1800) have been combined, and the results for these two subprojects have been presented together. Throughout, the results are presented for each individual subproject in turn, but note that no word length analysis has been conducted in Subproject 3 (French), and no word class analysis in Subproject 5 (English). In Subprojects 1 (Latin) and 3 (French), the analysis of the verbs in the word class analysis has been omitted because of the large number of compound verbs in these languages. For a more detailed description of the theory and method used in the current project, see the relevant chapters in this volume.

In order to conduct several of the analyses below, a computer programme called the Tag Analysis Program (TAP) was developed under the auspices of the 'Women's language' project. The programme was developed in cooperation with computer linguist Maria Holmqvist of the University of Linköping. The variables registered by this programme are (see p. 55) rhetorical figures, number of words in the macrosyntagm, irregular clauses, embedded macrosyntagms, bases, asyndeton, polysyndeton, mother-tongue words, phrases or text passages, foreign-language phrases or text passages, and topics.

The abbreviations used generally refer to the different constituent corpora of the material studied. The letter texts have been divided into groups with designations signifying the gender of the writers and recipients of the letters, using the abbreviations F for female and M for male. The designation FF thus signifies letters that have both a female writer and a female recipient, FM denotes letters that have a female writer and a male recipient, and so on. The abbreviation M denotes all letters that have either a male writer and/or a male recipient and is thus made up of the corpora FM, MF, and MM. This means that the constituent corpora number five in total: FF, M, FM, MF, and MM.

Other abbreviations:
SCC subordinate clauses and clause equivalents
CP0 main clause(s) or expanded interjectional or vocative
phrase(s) on the 0 level

Word classes

The word class analysis has not been conducted in Subproject 5 because of the large number of homographs in the English language. The analysis of verbs (stative/dynamic) has not been conducted in Subprojects 1 (Latin) and 3 (French), because of the large number of compound verbs in these languages. Only the results of the analysis of the two major constituent corpora, FF and M, are presented.

Distribution concrete/abstract for the 100 most common nouns (FF, M)

Subproject 1

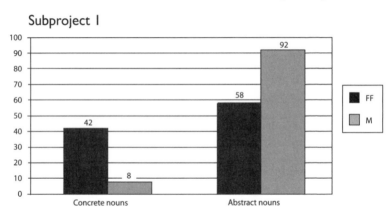

Subprojects 2 & 4

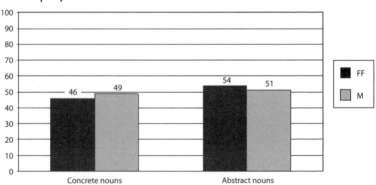

Subproject 3

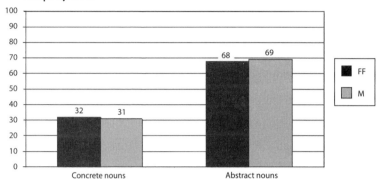

Subproject 6

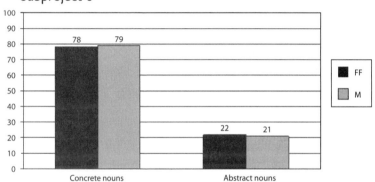

Distribution stative/dynamic for the 100 most common verbs (FF, M)

Subprojects 2 & 4

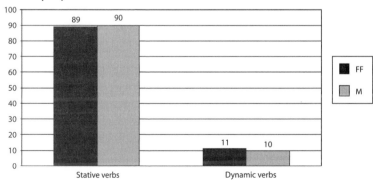

Subproject 6

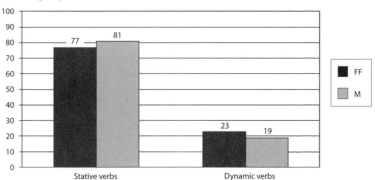

Distribution neutral/emotive for the 100 most common adjectives (FF, M)

Subproject 1

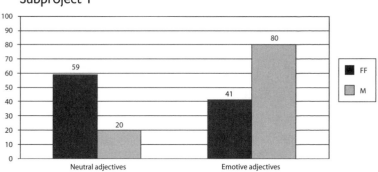

Subprojects 2 & 4

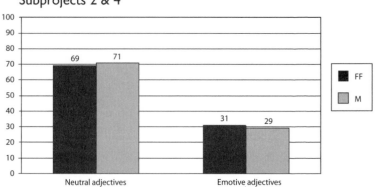

Subproject 3

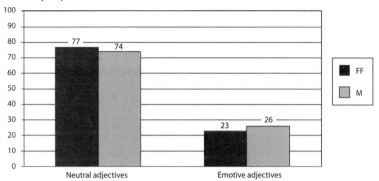

Subproject 6

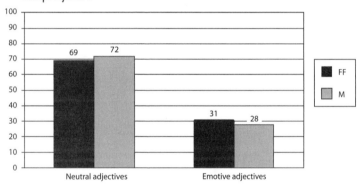

Length of words

The length of words has been determined using the concordance software Concordance (for more information, see <http://www.concordancesoftware.co.uk>).

The word length analysis has not been performed in Subproject 3.

The diagrams indicate the total number of words consisting of only one letter (graph), the total number of words consisting of two letters (graphs), and so on. The percentage given for each column indicates the relative occurrence of the particular word length in the constituent corpus under study. Only the results of the two major corpora, FF and M, have been presented.

Length of words (FF, M)

Length of words in the FF constituent corpus, Subproject I

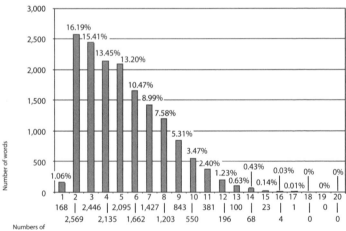

Length of words in the M constituent corpus, Subproject I

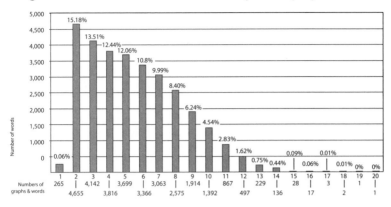

Length of words in the FF constituent corpus, Subprojects 2 & 4

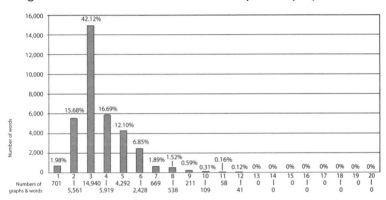

Length of words in the M constituent corpus, Subprojects 2 & 4

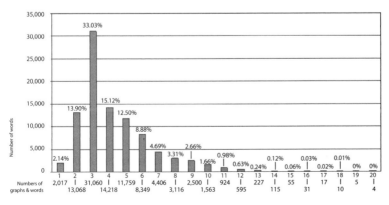

Length of words in the FF constituent corpus, Subproject 5

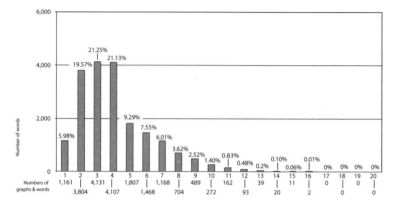

Length of words in the M constituent corpus, Subproject 5

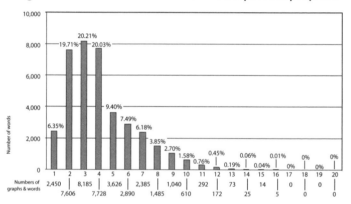

Length of words in the FF constituent corpus, Subproject 6

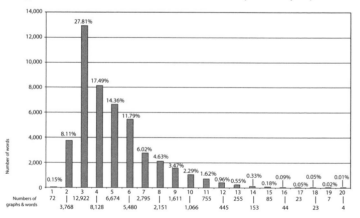

Length of words in the M constituent corpus, Subproject 6

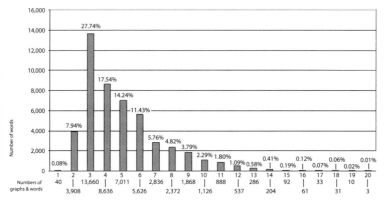

Hypotaxis (super- and subordination)

The following are included as part of this analysis:

- the most commonly occurring length of macrosyntagms in each constituent corpus, measured by the number of words
- the number of subordinate clauses and clause equivalents (SCC) per main clause or expanded interjectional and/or vocative macro-syntagm on the 0 level (CP0)
- the number of SCC on level 1 per 100 macrosyntagms and per CP0; number of SCC on level 2 per hundred macrosyntagms and per CP0, and so on. Only the first seven subordination levels have been included in the presentation below.

This analysis has been conducted for the two major corpora, FF and M, and on each of the four constituent corpora, FF, FM, MF, and MM.

Number of words per macrosyntagm (FF, M)

Subproject I

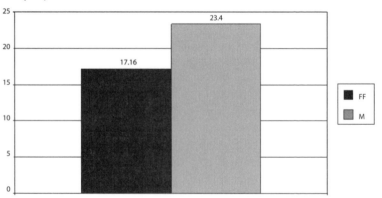

Subprojects 2 & 4

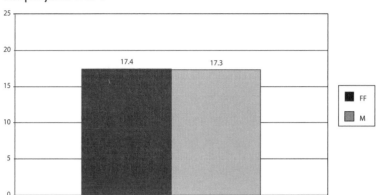

Subproject 3

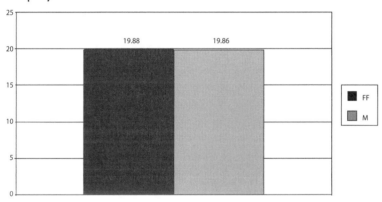

Subproject 6

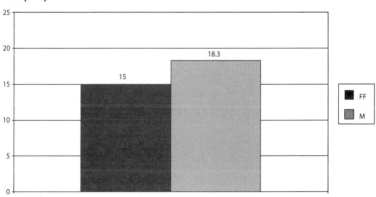

Number of words per macrosyntagm (FF, FM, MF, MM)

Subproject1

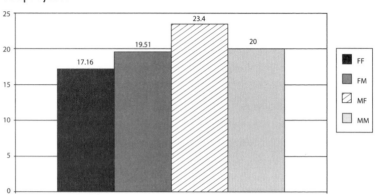

Subprojects 2 & 4

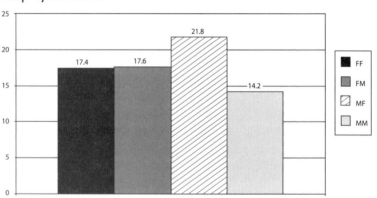

Subproject 3

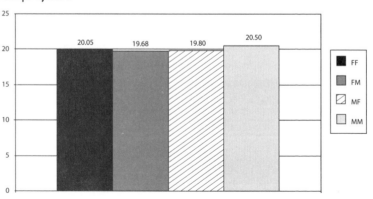

Subproject 6

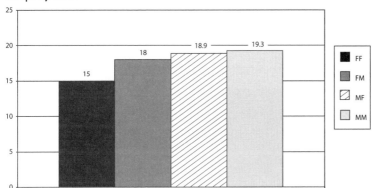

Number of SCC per CP0 (FF, M)

Subproject 1

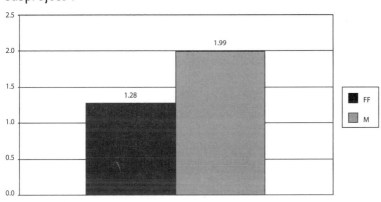

Subprojects 2 & 4

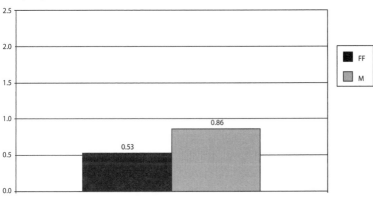

Subproject 3

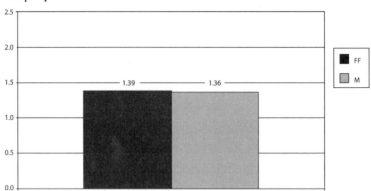

Subproject 6

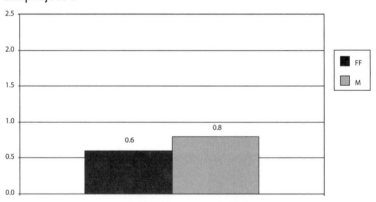

Number of SCC per CP0 (FF, FM, MF, MM)

Subproject 1

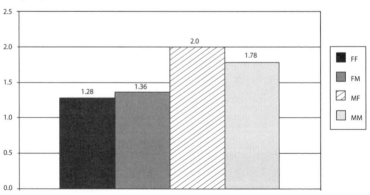

Subprojects 2 & 4

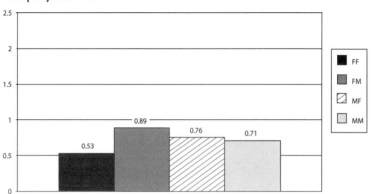

Subproject 3

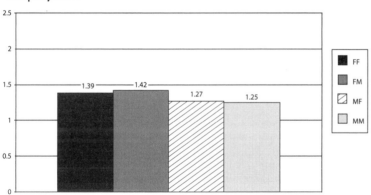

Subproject 6

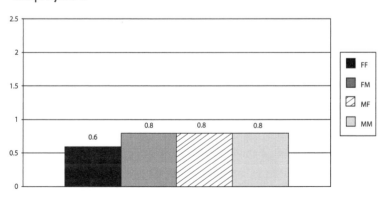

Levels of subordination 1–7
per hundred macrosyntagms (FF, M)

Subproject 1

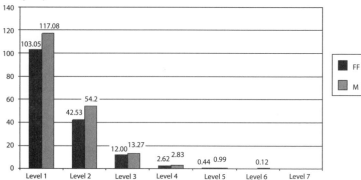

Subprojects 2 & 4

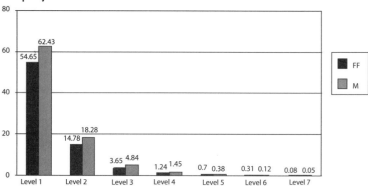

Subproject 3

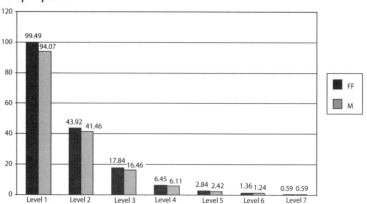

Subproject 6

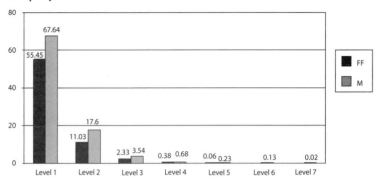

Levels of subordination 1–7
per hundred macrosyntagms (FF, FM, MF, MM)

Subproject 1

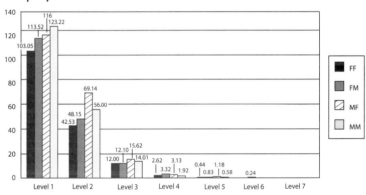

Subprojects 2 & 4

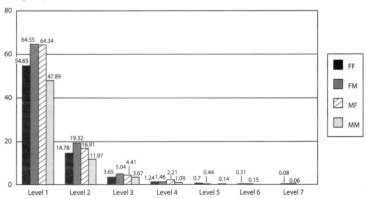

Subproject 3

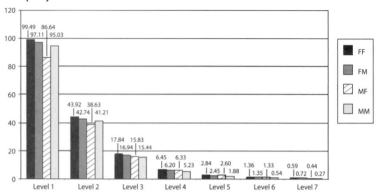

Subproject 6

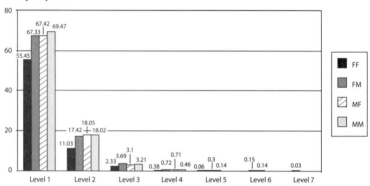

Levels of subordination 1–7 per CP0 (FF, M)

Subproject 1

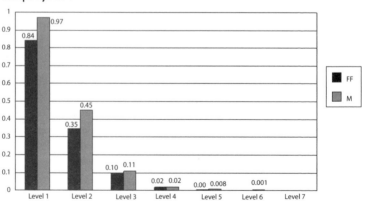

Subprojects 2 & 4

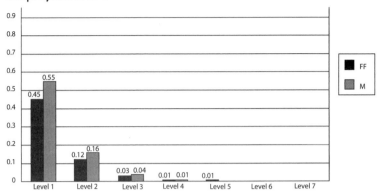

Subproject 3

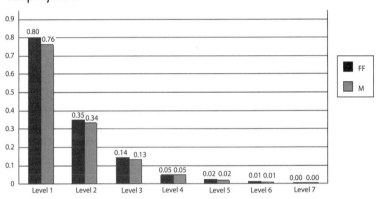

Subproject 6

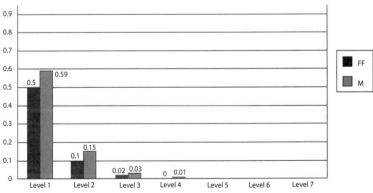

Levels of subordination 1–7 per CP0 (FF, FM, MF, MM)

Subproject 1

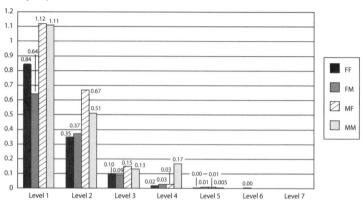

Subprojects 2 & 4

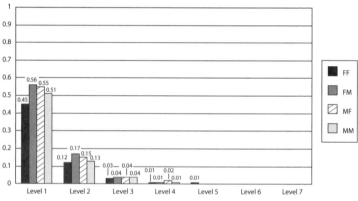

Subproject 3

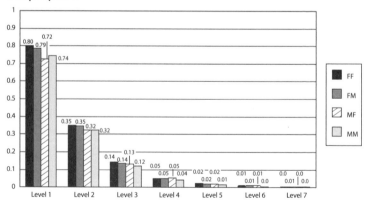

Subproject 6

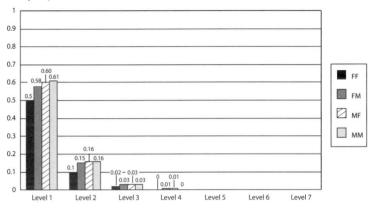

Other stylistic variables on the syntactic level

This analysis brings to light certain syntactic elements in the text: embedded macrosyntagms, irregular macrosyntagms, the most common length of the macrosyntagms, long bases, and polysyndeton/asyndeton. The length of the base has not been investigated in Subproject 1.

This analysis has been conducted for the two major corpora, FF and M, and for each of the four constituent corpora, FF, FM, MF, and MM.

Other syntactic variables
per hundred macrosyntagms (FF, M)

Subproject I

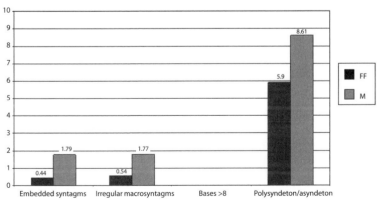

Subprojects 2 & 4

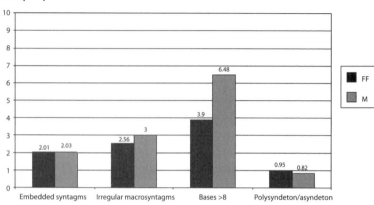

Subproject 3

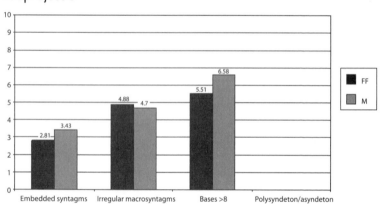

Subproject 5

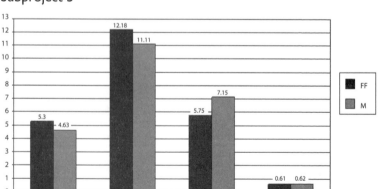

Subproject 6

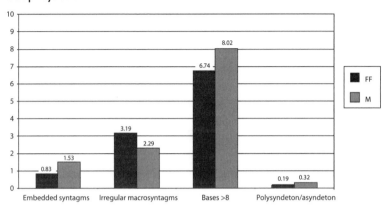

Other syntactic variables
per hundred macrosyntagms (FF, FM, MF, MM)

Subproject I

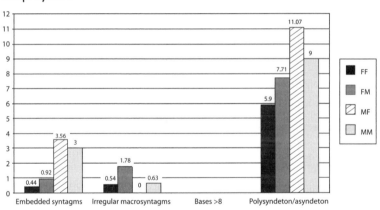

Subprojects 2 & 4

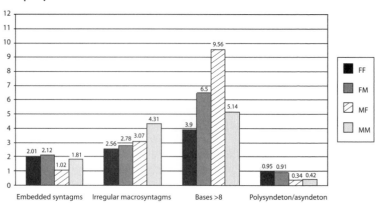

Subproject 3

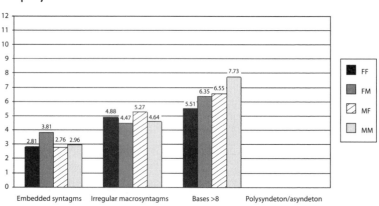

Subproject 5

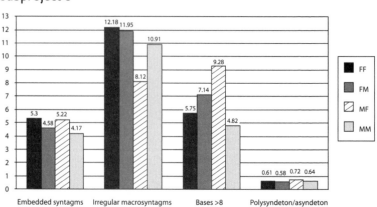

Subproject 6

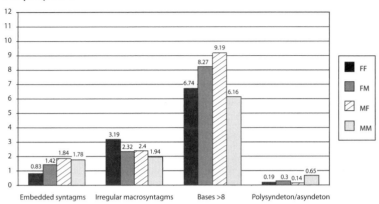

The most common length
of the macrosyntagm (FF, M)

Subproject 1

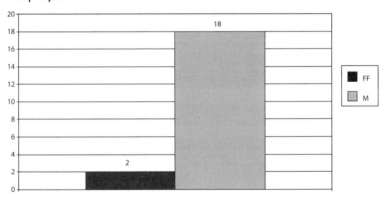

Subprojects 2 & 4

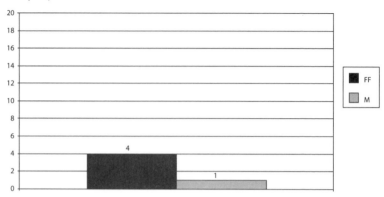

Subproject 3

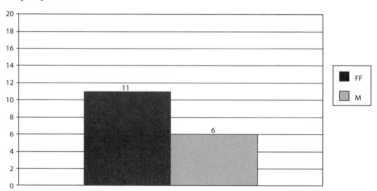

Subproject 5

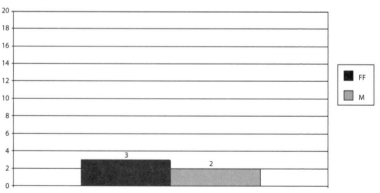

Subproject 6

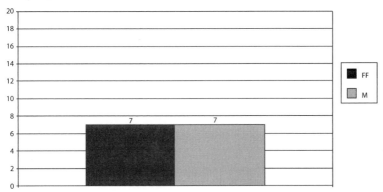

The most common length
of the macrosyntagm (FF, FM, MF, MM)
Where the analysis has resulted in more than
one value per corpus, this has been indicated.

Subproject 1

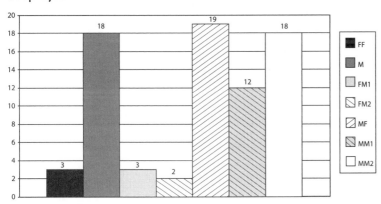

FM1 = 3 words
FM2 = 2 words

Subprojects 2 & 4

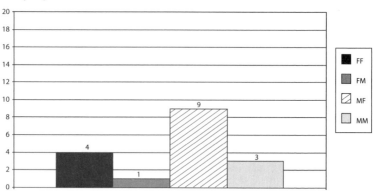

Subproject 3

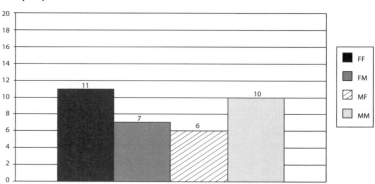

Subproject 5

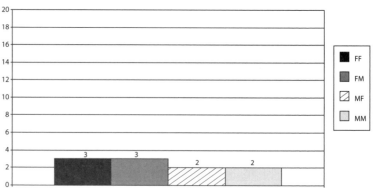

Subproject 6

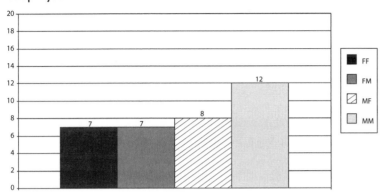

Code-switching

For the definition of code-switching, see p. 52.

Instances of code-switching
per hundred macrosyntagms (FF, M)

Subproject 1

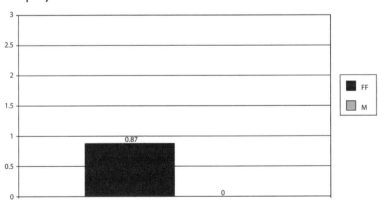

Subprojects 2 & 4

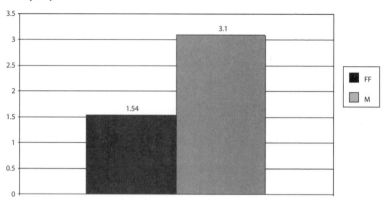

Subproject 3

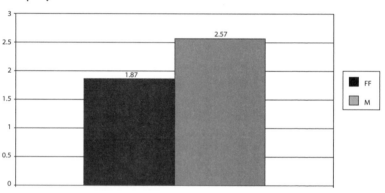

Subproject 5

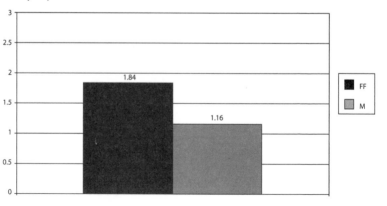

Subproject 6

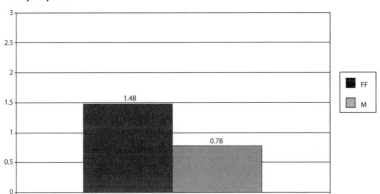

Instances of code-switching
per hundred macrosyntagms (FF, FM, MF, MM)

Subproject 1

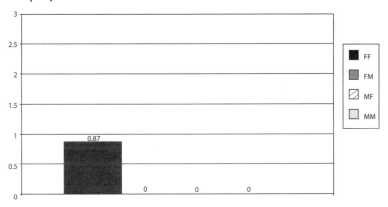

Subprojects 2 & 4

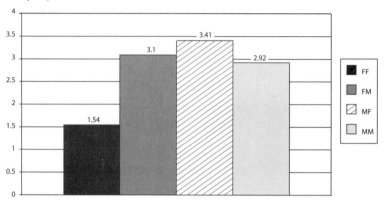

Subproject 3

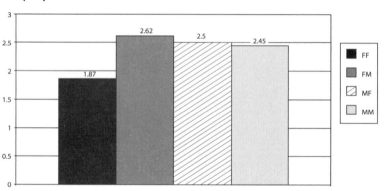

Subproject 5

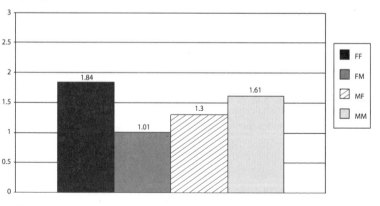

Subproject 6

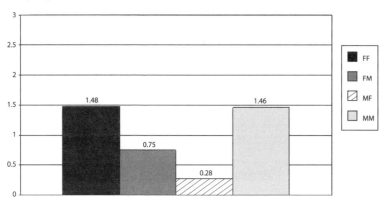

Rhetorical figures

The presentation of the results regarding rhetorical figures is divided by the total number of rhetorical figures, tropes, metaphors, and other rhetorical figures. In addition, for each subproject the most important language- and corpus-specific rhetorical figures or other stylistically significant elements have been selected for separate presentation and internal comparisons.

**Rhetorical figures per hundred
macrosyntagms (FF, M)**

Subproject 1

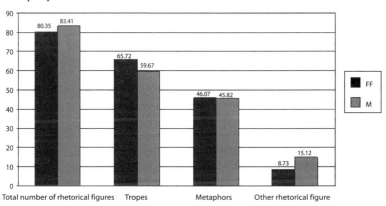

Subprojects 2 & 4

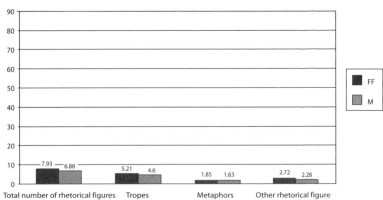

Subproject 3

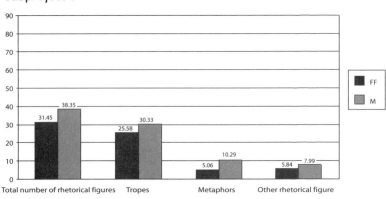

Subproject 5

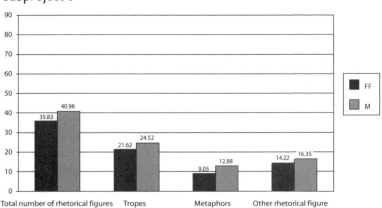

Subproject 6

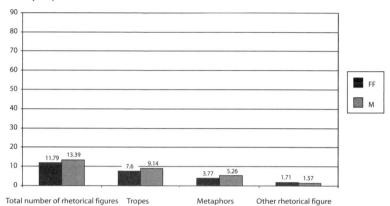

Rhetorical figures per hundred macrosyntagms (FF, FM, MF, MM)

Subproject 1

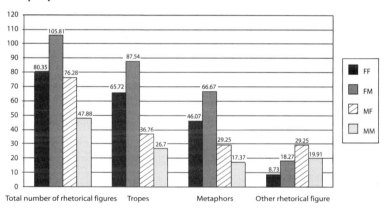

Subprojects 2 & 4

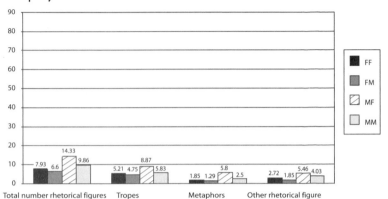

Subproject 3

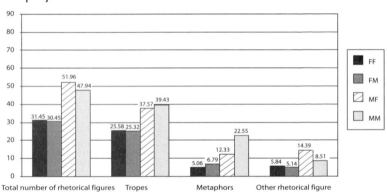

Subproject 5

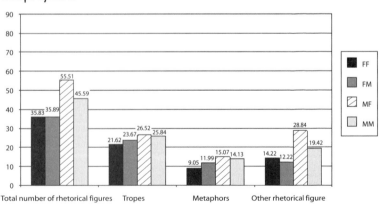

Subproject 6

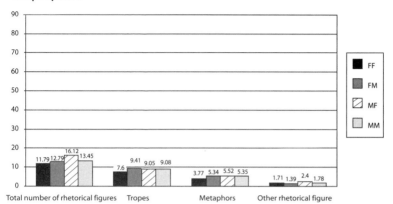

Individual rhetorical figures
per hundred macrosyntagms (FF, M)

Subproject 1

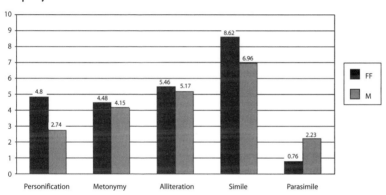

Subprojects 2 & 4

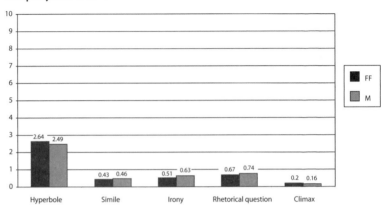

Subproject 3

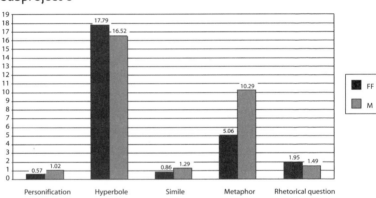

Subproject 5

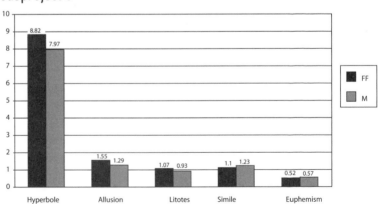

Subproject 6

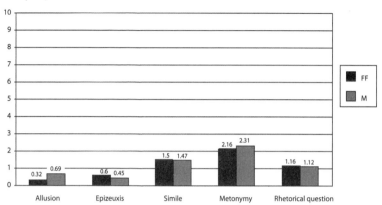

**Individual rhetorical figures
per hundred macrosyntagms (FF, FM, MF, MM)**

Subproject 1

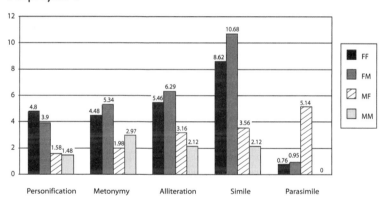

Subprojects 2 & 4

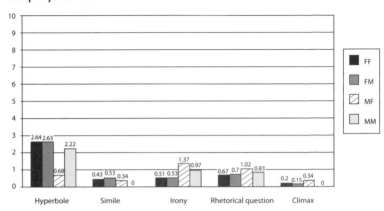

Subproject 3

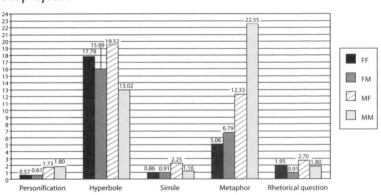

Subproject 5

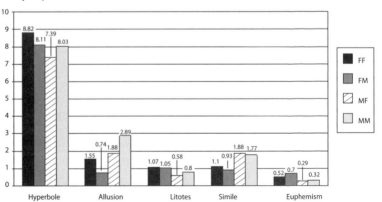

Subproject 6

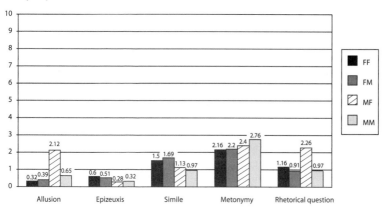

Addressing the reader

This analysis has been conducted for the two major corpora, FF and M, and on each of the four constituent corpora, FF, FM, MF, and MM.

Instances of address
per hundred macrosyntagms (FF, M)

Subproject 1

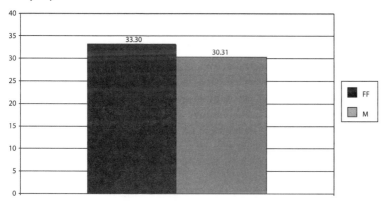

Subprojects 2 & 4

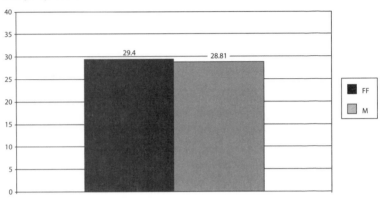

Subproject 3

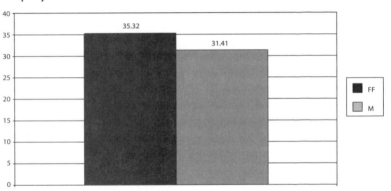

Subproject 5

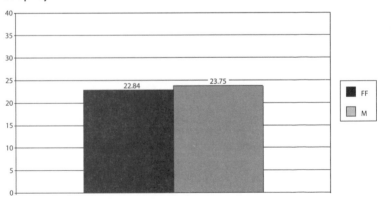

Subproject 6

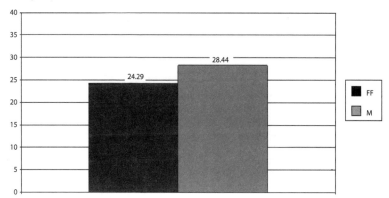

Instances of address
per hundred macrosyntagms (FF, FM, MF, MM)

Subproject 1

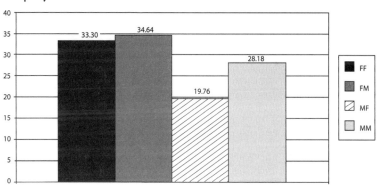

Subprojects 2 & 4

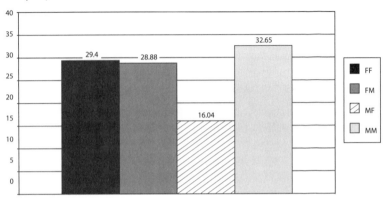

Subproject 3

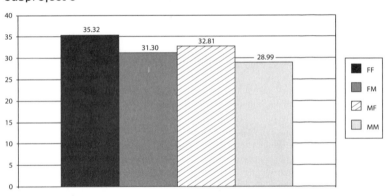

Subproject 5

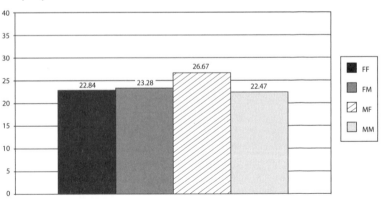

Subproject 6

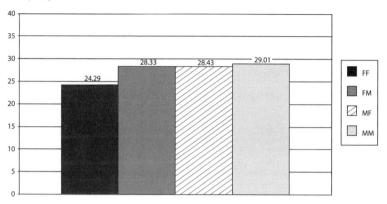

Topics

This analysis has been conducted for the two major corpora, FF and M, and on each of the four constituent corpora, FF, FM, MF, and MM. Note that an analysis of the topics of the letters has not been conducted for Subproject 1.

The percentual distribution of letter topics

Subprojects 2 & 4: Topics in the FF constituent corpus

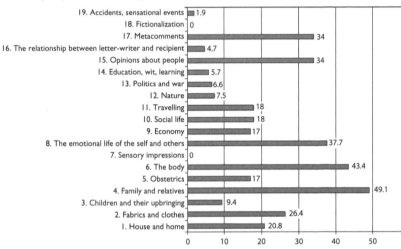

Subprojects 2 & 4: Topics in the M constituent corpus

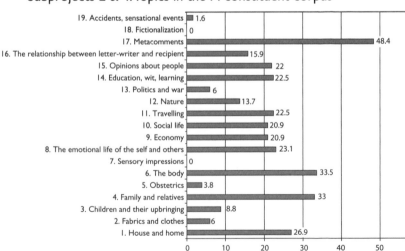

Subproject 3: Topics in the FF constituent corpus

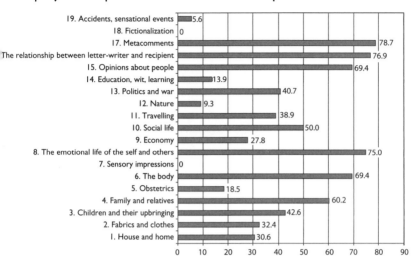

Topic	Value
19. Accidents, sensational events	5.6
18. Fictionalization	0
17. Metacomments	78.7
The relationship between letter-writer and recipient	76.9
15. Opinions about people	69.4
14. Education, wit, learning	13.9
13. Politics and war	40.7
12. Nature	9.3
11. Travelling	38.9
10. Social life	50.0
9. Economy	27.8
8. The emotional life of the self and others	75.0
7. Sensory impressions	0
6. The body	69.4
5. Obstetrics	18.5
4. Family and relatives	60.2
3. Children and their upbringing	42.6
2. Fabrics and clothes	32.4
1. House and home	30.6

Subproject 3: Topics in the M constituent corpus

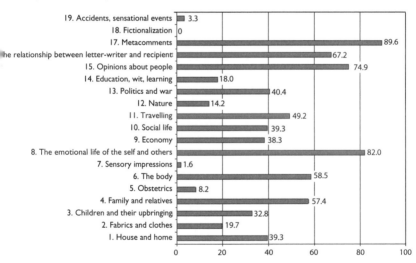

Topic	Value
19. Accidents, sensational events	3.3
18. Fictionalization	0
17. Metacomments	89.6
the relationship between letter-writer and recipient	67.2
15. Opinions about people	74.9
14. Education, wit, learning	18.0
13. Politics and war	40.4
12. Nature	14.2
11. Travelling	49.2
10. Social life	39.3
9. Economy	38.3
8. The emotional life of the self and others	82.0
7. Sensory impressions	1.6
6. The body	58.5
5. Obstetrics	8.2
4. Family and relatives	57.4
3. Children and their upbringing	32.8
2. Fabrics and clothes	19.7
1. House and home	39.3

Subproject 5: Topics in the FF constituent corpus

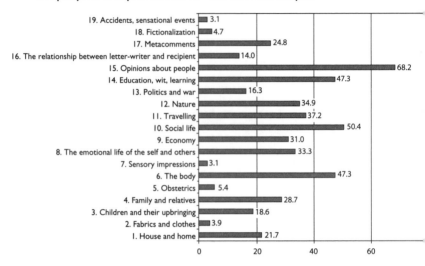

Subproject 5: Topics in the M constituent corpus

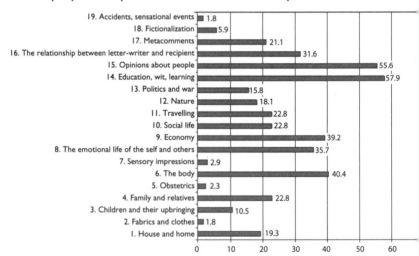

Subproject 6: Topics in the FF constituent corpus

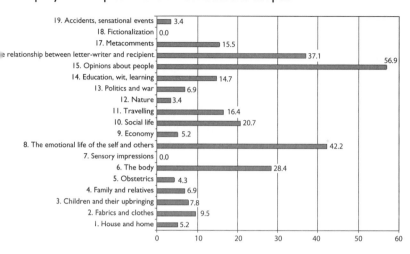

Subproject 6: Topics in the M constituent corpus

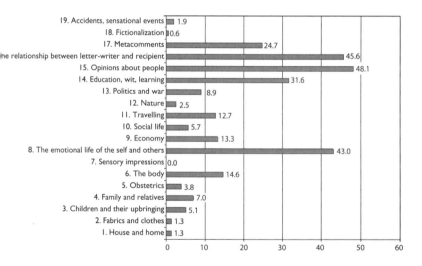

Subprojects 2 & 4: The percentual distribution of letter topics in the FF, FM, MF and MM constituent corpora

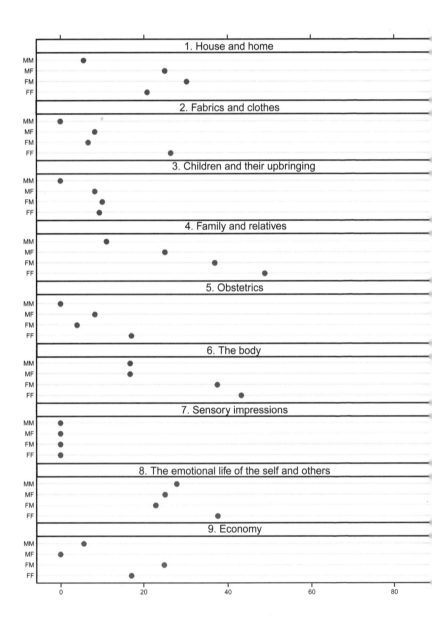

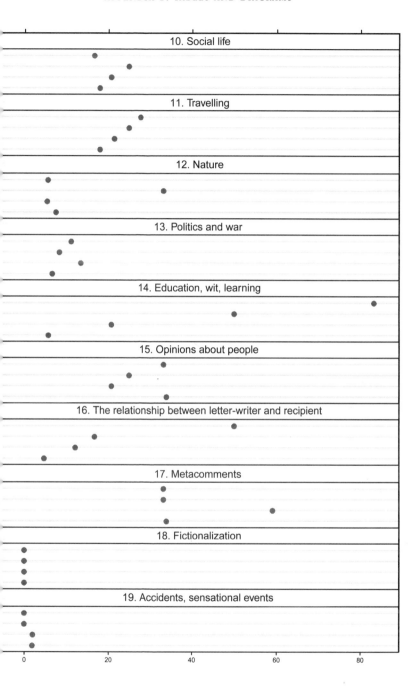

Subproject 3: The percentual distribution of letter topics in the FF, FM, MF, and MM constituent corpora

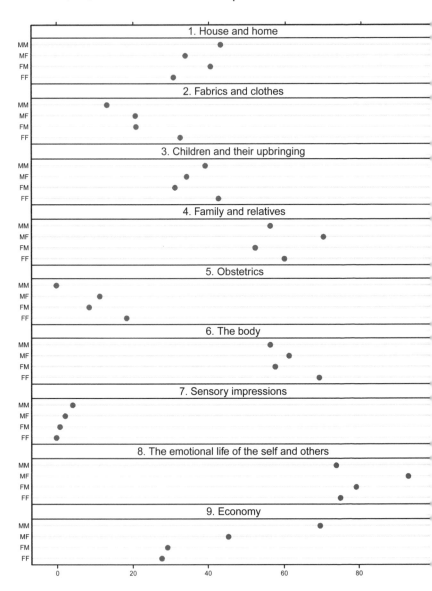

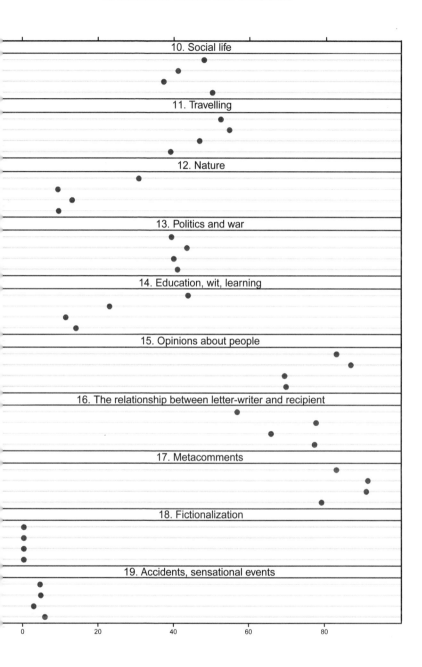

Subproject 5: The percentual distribution of letter topics in the FF, FM, MF, and MM constituent corpora

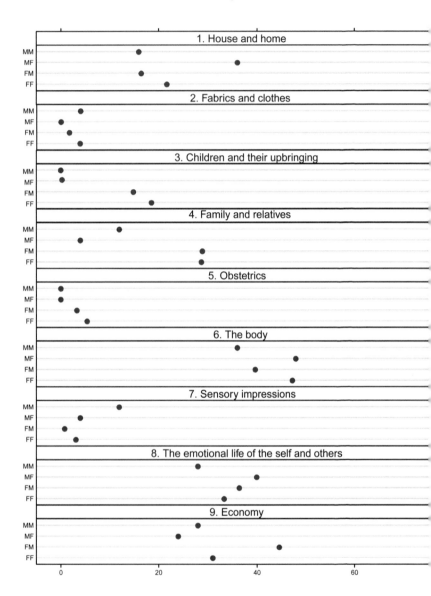

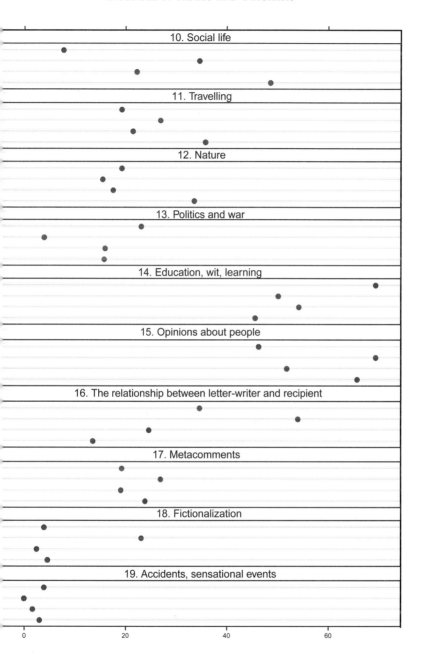

10. Social life

11. Travelling

12. Nature

13. Politics and war

14. Education, wit, learning

15. Opinions about people

16. The relationship between letter-writer and recipient

17. Metacomments

18. Fictionalization

19. Accidents, sensational events

Subproject 6: The percentual distribution of letter topics in the FF, FM, MF, and MM constituent corpora

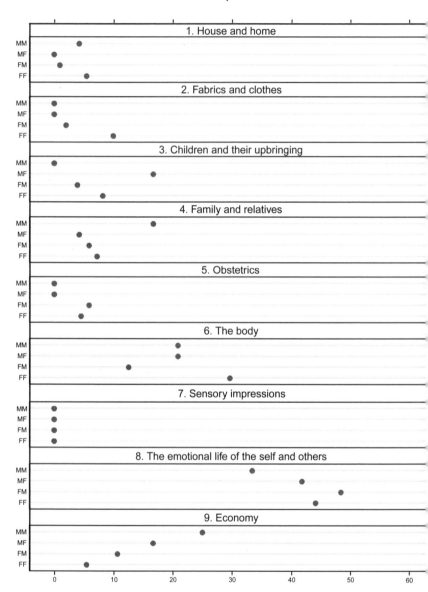

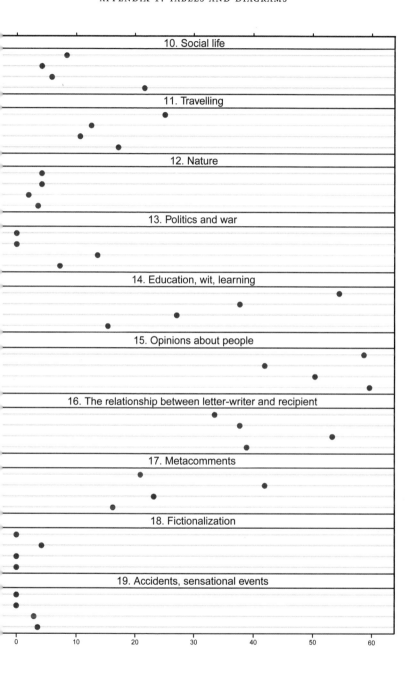

Appendix 2

Statistical analysis and hypothesis testing and statistical result tables

For this part of the investigation the project members received help from Ph.D. Mats Brodén, Mathematical Statistics, Centre for Mathematical Sciences, Lund University, and Professor Tobias Rydén, formerly of Mathematical Statistics, Centre for Mathematical Sciences, Lund University.

Introduction

Hypothesis testing is a central concept within statistical theory. Hypothesis testing is used to determine whether specific assumptions regarding the statistical properties of a number of observations should be rejected or not. Assume, for instance, that you wish to determine whether the population mean of a number of observations is greater than zero. You begin by stating a preliminary hypothesis called the null hypothesis (usually represented by H_0), and an alternative hypothesis that is true if the null hypothesis proves not to be true. In the above example, the null hypothesis would be that the population mean is less than or equal to zero. The alternative hypothesis is whatever you wish to establish, in this case that the population mean is greater than zero.

Assume that we have a number of observations, $\mathbf{x} = (x_1, \ldots, x_n)$. In order to test the null hypothesis we need to come up with a suitable *test statistic, $t = t(\mathbf{x})$*. The test statistic should be selected in such a way that it will say something about the property we wish to investigate in the population in question. Usually, the test statistic is chosen so that it tends to be small if the null hypothesis is valid, and large if the alternative hypothesis is valid. If the null hypothesis concerns the size of the population mean, the mean of the observations may be a suitable test statistic. In the above case, a large mean score indicates that the alternative hypothesis is valid.

We must also define a *critical region, C.* If *t* is within the critical region, then we reject H_0. The critical region is selected in such a way that if H_0 is true, then the probability that *t* is within *C* is equal to some small value α. The significance level of the test is called α, and is usually decided prior to the test. The significance level is, in other words, the probability of erroneously rejecting the null hypothesis even though it is true. For this reason, we choose to make this probability small.

In this case, when we want to test whether the population mean is greater than zero, *C* would be all values greater than some positive number *a*. If our test statistic *t*—in other words, the mean score of the observations $x_1, ..., x_n$—should prove to be greater than *a*, we reject the null hypothesis and conclude that the population mean is greater than zero. If the null hypothesis is rejected, we say that the result is statistically *significant.* In the event that the null hypothesis is not rejected, the result is said to be *non-significant.*

It is common to work with several different levels of significance, usually the levels 0.05, 0.01, and 0.001. When working with these levels, the designations *significant**, *significant***, and *significant****, respectively, are commonly used to indicate that a result is significant at the level in question.

All the tests in this report present the so-called *p-value.* The p-value can, somewhat imprecisely, be described as the probability that, given that H_0 is true, the test statistic deviates as much, or more, from the hypothetical value according to the null hypothesis, as does the test statistic calculated from the data. Using the direct method mentioned above, we can, using the p-value, directly determine at which significance level a null hypothesis can be rejected. If, for example, the p-value is between 0.01 and 0.05, the result is significant *, but not significant **.

Hypothesis testing in the 'Women's language' project

The data consists of measurements from letters in the following letter classes: letters written by women to women (FF), by women to men (FM), by men to women (MF), and by men to men (MM).

We have also defined a class M, which consists of FM and a combination of MF and MM. MF and MM are combined with FM, forming M in those cases where there is no significant difference between FM and MF on the one hand, and FM and MM on the other.

The observations from the FF class have been tested against the observations from the FM, MF, MM, and M classes.

Test of binominal properties

In the word class analysis we investigate, among other things, the distribution of concrete and abstract nouns. The probability that a randomly selected noun is concrete is indicated by p. The probability that a noun is abstract is then indicated by $1\text{-}p$.

In order to test whether there is a difference in the population of concrete and abstract nouns between the classes FF and M, we can state the null hypothesis

$$H_0 : \ p^{KK} = p^M$$

The alternative hypothesis is stated as

$$H_1 : \ p^{KK} \neq p^M$$

In order to test the null hypothesis against the alternative hypothesis, we have used Fisher's exact test. This test will result in a p-value that will then be used to determine whether the null hypothesis should be rejected or not.[1]

The above test, in which the aim is to investigate the difference in proportions between two populations, is also used regarding, for example, the analysis of linguistic variables and the subject analysis.

Normal approximation

In the hypotaxis analysis the ratio of two different quantities is compared among the different letter classes, for example, the number of subordinated clauses and phrases per macrosyntagm. For every class of letters we assign a simple linear regression model according to

$$y_i = \beta x_i + e_i$$

where e_i is a noise variable, i.e., a deviation from the expected regression line. $y = \beta x$. We now want to test whether the β-value differs between the two different classes FF and M. The test is formulated as follows:

$$H_0 : \ \beta^{KK} = \beta^M$$

The alternative hypothesis is formulated as

$$H_1: \ \beta^{KK} \neq \beta^M$$

In this test we will make use of the fact that the estimations of β are approximately normally distributed, and apply the methods in chapters eight and ten in Montgomery and Runger's *Applied Statistics and Probability for Engineers* (the method of estimating β and its standard deviation is described in Method 1).[2]

Another investigation that is part of the hypotaxis analysis concerns the number of words per macrosyntagm. We let m represent the population mean of the number of words per macrosyntagm. In order to test whether m differs between the classes FF and M, we formulate the null hypothesis

$$H_0: \ m^{KK} = m^M$$

with the alternative hypothesis

$$H_1: \ m^{KK} \neq m^M$$

Also in this case, we can make use of the fact that the estimations of m are approximately normally distributed. The method of estimating m and the standard deviation of the estimation is described on the next page, 199.

Test of Poisson-distributed random variables

In some cases when we want to compare the ratio of two different quantities among the different letter classes, there is insufficient data for a test of the above kind. Instead, we have chosen to assign a model built on the assumption that the data have a Poisson distribution. For every class we assign a model according to

$$X_i \in \text{Po} \ (\lambda_i n_i)$$

where X_i signifies one quantity, n_i signifies the other, and λ_i can be interpreted as the ratio between these quantities. We now want to test whether the value of λ_i differs among the different classes. The test is formulated as:

$$H_0: \lambda^{KK} = \lambda^M$$

The alternative hypothesis is formulated as

$$H_1: \lambda^{KK} \neq \lambda^M$$

Under the assumption that the value of λ is the same for both classes, it is possible to show that the conditional distribution of X_1, given $X_1 + X_2$, is conditionally binomially distributed with the parameters $X_1 + X_2$ and $n_1 /(n_1 + n_2)$. Under this assumption, it is possible, with the aid of the direct method, to calculate a p-value that can then be used to determine whether the null hypothesis should be rejected or not.

Estimating the regression coefficients
As mentioned earlier, we adopt a simple linear regression model

$$y_i = \beta x_i + e_i .$$

where $E[e_i]=0$ for every letter class. In addition, we have $m_i=\beta x_i$ where $E[Y_i]=m_i$ and $V[Y_i]=\sigma^2$.

We estimate β by

$$\beta^* = \frac{\sum_{i=1}^{N} y_i}{\sum_{j=1}^{N} x_j} = \sum_{i=1}^{N} \frac{1}{\sum_{j=1}^{N} x_j} y_i = \sum_{i=1}^{N} c y_i$$

The variance is given by

$$V\left[\beta^*\right] = \sum_{i=1}^{N} c^2 V[Y_i] = \sum_{i=1}^{N} c^2 \sigma^2 = \sigma^2 \sum_{i=1}^{N} \left(\frac{1}{\sum_{j=1}^{N} x_j}\right)^2 = \frac{N\sigma^2}{\left(\sum_{j=1}^{N} x_j\right)^2}$$

Estimation of the population mean and the standard deviation
We let x_{ij} be a sample of some distribution with the population mean m and the variance σ^2. In our case, x_{ij} is the number of words in macrosyntagm j in letter i. We let n_i represent the number of macrosyntagms in letter number i and N represent the total number of letters. The observations are organized in such a way that we only have access to the sums $\tilde{x}_i = \sum_{j=1}^{n_i} x_{ij}$ and n_i. To estimate of m we use

$$m^* = \frac{\sum_{i=1}^{N} \tilde{x}_i}{\sum_{i=1}^{N} n_i}$$

The variance σ^2 is estimated by

$$s^2 = \frac{1}{N-1} \sum_{i=1}^{N} n_i \left(\overline{x}_i - m^* \right)^2$$

where $\overline{x}_i = \left(\sum_{j=1}^{n_i} x_{ij} \right) / n_i$

Results of the statistical analysis

In the report, the p-value is provided for each test. The p-value determines at what level a certain null hypothesis can be rejected. The most common significance levels are

0 < p-value < 0.001 *Significant****
0.001 < p-value < 0.01 *Significant***
0.01 < p-value < 0.05 *Significant**

This is to say that, in order to determine that a result is statistically significant, the p-value of the test must be smaller than 0.05, and the null hypothesis must then be rejected.

In all the tests the null hypothesis is of the type that there is no difference between the classes concerning, for example, the expectation of a certain parameter or distribution.

In some cases, when it has not been possible to conduct one or more parts of an analysis (for instance, the word class analysis of Subproject 5), no statistical analysis has been performed.

Notes

1 For a description of Fisher's exact test, see Alan Agresti, 'A Survey of Exact Inference for Contingency Tables', *Statistical Science*, 7 (1992), 131–53.
2 Douglas C. Montgomery and George C. Runger, *Applied Statistics and Probability for Engineers* (2nd edn. New York: Wiley, 1999).

References

Agresti, Alan, 'A Survey of Exact Inference for Contingency Tables', *Statistical Science*, 7 (1992), 131–53.
Montgomery, Douglas C. and George C. Runger, *Applied Statistics and Probability for Engineers* (2nd edn., New York: Wiley, 1999).

Word classes

Subproject 1

	FF	P-value	FM	P-value	MF	P-value	MM	P-value	M	P-value	Constituent corpora in M
Noun										0.8857	
Adjective										0.4665	

Subprojects 2 & 4

	FF	P-value	FM	P-value	MF	P-value	MM	P-value	M	P-value	Constituent corpora in M
Noun										0.7771	
Verb										1	
Adjective										0.8775	

Subproject 3

	FF	P-value	FM	P-value	MF	P-value	MM	P-value	M	P-value	Constituent corpora in M
Noun										1	
Adjective										0.7425	

Subproject 6

	FF	P-value	FM	P-value	MF	P-value	MM	P-value	M	P-value	Constituent corpora in M
Noun										1	
Verb										0.6029	
Adjective										0.7566	

Hypotaxis

Subproject 1

Hypotaxis	FF	FM	P-value	MF	P-value	MM	P-value	M	P-value	Constituent corpora in M
Words/macrosyntagm	17.1636	19.5113	0.0144	23.4336	0.0061	20.0269	0.0466	20.2969	0.0003	FM MF MM
SCC/macrosyntagm	1.6063	1.7817	0.5435	2.0508	0.4335	1.9635	0.5195	1.8827	0.3433	FM MF MM
SCC/CP0	1.314	1.3605	0.8375	1.9811	0.2169	1.776	0.3523	1.5681	0.2922	FM MF MM
SCC1/macrosyntagm	1.0305	1.1352	0.5588	1.1602	0.6889	1.2322	0.4947	1.1704	0.4076	FM MF MM
SCC2/macrosyntagm	0.4253	0.4816	0.5014	0.6914	0.1699	0.5662	0.4414	0.542	0.2036	FM MF MM
SCC3/macrosyntagm	0.12	0.121	0.9721	0.1563	0.4731	0.1401	0.7599	0.1327	0.6863	FM MF MM
SCC4/macrosyntagm	0.0262	0.0332	0.4944	0.0313	0.7791	0.0192	0.6128	0.0284	0.8073	FM MF MM
SCC5/macrosyntagm	0.0044	0.0083	0.2837	0.0117	0.398	0.0058	0.8201	0.008	0.2903	FM MF MM
SCC6/macrosyntagm	0	0.0024	0.1542	0	1	0	1	1	0.1553	FM MF MM
SCC1/CP0	0.843	0.8668	0.8651	1.1208	0.3668	1.1146	0.3034	0.9748	0.3451	FM MF MM
SCC2/CP0	0.3479	0.3678	0.7634	0.6679	0.0839	0.5122	0.3172	0.4514	0.173	FM MF MM
SCC3/CP0	0.0981	0.0924	0.8068	0.1509	0.2691	0.1267	0.6287	0.1105	0.6347	FM MF MM
SCC4/CP0	0.0214	0.0254	0.6262	0.0302	0.6086	0.0174	0.7399	0.0237	0.7656	FM MF MM
SCC5/CP0	0.0036	0.0063	0.3351	0.0113	0.3524	0.0052	0.7653	0.0067	0.277	FM MF MM
SCC6/CP0	0	0.0018	0.1542	0	1	0	1	0.001	0.1553	FM MF MM

Subprojects 2 & 4

Hypotaxis	FF	FM	P-value	MF	P-value	MM	P-value	M	P-value	Constituent corpora in M
Words/macrosyntagm	17.4162	17.5621	0.8423	21.8456	0.0256	14.2395	0.0025	17.5621	0.8423	FM
SCC/macrosyntagm	0.9915	1.2066	0.0195	0.8787	0.6103	0.683	0.016	1.189	0.0301	FM MF
SCC/CP0	0.8099	1.0476	0.0021	0.7563	0.7776	0.7286	0.5254	1.0318	0.0037	FM MF
SCC1/macrosyntagm	0.7033	0.7792	0.2116	0.6434	0.6831	0.4952	0.0069	0.7719	0.2513	FM MF
SCC2/macrosyntagm	0.2106	0.3126	0	0.1691	0.4763	0.1333	0.0385	0.3126	0	FM
SCC3/macrosyntagm	0.0516	0.0855	0.0012	0.0441	0.6937	0.0408	0.5116	0.0855	0.0012	FM
SCC4/macrosyntagm	0.0144	0.0211	0.1262	0.0221	0.5598	0.0122	0.787	0.02	0.1851	FM MF MM
SCC5/macrosyntagm	0.0074	0.0056	0.5679	0	0.0061	0.0014	0.0461	0.0056	0.5679	FM
SCC6/macrosyntagm	0.0031	0.0015	0.2693	0	0.0183	0	0.0183	0.0015	0.2693	FM
SCC7/macrosyntagm	0.0008	0.0006	0.8204	0	0.1553	0	0.1553	0.0005	0.6787	FM MF MM
SCC8/macrosyntagm	0.0004	0.0002	0.685	0	0.3173	0	0.3173	0.0002	0.6124	FM MF MM
SCC9/macrosyntagm	0	0	0.3173	0	1	0	1	1	0.3173	FM MF MM
SCC1/CP0	0.5745	0.6765	0.0463	0.5538	0.8694	0.5283	0.5464	0.6548	0.0956	FM MF MM
SCC2/CP0	0.1721	0.2714	0	0.1456	0.5957	0.1422	0.4303	0.2714	0	FM
SCC3/CP0	0.0421	0.0743	0.0003	0.038	0.7968	0.0435	0.9329	0.0708	0.0008	FM MM
SCC4/CP0	0.0117	0.0183	0.0739	0.019	0.5217	0.0131	0.8664	0.0178	0.0915	FM MF MM
SCC5/CP0	0.006	0.0049	0.6544	0	0.0061	0.0015	0.0826	0.0045	0.5389	FM MF MM
SCC6/CP0	0.0025	0.0013	0.3037	0	0.0183	0	0.0183	0.0013	0.3037	FM
SCC7/CP0	0.0006	0.0005	0.8701	0	0.1553	0	0.1553	0.0005	0.7385	FM MF MM
SCC8/CP0	0.0003	0.0002	0.711	0	0.3173	0	0.3173	0.0002	0.6428	FM MF MM
SCC9/CP0	0	0	0.3173	0	1	0	1	1	0.3173	FM MF MM

Subproject 3

Hypotaxis	FF	FM	P-value	MF	P-value	MM	P-value	M	P-value	Constituent corpora in M
Words/macrosyntagm	20.0527	19.6844	0.5585	19.8005	0.8407	20.498	0.7278	19.8167	0.7037	FM MF MM
SCC/macrosyntagm	1.7307	1.7481	0.8944	1.5187	0.3207	1.5973	0.4561	1.6686	0.6235	FM MF MM
SCC/CP0	1.3876	1.4209	0.7517	1.2708	0.5089	1.25	0.33	1.4021	0.8881	FM MF MM
SCC1/macrosyntagm	0.9949	1.0052	0.8991	0.8664	0.2637	0.9503	0.7101	0.9616	0.6716	FM MF MM
SCC2/macrosyntagm	0.4392	0.4484	0.7865	0.3863	0.3757	0.4121	0.5873	0.4274	0.7238	FM MF MM
SCC3/macrosyntagm	0.1784	0.1745	0.8094	0.1583	0.519	0.1544	0.234	0.1677	0.4898	FM MF MM
SCC4/macrosyntagm	0.0645	0.0637	0.9256	0.0633	0.9284	0.0523	0.3014	0.0622	0.7676	FM MF MM
SCC5/macrosyntagm	0.0284	0.0255	0.5616	0.026	0.7676	0.0188	0.1414	0.0248	0.4189	FM MF MM
SCC6/macrosyntagm	0.0136	0.0134	0.9752	0.0133	0.9573	0.0054	0.0198	0.0134	0.9623	FM MF
SCC7/macrosyntagm	0.0059	0.0071	0.6135	0.0044	0.5249	0.0027	0.1694	0.0059	0.9909	FM MM
SCC8/macrosyntagm	0.0028	0.0049	0.3179	0.0006	0.0452	0.0013	0.3597	0.0043	0.4132	FM MM
SCC9/macrosyntagm	0.0015	0.0025	0.5535	0	0.0548	0	0.0548	0.0015	0.9809	FM MF MM

	FF	FM	P-value	MF	P-value	MM	P-value	M	P-value	Constituent corpora in M
SCC1/CP0	0.7977	0.8171	0.7671	0.725	0.4431	0.9672	0.1374	0.8081	0.8699	FM MF MM
SCC2/CP0	0.3521	0.3645	0.6519	0.3233	0.5599	0.4194	0.1609	0.3592	0.795	FM MF MM
SCC3/CP0	0.143	0.1419	0.9283	0.1325	0.6838	0.1571	0.4655	0.1409	0.8691	FM MF MM
SCC4/CP0	0.0517	0.0518	0.9958	0.053	0.9055	0.0533	0.8906	0.0522	0.9353	FM MF MM
SCC5/CP0	0.0228	0.0207	0.6133	0.0217	0.8786	0.0191	0.5656	0.0208	0.5972	FM MF MM
SCC6/CP0	0.0109	0.0109	0.986	0.0111	0.951	0.0055	0.0933	0.0104	0.8643	FM MF MM
SCC7/CP0	0.0047	0.0058	0.5892	0.0037	0.5916	0.0027	0.3664	0.0049	0.8964	FM MF MM
SCC8/CP0	0.0023	0.004	0.3081	0.0005	0.0513	0.0014	0.5628	0.0036	0.3681	FM MM
SCC9/CP0	0.0012	0.002	0.5432	0	0.0548	0	0.0548	0.0013	0.9698	FM MF MM
SCC10/CP0	0.0008	0.0018	0.4633	0	0.0998	0	0.0998	0.0011	0.7388	FM MF MM
SCC11/CP0	0.0004	0.0004	0.953	0	0.3173	0	0.3173	0.0003	0.7958	FM MF MM

Subproject 6

Hypotaxis

	FF	FM	P-value	MF	P-value	MM	P-value	M	P-value	Constituent corpora in M
Words/macrosyntagm	15.0374	17.9619	0	18.8519	0.0173	19.3481	0.0027	18.2897	0	FM MF MM
SCC/macrosyntagm	0.6925	0.8964	0.0241	0.8956	0.0574	0.9115	0.0041	0.8984	0.0044	FM MF MM
SCC/CP0	0.6183	0.7747	0.0466	0.8018	0.0551	0.8068	0.0054	0.7831	0.0094	FM MF MM
SCC1/macrosyntagm	0.5545	0.6733	0.052	0.6742	0.1172	0.6947	0.0129	0.6764	0.015	FM MF MM
SCC2/macrosyntagm	0.1103	0.1742	0.004	0.1805	0.0111	0.1802	0.0044	0.176	0.0002	FM MF MM
SCC3/macrosyntagm	0.0233	0.0369	0.0956	0.031	0.3947	0.0321	0.3472	0.0354	0.0631	FM MF MM
SCC4/macrosyntagm	0.0038	0.0072	0.2311	0.0071	0.5028	0.0046	0.8022	0.0068	0.2102	FM MF MM
SCC5/macrosyntagm	0.0006	0.003	0.1766	0.0014	0.6053	0	0.1782	0.0023	0.1915	FM MF MM
SCC6/macrosyntagm	0	0.0015	0.0928	0.0014	0.3173	0	1	0.0013	0.0557	FM MF MM
SCC7/macrosyntagm	0	0.0003	0.3173	0	1	0	1	0.0002	0.3173	FM MF MM
SCC1/CP0	0.495	0.5819	0.1032	0.6035	0.1125	0.6149	0.0166	0.5896	0.0321	FM MF MM
SCC2/CP0	0.0984	0.1505	0.007	0.1616	0.0108	0.1595	0.0051	0.1534	0.0004	FM MF MM
SCC3/CP0	0.0208	0.0319	0.1178	0.0278	0.3907	0.0284	0.3589	0.0308	0.0783	FM MF MM
SCC4/CP0	0.0034	0.0062	0.2536	0.0063	0.5014	0.0041	0.8114	0.0059	0.2293	FM MF MM
SCC5/CP0	0.0006	0.0026	0.1816	0.0013	0.6043	0	0.1782	0.002	0.1971	FM MF MM
SCC6/CP0	0	0.0013	0.0928	0.0013	0.3173	0	1	0.0011	0.0557	FM MF MM
SCC7/CP0	0	0.0003	0.3173	0	1	0	1	0.0002	0.3173	FM MF MM

Other stylistic variables on the syntactic level. Code-switching and rhetorical figures (for the acronym TAP, see p. 55 and 137)

Subproject 1

TAP	FF	FM	P-value	MF	P-value	MM	P-value	M	P-value	Constituent corpora in M
Embedded macrosyntagms	0.44	0.95	0.2497	3.52	0.0003	3.07	0.0001	0.95	0.2497	FM
Irregular macrosyntagms	0.55	1.78	0.0221	0	0.5916	0.58	1	1.32	0.0868	FM MM
Polysyndeton/asyndeton	5.89	7.71	0.1298	10.94	0.008	9.02	0.0314	8.64	0.0127	FM MF MM
Code-switching	0.87	0	0.0081		0.2124	0	0.0569	0	0.0003	FM MF MM
Total number of rhetorical figures	80.35	105.81		76.28	0.1613	47.88		83.41		
Tropes	65.76	87.54	0	36.72	0	26.68	0	87.54	0	FM
Metaphors	46.02	66.67	0	29.3	0	17.27	0	66.67	0	FM
Other rhetorical figures	8.72	18.27	0	29.3	0	19.96	0	18.91	0	FM MM
Simile	8.62	10.68	0.1458	3.52	0.0046	2.11	0	10.68	0.1458	FM
Personification	4.8	3.91	0.4146	1.56	0.0195	1.54	0.0011	3.37	0.1114	FM MF
Metonymy	4.47	5.34	0.4391	1.95	0.0697	2.88	0.1565	5.34	0.4391	FM
Alliteration	5.45	6.29	0.4779	3.12	0.1441	2.11	0.0025	5.55	1	FM MF
Polysyndeton on the phrasal level	5.34	7.83	0.0422	0.78	0.0007	4.03	0.3084	7.83	0.0422	FM

Subprojects 2 & 4

TAP	FF	FM	P-value	MF	P-value	MM	P-value	M	P-value	Constituent corpora in M
Embedded macrosyntagms	2.01	2.12	0.7962	1.02	0.3637	1.81	0.8791	2.03	1	FM MF MM
Irregular macrosyntagms	2.56	2.78	0.6488	3.07	0.5625	4.31	0.0177	2.8	0.6001	FM MF
Polysyndeton/asyndeton	0.95	0.91	0.898	0.34	0.5073	0.42	0.2425	0.82	0.6055	FM MF MM
Unknown	0.35	0.25	0.4943	4.1	0	1.67	0.0005	0.25	0.4943	FM
Bases >8	3.93	6.77	0	9.52	0.0001	6.85	0.0054	6.93	0	FM MF MM
Code-switching	1.54	3.1	0	3.41	0.0301	2.92	0.0264	3.09	0	FM MF MM
Total number of rhetorical figures	7.93	6.6	0.0387	14.33	0.0006	9.86	0.1087	6.6	0.0387	FM
Tropes	5.21	4.75	0.3934	8.87	0.0148	5.83	0.5114	4.9	0.581	FM MM
Metaphors	1.85	1.29	0.0673	5.8	0.0002	2.5	0.2903	1.29	0.0673	FM
Other rhetorical figures	2.72	1.85	0.0173	5.46	0.0169	4.03	0.0827	1.85	0.0173	FM
Hyperbole	2.64	2.63	1	0.68	0.0425	2.22	0.5937	2.58	0.8799	FM MM
Simile	0.43	0.53	0.7265	0.34	1	0	0.137	0.45	1	FM MF MM
Irony	0.51	0.53		1.37	0.0909	0.97	0.1768	0.63	0.6416	FM MF MM
Rhetorical question	0.67	0.7	1	1.02	0.4548	0.83	0.6175	0.73	0.8874	FM MF MM
Climax	0.2	0.15	0.7631	0.34	0.4814	0	0.5928	0.14	0.5542	FM MF MM

TAP	FF	FM	P-value	MF	P-value	MM	P-value	M	P-value	Constituent corpora in M
Embedded macrosyntagms	2.82	3.81	0.0169	2.79	1	2.95	0.81	3.43	0.0896	FM MF MM
Irregular macrosyntagms	4.89	4.47	0.414	5.26	0.5841	4.7	0.9259	4.71	0.6997	FM MF MM
Code-switching	1.87	2.61	0.0348	2.47	0.1701	2.42	0.3132	2.55	0.0274	FM MF MM
Bases >8	13.98	15.11	0.3842	15.85	0.2597	16.76	0.2045	15.52	0.1884	FM MF MM
Total number of rhetorical figures	31.46	30.46	0.3569	51.93	0	47.92	0	30.46	0.3569	FM
Tropes	25.57	25.33	0.812	37.56	0	39.46	0	25.33	0.812	FM
Metaphors	5.07	6.78	0.0017	12.35	0	22.55	0	6.78	0.0017	FM
Other rhetorical figures	5.84	5.13	0.189	14.38	0	8.46	0.0102	5.13	0.189	FM
Personification	0.56	0.6	0.8802	1.71	0.0001	1.74	0.0019	0.6	0.8802	FM
Hyperbole	17.79	16	0.0396	19.51	0.1427	13.02	0.0014	16	0.0396	FM
Simile	0.87	0.91	0.9027	2.28	0.0001	1.21	0.4009	0.96	0.7297	FM MM
Metaphor	5.07	6.78	0.0017	12.35	0	22.55	0	6.78	0.0017	FM
Rhetorical question	1.95	0.91	0.0001	2.72	0.0816	1.74	0.8838	0.91	0.0001	FM

Subproject 5

TAP	FF	FM	P-value	MF	P-value	MM	P-value	M	P-value	Constituent corpora in M
Embedded macrosyntagms	5.3	4.58	0.2204	5.22	1	4.17	0.2731	4.63	0.2009	FM MF MM
Irregular macrosyntagms	12.18	11.95	0.8061	8.12	0.0023	10.91	0.4169	11.75	0.6136	FM MM
Polysyndeton/asyndeton	0.61	0.58	1	0.72	0.7898	0.64	1	0.62	1	FM MF MM
Code-switching	1.84	1.01	0.0103	1.3	0.421	1.61	0.8687	1.16	0.0206	FM MF MM
Bases >8	7.48	9.32	0.0315	11.87	0.0013	6.12	0.3385	9.86	0.0032	FM MF
Total number of rhetorical figures	35.83	35.89	0.9778	55.51	0	45.59	0	35.89	0.9778	FM
Tropes	21.62	23.67	0.0689	26.52	0.0064	25.84	0.0233	24.52	0.0043	FM MF MM
Metaphors	9.05	11.99	0.0003	15.07	0	14.13	0.0002	12.41	0	FM MM
Other rhetorical figures	14.22	12.22	0.028	28.84	0	19.42	0.0014	12.22	0.028	FM
Hyperbole	8.82	8.11	0.3636	7.39	0.2588	8.03	0.5852	7.97	0.2068	FM MF MM
Allusion	1.55	0.74	0.0045	1.88	0.5054	2.89	0.0292	0.74	0.0045	FM
Litotes	1.07	1.05	1	0.58	0.2904	0.8	0.6667	0.93	0.6265	FM MF MM
Simile	1.1	0.93	0.5968	1.88	0.1249	1.77	0.1621	1.09	1	FM MM
Euphemism	0.52	0.7	0.3928	0.29	0.758	0.32	0.7542	0.57	0.8705	FM MF MM

Subproject 6

TAP	FF	FM	P-value	MF	P-value	MM	P-value	M	P-value	Constituent corpora in M
Embedded macrosyntagms	0.83	1.42	0.0152	1.84	0.0204	1.78	0.0415	1.53	0.002	FM MF MM
Irregular macrosyntagms	3.19	2.32	0.0237	2.4	0.2946	1.94	0.1041	2.28	0.0077	FM MF MM
Polysyndeton/asyndeton	0.19	0.3	0.3566	0.14	1	0.65	0.0555	0.32	0.2273	FM MF MM
Code-switching	1.48	0.75	0.0031	0.28	0.0068	1.46	1	0.78	0.0016	FM MF MM
Bases >8	6.89	8.02	0.0571	9.21	0.0343	6.55	0.8614	8.02	0.0399	FM MF MM
Total number of rhetorical figures	11.79	12.79	0.1875	16.12	0.0017	13.45	0.2353	12.9	0.1215	FM MM
Tropes	7.6	9.41	0.0041	9.05	0.1758	9.08	0.2004	9.31	0.0032	FM MF MM
Metaphors	3.77	5.34	0.0009	5.52	0.0305	5.35	0.0617	5.37	0.0002	FM MF MM
Other rhetorical figures	1.71	1.39	0.2746	2.4	0.2227	1.78	0.8691	1.59	0.685	FM MF MM
Allusion	0.32	0.39	0.7015	2.12	0	0.65	0.2676	0.43	0.4778	FM MM
Epizeuxis	0.6	0.51	0.6519	0.28	0.4188	0.32	0.5708	0.45	0.3905	FM MF MM
Simile	1.5	1.69	0.524	1.13	0.6112	0.97	0.3703	1.51	1	FM MF MM
Metonymy	2.16	2.2	0.938	2.4	0.679	2.76	0.3823	2.31	0.6741	FM MF MM
Rhetorical question	1.16	0.91	0.3169	2.26	0.0206	0.97	0.8406	0.92	0.2892	FM MM

Addressing the reader	FF	FM	P-value	MF	P-value	MM	P-value	M	P-value	M
Subproject 1	33.26	34.64	0.5458	19.92	0	28.21	0.0512	34.64	0.5458	FM
Subprojects 2 & 4	29.42	28.89	0.6448	16.04	0	32.64	0.0978	28.89	0.6448	FM
Subproject 3	35.32	31.31	0.0002	32.81	0.0792	28.99	0.0009	31.42	0.0001	FM MF MM
Subproject 5	22.84	23.28	0.704	26.67	0.0371	22.47	0.8753	23.75	0.3776	FM MF MM
Subproject 6	24.29	28.33	0.0001	28.36	0.029	29	0.0078	28.44	0	FM MF MM

Subprojects 2 & 4

Topics	FF	FM	P-value	MF	P-value	MM	P-value	M	P-value	Constituent corpora in M
House and home	20.75	30.41	0.1119	25	0.7159	5.56	0.191	30	0.1175	FM MF
Fabrics and clothes	26.42	6.76	0	8.33	0.2892	0	0.012	6.18	0	FM MF MM
Children and their upbringing	9.43	10.14	1	8.33	0.1365	11.11	0.355	8.99	1	FM MF MM
Family and relatives	49.06	37.16	0.0712	25	0.6877	11.11	0.0037	36.25	0.0424	FM MF
Obstetrics	16.98	4.05	0.0008	8.33	0.1192	0	0.072	3.93	0.0003	FM MF MM
The body	43.4	37.84	0.4363	16.67	1	16.67	0.0378	34.27	0.1308	FM MF MM
Sensory impressions	0	0	1	0	1	0	1	0	1	FM MF MM
The emotional life of the self and others	37.74	22.97	0.012	25	0.532	27.78	0.5969	23.6	0.0146	FM MF MM
Economy	16.98	25	0.1641	0	0.2088	5.56	0.303	21.35	0.4415	FM MF MM
Social life	17.92	20.95	0.6321	25	0.6946	22.22	0.7433	21.35	0.5419	FM MF MM
Travelling	17.92	21.62	0.5269	25	0.6946	33.33	0.199	23.03	0.3678	FM MF MM
Nature	7.55	14.19	0.1129	33.33	0.02	5.56	1	14.61	0.0899	FM MF MM
Politics and war	6.6	5.41	0.7892	8.33	0.5877	11.11	0.6174	6.18	1	FM MF MM
Education, wit, learning	5.66	13.51	0.0575	50	0.0002	83.33	0	13.51	0.0575	FM
Opinions about people	33.96	20.95	0.0218	25	0.7485	33.33	1	22.47	0.0383	FM MF MM
The relationship between letter-writer and recipient	4.72	12.16	0.047	16.67	0.1495	50	0	12.5	0.0339	FM MF
Meta-comments	33.96	59.46	0.0001	33.33	1	33.33	1	57.5	0.0002	FM MF
Fictionalisation	0	0	1	0	1	0	1	0	1	FM MF MM
Accidents and sensational events	1.89	2.03	1	0	1	0	1	1.69	1	FM MF MM

Subproject 3

Topics	FF	FM	P-value	MF	P-value	MM	P-value	M	P-value	Constituent corpora in M
House and home	30.56	40.52	0.1273	34.09	0.7028	43.48	0.2336	39.34	0.1645	FM MF MM
Fabrics and clothes	32.41	20.69	0.05	20.45	0.1697	13.04	0.0779	19.67	0.0166	FM MF MM
Children and their upbringing	42.59	31.03	0.0956	34.09	0.3662	39.13	0.8194	32.79	0.1022	FM MF MM
Family and relatives	60.19	52.59	0.282	70.45	0.2692	56.52	0.8166	53.24	0.3023	FM MM
Obstetrics	18.52	8.62	0.0324	11.36	0.3413	0	0.0235	8.2	0.0143	FM MF MM
The body	69.44	57.76	0.0732	61.36	0.3474	56.52	0.2336	58.47	0.079	FM MF MM
Sensory impressions	0	0.86	1	2.27	0.2895	4.35	0.1756	1.64	0.2974	FM MF MM
The emotional life of the self and others	75	79.31	0.524	93.18	0.0124	73.91	1	81.97	0.1778	FM MF MM
Economy	27.78	29.31	0.8825	45.45	0.056	69.57	0.0002	33.75	0.348	FM MF
Social life	50	37.07	0.0593	40.91	0.3715	47.83	1	39.34	0.0869	FM MF MM
Travelling	38.89	46.55	0.2806	54.55	0.1041	52.17	0.2532	49.18	0.1129	FM MF MM

Contd.

	FF	FM	P-value	MF	P-value	MM	P-value	M	P-value	Constituent corpora in M
Nature	9.26	12.93	0.4049	9.09	1	30.43	0.0125	14.21	0.2698	FM MF MM
Politics and war	40.74	39.66	0.8922	43.18	0.8565	39.13	1	40.44	1	FM MF MM
Education, wit, learning	13.89	11.21	0.5525	22.73	0.2277	43.48	0.0026	14.38	1	FM MF
Opinions about people	69.44	68.97	1	86.36	0.0398	82.61	0.3074	71.22	0.7801	FM MM
The relationship between letter-writer and recipient	76.85	65.52	0.077	77.27	1	56.52	0.0672	67.21	0.0847	FM MF MM
Meta-comments	78.7	90.52	0.0157	90.91	0.1008	82.61	0.7833	89.62	0.015	FM MF MM
Fictionalisation	0	0	1	0	1	0	1	0	1	FM MF MM
Accidents and sensational events	5.56	2.59	0.3192	4.55	1	4.35	1	3.28	0.3714	FM MF MM

Subproject 5

Topics	FF	FM	P-value	MF	P-value	MM	P-value	M	P-value	Constituent corpora in M
House and home	21.71	16.53	0.337	36	0.1326	16	0.6022	16.44	0.2834	FM MM
Fabrics and clothes	3.88	1.65	0.4482	0	1	4	1	1.75	0.2962	FM MF MM
Children and their upbringing	18.6	14.88	0.4995	0	0.0146	0	0.0146	14.88	0.4995	FM
Family and relatives	28.68	28.93	1	4	0.0095	12	0.1324	26.03	0.6845	FM MM
Obstetrics	5.43	3.31	0.542	0	0.5993	0	0.5993	2.34	0.2162	FM MF MM
The body	47.29	39.67	0.2517	48	1	36	0.3816	40.35	0.2413	FM MF MM
Sensory impressions	3.1	0.83	0.3712	4	1	12	0.0851	1.37	0.424	FM MF
The emotional life of the self and others	33.33	36.36	0.6905	40	0.646	28	0.6498	35.67	0.714	FM MF MM
Economy	31.01	44.63	0.0274	24	0.6344	28	1	39.18	0.1468	FM MF MM
Social life	50.39	23.14	0	36	0.1991	8	0	22.81	0	FM MF MM
Travelling	37.21	22.31	0.0128	28	0.4954	20	0.112	22.81	0.0072	FM MF MM
Nature	34.88	18.18	0.0041	16	0.0986	20	0.1683	18.13	0.0012	FM MF MM
Politics and war	16.28	16.53	1	4	0.1296	24	0.39	15.79	1	FM MF MM
Education, wit, learning	47.29	56.2	0.1661	52	0.8273	72	0.029	57.89	0.0797	FM MF MM
Opinions about people	68.22	44.63	0.0002	72	0.816	48	0.0672	45.21	0.0002	FM MM
The relationship between letter-writer and recipient	13.95	24.79	0.0366	56	0	36	0.0177	26.71	0.0111	FM MM
Meta-comments	24.81	22.31	0.658	28	0.8024	20	0.799	22.81	0.6836	FM MF MM
Fictionalisation	4.65	2.48	0.5019	24	0.0048	4	1	2.74	0.5232	FM MM
Accidents and sensational events	3.1	1.65	0.6847	0	1	4	1	1.75	0.4683	FM MF MM

Subproject 6

Topics	FF	FM	P-value	MF	P-value	MM	P-value	M	P-value	Constituent corpora in M
House and home	5.17	0.93	0.1208	0	0.5908	4	1	1.27	0.0744	FM MF MM
Fabrics and clothes	9.48	1.85	0.0198	0	0.2129	0	0.2129	1.27	0.0025	FM MF MM
Children and their upbringing	7.76	3.7	0.2567	16	0.2468	0	0.3614	3.01	0.1511	FM MM
Family and relatives	6.9	5.56	0.7857	4	1	16	0.226	6.96	1	FM MF MM
Obstetrics	4.31	5.56	0.7622	0	0.5859	0	0.5859	3.8	1	FM MF MM
The body	28.45	12.04	0.0028	20	0.464	20	0.464	14.56	0.0062	FM MF MM
Sensory impressions	0	0	1	0	1	0	1	0	1	FM MF MM
The emotional life of the self and others	42.24	46.3	0.5911	40	1	32	0.3782	43.04	0.9024	FM MF MM
Economy	5.17	10.19	0.2079	16	0.0769	24	0.0077	13.29	0.0385	FM MF MM
Social life	20.69	5.56	0.0008	4	0.0479	8	0.1658	5.7	0.0003	FM MF MM
Travelling	16.38	10.19	0.2386	12	0.7652	24	0.3903	12.66	0.3882	FM MF MM
Nature	3.45	1.85	0.6845	4	1	4	1	2.53	0.7255	FM MF MM
Politics and war	6.9	12.96	0.1771	0	0.3505	0	0.3505	8.86	0.6555	FM MF MM
Education, wit, learning	14.66	25.93	0.0449	36	0.0209	52	0.0002	27.82	0.0137	FM MF
Opinions about people	56.9	48.15	0.2283	40	0.1838	56	1	48.1	0.1784	FM MF MM
The relationship between letter-writer and recipient	37.07	50.93	0.0434	36	1	32	0.8189	45.57	0.1742	FM MF MM
Meta-comments	15.52	22.22	0.2319	40	0.0108	20	0.5596	24.68	0.0718	FM MF MM
Fictionalisation	0	0	1	4	0.1773	0	1	0.63	1	FM MF MM
Accidents and sensational events	3.45	2.78	1	0	1	0	1	1.9	0.4614	FM MF MM

Appendix 3
Register of letters

The letters are listed for each subproject, and are arranged in each corpus by writer (female writers followed by male writers) arranged alphabetically by the writers' surnames. Usually the women can be found under their maiden names with their married names in parentheses. If the writer is well-known or exclusively known by her married name, she has been listed under this name followed by her maiden name in parentheses.

If the letters are available in published editions, these references have been given in agreement with standard bibliographic practice. Individual letter numbers or page references have not been provided unless necessary, however. Where applicable, the archival information for the source material has been provided according to the following format: the name of the repository, followed by the name of the collection. In the case of the National Archives of Sweden (Riksarkivet, RA), the so-called E number is also provided.

It is explicitly indicated in the tables when more than one value per corpus has been obtained.

Letters, Subproject 1

Hildegard of Bingen (1098–1179)

Recipient	Date	Corpus	Source
			Hildegardis Bingensis epistolarium, eds. L. Van Acker & M. Klaes Hachmüller, 3 vols (Turnhout: Brepols, 1999–2001)
The abbess of Altena	before 1170	FF	No. 49
Sophia, abbess of Altwik	1164–1170	FF	No. 50R
The nuns of Andernach	1148–1150	FF	No. 52R
An abbess in Bamberg	after 1157	FF	No. 61R
The nun Gertrude in Bamberg	after 1161	FF	No. 62R
The nuns in Bamberg	1157–1170	FF	No. 63
Richardis, abbess of Bassum	1151–1152	FF	No. 64
The nuns of Clusin	1161–1163(?)	FF	No. 73
An abbess in Erfurt	before 1173	FF	No. 94R
A "magistra" in Erlesbüren	1166–1170(?)	FF	No. 95
Adelheid, abbess of Gandersheim	1152–1173	FF	No. 99
Adelheid, abbess of Gandersheim	1152–1173	FF	No. 101
The abbess of Gerbstädt	before 1173	FF	No. 110R
The abbess of Herkenrode (?)	before 1173	FF	No. 117R
The prioress of Ilbenstadt	before 1173	FF	No. 140R
The abbess of Kaufungen	before 1173	FF	No. 147R

211

Sophia, abbess of Kitzingen	1153–1155(?)	FF	No. 150R
Sophia, abbess of Kitzingen	1153–1155(?)	FF	No. 151
Rumunda, lay sister of Kitzingen	before 1170	FF	No. 152
An abbess in Cologne/Bonn	1163(?)–1173	FF	No. 156R
Hazzecha, abbess of Krauftal	1160–1173(?)	FF	No. 159R
Hazzecha, abbess of Krauftal	1160–1173(?)	FF	No. 160R
Hazzecha, abbess of Krauftal	1160–1173(?)	FF	No. 161
The nuns of Krauftal	1161–1170	FF	No. 162
The abbess of Lubolzberg(?)	before 1173	FF	No. 163R
An abbess in Metz	before 1173	FF	No. 174R
An abbess in Neuss	before 1173	FF	No. 177R
An abbess in Regensburg	c.1162–1173	FF	No. 184
An abbess in Regensburg	c.1162–1173	FF	No. 185R
An abbess in Regensburg	before 1173	FF	No. 186R
The nuns of Mount St Rupert	c.1153–1170	FF	No. 192
The nuns of Mount St Rupert	c.1153–1170	FF	No. 193
The nuns of Mount St Rupert	c.1153–1170	FF	No. 194
The nuns of Mount St Rupert	c.1153–1170	FF	No. 195R
Elisabeth, abbess of St Thomas an der Kyll(?)	c.1175	FF	No. 198
Elisabeth, nun of Schönau	1152–1156	FF	No. 201R
Luitburga, nun of Trier	before 1170	FF	No. 222
Gertrude, nun of Wechterswinkel	1156–1157	FF	No. 232
Gertrude, nun of Wechterswinkel	1156–1157	FF	No. 233
Jutta, lay-sister of Wechterswinkel	1153–1154	FF	No. 234
The nuns of Wechterswinkel	1157–1170	FF	No. 235
The abbess of Widersdorf	before 1173	FF	No. 237R
Christina, prioress of Woffenheim	before 1170	FF	No. 238
The nuns of Woffenheim	before 1170	FF	No. 239
The nuns in Zwiefalten	1153–1154	FF	No. 250R
Unidentified abbess	c.1170–1179	FF	No. 266
Unidentified abbess	c.1170–1179	FF	No. 267
Unidentified abbess	c.1170–1179	FF	No. 268
Unidentified abbess	1173–1179(?)	FF	No. 269R
Unidentified nun	1173–1179(?)	FF	No. 275
Eleanor, Queen of England	1154–1170	FF	No. 318
Bertha, Queen of the Greeks	1146–1160	FF	No. 319

The Margravine Richardis	1151	FF	No. 323
The Countess Oda of Eberstein	1153–1154	FF	No. 326
Luthgard, Countess of Neuffen	before 1160	FF	No. 327
A., Countess of Regensburg	1155–1170	FF	No. 328
Countess Irmintrude of Widen	before 1170	FF	No. 329
Unidentified married woman of Bassum	before 1170	FF	No. 333
Bertha, a married woman of Fulda	before 1170	FF	No. 335
Luthgard of Karlsburg	before 1170	FF	No. 336
Sibyl, a married woman of Lausanne	c.1153–1170	FF	No. 338
Sibyl, a married woman of Lausanne	c.1153–1170	FF	No. 339
Cuneza, a married woman of Strassburg	before 1170	FF	No. 341
Luitgard, a married woman of Strassburg	before 1170	FF	No. 342
Otilia of Trier	before 1170	FF	No. 343
Unidentified laywoman	c.1170–1179	FF	No. 346
Unidentified laywoman	c.1170–1179	FF	No. 354
Unidentified laywoman	c.1170–1179	FF	No. 356
Unidentified laywoman	c.1170–1179	FF	No. 368
Bernard of Clairvaux	1146–1147	FM	Anhang 4R
Pope Eugenius	c.1148–1153	FM	No. 2
Pope Eugenius	c.1148–1153	FM	No. 3
Pope Eugenius	c.1148–1153	FM	No. 5
Pope Eugenius	c.1148–1153	FM	No. 6
The abbot of Himmerod	c.1171	FM	No. 118
Pope Anastasius	1153–1154	FM	No. 8
Pope Hadrian	1154–1159	FM	No. 9
Pope Alexander III	1173	FM	No. 10
Hartwig, Archbishop of Bremen	before 1148–1152	FM	No. 11
Hartwig, Archbishop of Bremen	before 1148–1152	FM	No. 12
Hartwig, Archbishop of Bremen	before 1148–1152	FM	No. 13R
Heinrich, Archbishop of Mainz	1151–1153	FM	No. 18R
Heinrich, Archbishop of Mainz	1151–1153	FM	No. 19
Arnold, Archbishop of Mainz	1158–1160	FM	No. 20R
Conrad, Archbishop of Mainz	before 1165	FM	No. 21
Conrad, Archbishop of Mainz	before 1165	FM	No. 22R
Christian, Archbishop of Mainz	1179	FM	No. 24

Odo of Soissons	1148–1149	FM	No. 39R
Odo of Paris	1148–1149	FM	No. 40R
Kuno, abbot of St. Disibod	before 1155	FM	No. 74R
Guibert of Gembloux	1175–1176	FM	No. 103R
Guibert of Gembloux	1175–1176	FM	No. 106R
Guibert of Gembloux	1175–1176	FM	No. 109R
The abbot of Himmerod (?)	c.1171	FM	No. 118
The abbot Otto	before 1170	FM	No. 251
Unidentified abbot	before 1170	FM	No. 252
Unidentified abbot	before 1170–1179	FM	No. 253
Unidentified abbot	before 1170	FM	No. 254
Unidentified abbot	before 1170	FM	No. 255
Unidentified abbot	before 1170	FM	No. 256
Unidentified abbot	1173–1179(?)	FM	No. 257
Unidentified abbot	1173–1179(?)	FM	No. 258
Unidentified abbot	1173–1179(?)	FM	No. 260
Unidentified abbot	before 1170	FM	No. 261
Unidentified prelate	1173–1179(?)	FM	No. 262
Unidentified prelate	1173–1179(?)	FM	No. 263
Unidentified prelate	1173–1179(?)	FM	No. 264
Unidentified monk	before 1170	FM	No. 270R
Count Zeizolf, later monk	before 1170	FM	No. 271
Unidentified monk	before 1170	FM	No. 272
Unidentified monk	before 1170	FM	No. 273
Unidentified monk	before 1170	FM	No. 274
Radulfus, teacher	before 1170	FM	No. 279
Unidentified teacher	1173–1179(?)	FM	No. 280
The priest Eberold	before 1170	FM	No. 282
The priest Eberold	before 1170	FM	No. 283
The priest Reginbert	before 1170	FM	No. 286
Unidentified priest	before 1170	FM	No. 284
Unidentified priest	before 1170	FM	No. 285
Unidentified priest	1173–1179(?)	FM	No. 289
Unidentified priest	1173–1179(?)	FM	No. 291
Unidentified priest	1173–1179(?)	FM	No. 293
Unidentified priest	1173–1179(?)	FM	No. 294

Recipient	Date	Corpus	Source
Hartmut, layman of Kumtich	before 1170	FM	No. 337
Unidentified layman	before 1170	FM	No. 345
Fredrick, a layman	before 1170	FM	No. 347
Unidentified layman	before 1170	FM	No. 348
Unidentified layman	before 1170	FM	No. 349
Unidentified layman	before 1170	FM	No. 350
Unidentified layman	before 1170	FM	No. 351
Unidentified excommunicated layman	1173–1177(?)	FM	No. 352
Unidentified layman	1173–1177(?)	FM	No. 353
Unidentified layman	1173–1177(?)	FM	No. 355
Unidentified man	before 1170	FM	No. 362
Unidentified man	before 1170	FM	No. 363
Unidentified man	before 1170	FM	No. 364
Heidenric	before 1170	FM	No. 361

Guibert of Gembloux (c.1125–1213)

Recipient	Date	Corpus	Source
Hildegard of Bingen	1175–1179	MF	*Guiberti Gemblacensis Epistolae quae en codice B.R. BRUX. 5527-5534 inueniuntur. Pars 1, Epistolae I–XXIV*, ed. Alberti Derolez (Turnhout: Brepols, 1988), no. 16
Hildegard of Bingen	1175–1179	MF	No. 20
Hildegard of Bingen	1175–1179	MF	No. 21
Hildegard of Bingen	1175–1179	MF	No. 22
Hildegard of Bingen	1175–1179	MF	No. 24
Philip of Heinsberg, Archbishop of Cologne	1177–1179	MM	No. 7
The monks of Marmoutier	1183(?)	MM	No. 13

Bernard of Clairvaux (1090–1153)

Recipient	Date	Corpus	Source
Ermengarde, formerly Countess of Brittany	1121–1153	MF	*S. Bernardi opera* ed. J. Leclercq, Henri M. Rochais, 9 vols (Rome: Editiones Cistercienses, 1957–1998), no. 116
Ermengardie, formerly Countess of Brittany	1121–1153	MF	No. 117
Beatrice, a noble lady	1121–1153	MF	No. 118

The Duchess of Lorraine	1121–1153	MF	No. 120
Hildegard of Bingen	1121–1153	MF	*Hildegardis Bingensis epistolarium*, 3 vols, ed. by L. Van Acker (Turnhout: Brepols, 1999–2001), Anhang 4
Peter the Venerable, abbot of Cluny	1121–1153	MM	*S. Bernardi opera*, 9 vols, ed. by J. Leclercq, Henri M. Rochais (Rome: Editiones Cistercienses, 1957–1998), no. 387
Peter the Venerable, abbot of Cluny	1121–1153	MM	No. 389
Eskil, Archbishop of Lund	1121–1153	MM	No. 390
Alvisus, Bishop of Arras	1121–1153	MM	No. 395
An abbot	1121–1153	MM	No. 396

Peter the Venerable, abbot of Cluny (1092–1156)

Recipient	Date	Corpus	Source
The nun Adela, former Countess of Blois	1122–1156	MF	*The Letters of Peter the Venerable* ed. Giles Constable, 2 vols (Cambridge, Mass: Harvard University Press, 1967), no. 15
Heloise, abbess of the Paraklet convent	1122–1156	MF	No. 115
Bernard of Clairvaux	1122–1156	MM	No. 29
Bernard of Clairvaux	1122–1156	MM	No. 65
Bernard of Clairvaux	1122–1156	MM	No. 73
Suger, abbot of St. Denis	1122–1156	MM	No. 109
Étienne, nobleman of Auvergne	1122–1156	MM	No. 140

Peter Damian, saint (1007–1072)

Recipient	Date	Corpus	Source
Margrave Boniface of Tuscany	1042–1043	MM	*Die Briefe des Petrus Damiani*, vol. 1, ed. Kurt Reindel (Monumenta Germaniae historica: Die Briefe der deutschen Kaiserzeit; Munich: n. pub., 1983), no. 2
Gebhard, archbishop of Ravenna	1043	MM	No. 3
L[awrence, archbishop of Amalfi?]	1043	MM	No. 4
A bishop	1043	MM	No. 5
The monks of Pomposa	c.1044	MM	No. 6

John of Salisbury (1115/20–1180)

Recipient	Date	Corpus	Source
Adelidis, abbess of Barking	1156–1166	MF	*The Letters of John of Salisbury* ed. W.J. Millor, H.E. Butler & C.N.L. Brooke, 2 vols (Oxford: Clarendon, 1955–79), no. 69

Thomas Becket, Lord Chancellor of England	1156–1157	MM	No. 28
Peter, abbot of Celle	1157	MM	No. 31
Henry, Bishop of Winchester	1157	MM	No. 36
Henry, Bishop of Winchester	1157–1158	MM	No. 37

Letters, Subprojects 2 & 4

De la Gardie, Hedvig Ulrika, m. Armfelt (1761–1832)

Recipient	Date	Corpus	Source
Armfelt, Gustaf Mauritz	1 Jul 1788	FM	Riksarkivet, Stockholm (RA), Armfeltska samlingen, E 3135
Armfelt, Gustaf Mauritz	22 Aug 1788	FM	
Armfelt, Gustaf Mauritz	2 Apr 1790	FM	
Armfelt, Gustaf Mauritz	15 Jun 1790	FM	
Armfelt, Gustaf Mauritz	2 Jul 1790	FM	
Armfelt, Gustaf Mauritz	27 ? 1791	FM	
Armfelt, Gustaf Mauritz	25 Oct 1792	FM	
Armfelt, Gustaf Mauritz	10 Nov 1792	FM	
Armfelt, Gustaf Mauritz	15 Feb 1793	FM	
Armfelt, Gustaf Mauritz	19 Feb 1793	FM	
Armfelt, Gustaf Mauritz	20 Feb 1793	FM	
Armfelt, Gustaf Mauritz	26 Feb 1793	FM	
Armfelt, Gustaf Mauritz	4 Mar 1793	FM	
Armfelt, Gustaf Mauritz	11 Mar 1793	FM	
Armfelt, Gustaf Mauritz	20 Mar 1793	FM	
Armfelt, Gustaf Mauritz	24 Mar 1793	FM	
Armfelt, Gustaf Mauritz	8 Apr 1793	FM	
Armfelt, Gustaf Mauritz	19 Apr 1793	FM	
Armfelt, Gustaf Mauritz	25 Apr 1793	FM	
Armfelt, Gustaf Mauritz	28 Apr 1793	FM	
Armfelt, Gustaf Mauritz	5 May 1793	FM	

Armfelt, Gustaf Mauritz	9 May 1793	FM	RA, Armfeltska samlingen, E 3135
Armfelt, Gustaf Mauritz	17 May 1793	FM	
Armfelt, Gustaf Mauritz	21 May 1793	FM	
Armfelt, Gustaf Mauritz	15 Aug 1793	FM	

Ekerman, Julie, m. Björckegren (1765–1800)

Recipient	Date	Corpus	Source
Carl Sparre	16 Mar 1784	FM	RA, Börstorpssamlingen, E 3052
Carl Sparre	11 May 1784		
Carl Sparre	6 Sep 1789		
Carl Sparre	20 Sep 1789		
Carl Sparre	24 Sep 1789		
Carl Sparre	28 Sep 1789		
Carl Sparre	12 Oct 1789		
Carl Sparre	26 Oct 1789		
Carl Sparre	2 Nov 1789		
Carl Sparre	12 Nov 1789		
Carl Sparre	26 Nov 1789		
Carl Sparre	3 Dec 1789		
Carl Sparre	10 Dec 1789		
Carl Sparre	28 Dec 1789		
Carl Sparre	4 Jan 1790		
Carl Sparre	11 Jan 1790		
Carl Sparre	25 Jan 1790		
Carl Sparre	28 Jan 1790		
Carl Sparre	1 Feb 1790		
Carl Sparre	18 Feb 1790		
Carl Sparre	13 Dec 1790		
Carl Sparre	14 Mar 1791		
Carl Sparre	4 Apr 1791		
Carl Sparre	9 May 1791		
Carl Sparre	13 Jun 1791		

Gjörwell, Brite Louise, m. Almqvist (1768–1806)

Recipient	Date	Corpus	Source
Bergman, Hedvig Cecilia (m. Almqvist)	26 Sep 1791	FF	National Library of Sweden (KB), C. C. Gjörwell, Correspondence, Family letters, Supp. II, EpG 12:1–7
Gjörwell, Gustafva Eleonora (m. Lindahl)	29 Dec 1791	FF	KB, C. C. Gjörwell, Brevväxling, Familjebrev, Supp, Supp. II, EpG 12:1–7
Gjörwell, Gustafva Eleonora (m. Lindahl)	7 Aug 1796	FF	
Müllern, Brita Eleonora (m. Gjörwell)	25 Dec 1791	FF	
Carl Christoffer Gjörwell	9 Jan 1797	FM	
Linnerhielm, Jonas Carl	5 Jul 1791	FM	
Linnerhielm, Jonas Carl	20 Sep 1791	FM	
Linnerhielm, Jonas Carl	10 May 1793	FM	
Wallenius, Jacob	4 Sep 1792	FM	

Gjörwell, Gustafva Eleonora, m. Lindahl (1769–1840)

Recipient	Date	Corpus	Source
Gjörwell, Brite Louise (m. Almqvist)	16 Jan 1792	FF	KB, C. C. Gjörwell, Brevväxling, Familjebrev, Supp. II, EpG 12:1–7
Müllern, Brita Eleonora (m. Gjörwell)	13 Dec 1791	FF	
Müllern, Brita Eleonora (m. Gjörwell)	9 Jul 1792	FF	
Müllern, Brita Eleonora (m. Gjörwell)	26 Sep 1796	FF	
Gjörwell, Carl Christoffer	26 Dec 1791	FM	
Gjörwell, Carl Christoffer	16 jan 1792	FM	
Gjörwell, Carl Christoffer	12 Feb 1792	FM	
Gjörwell, Carl Christoffer	4 Mar 1792	FM	
Gjörwell, Carl Christoffer	22 Mar 1792	FM	
Gjörwell, Carl Christoffer	20 Oct 1796	FM	
Gjörwell, Carl Christoffer	26 Mar 1798	FM	
Gjörwell, Carl Christoffer	26 Apr 1798	FM	
Gjörwell, Carl Christoffer	4 Jun 1800	FM	
Gjörwell, Carl Christoffer	6 Sep 1800	FM	
Gjörwell, Carl Christoffer the Younger	26 Dec 1791	FM	
Gjörwell, Carl Christoffer the Younger	16 Jan 1792	FM	
Gjörwell, Carl Christoffer the Younger	31 Jul 1796	FM	
Gjörwell, Carl Christoffer the Younger	8 Jun 1797	FM	
Lindahl, Johan Niklas	2 Feb 1797	FM	
Lindahl, Johan Niklas	6 Apr 1797	FM	

Recipient	Date	Corpus	Source
Lindahl, Johan Niklas	10 Apr 1797	FM	
Lindahl, Johan Niklas	12 Apr 1797	FM	
Lindahl, Johan Niklas	17 Apr 1797	FM	
Lindahl, Johan Niklas	20 Apr 1797	FM	
Lindahl, Johan Niklas	21 Jun 1797	FM	KB, C. C. Gjörwell, Brevväxling, Familjebrev, Supp. II, EpG 12:1–7

Lenngren, Anna Maria, b. Malmstedt (1754–1817)

Recipient	Date	Corpus	Source
Malmstedt, Lisa Maja (1)	undated	FF	Source 1. Olle Holmberg, 'Några ord till hennes kära guddotter: Nio nyfunna brev från fru Lenngren', Svensk litteraturtidskrift 1954, No. 3 (Lund: Gleerup)
Malmstedt, Lisa Maja (2)	3 Jun 1790	FF	
Malmstedt, Lisa Maja (1)	10 Dec 1795	FF	
Malmstedt, Lisa Maja (1)	27 Jul 1796	FF	
Malmstedt, Lisa Maja (2)	16 Oct 1797	FF	Source 2. Samlade skrifter ed. Theodor Hjelmqvist & Karl Warburg, vol. 2 (Stockholm: Bonniers, 1917–19)
Malmstedt, Lisa Maja (1)	24 Jan 1799	FF	
Malmstedt, Lisa Maja (1)	29 Jan 1799	FF	
Malmstedt, Lisa Maja (1)	20 Jun 1799	FF	
Malmstedt, Lisa Maja (2)	23 Sep 1799	FF	
Malmstedt, Lisa Maja (1)	27 Nov 1806	FF	
Malmstedt, Lisa Maja (1)	4 Feb 1807	FF	
Malmstedt, Lisa Maja (1)	24 Jun 1813	FF	
Malmstedt, Lisa Maja (2)	30 Sep 1815	FF	
Rosén, Anna (2)	2 Nov 1778	FF	
Wrangel, Eleonora Charlotta (m. d'Albedyhll) (2)	2 Nov 1798	FF	
Ifvarsson, Jonas (2)	26 Feb 1777	FM	
Ifvarsson, Jonas (2)	7 Jun 1777	FM	
Ifvarsson, Jonas (2)	10 Mar 1778	FM	

Nordenflycht, Hedvig Charlotta (1718–63)

Recipient	Date	Corpus	Source
Ahlgren, Catharina	8 Mar 1763	FF	Samlade skrifter ed. Hilma Borelius & Theodor Hjelmqvist, vol. 3 (Stockholm: Bonniers, 1938)
Johanna Burman (m. Benzelstjerna)	23 Nov 1748	FF	
Beurelholm, Maria	21 Oct 1757	FF	

Recipient	Date	Corpus	Source
Wrangel, Ingeborg Catharina	5 Jul 1748	FF	
Reuterholm, Axel	15 Jul 1751	FM	
Reuterholm, Axel	13 Aug 1752	FM	
Reuterholm, Axel	3 Jun 1754	FM	
Reuterholm, Gustaf Gottfrid	12 Jun 1746	FM	
Reuterholm, Gustaf Gottfrid	30 Jun 1746	FM	
Reuterholm, Gustaf Gottfrid	2 Jul 1747	FM	
Reuterholm, Gustaf Gottfrid	12 Feb 1748	FM	
Reuterholm, Gustaf Gottfrid	28 Apr 1748	FM	
Reuterholm, Gustaf Gottfrid	undated	FM	
Reuterholm, Gustaf Gottfrid	21 Jul 1748	FM	
Reuterholm, Gustaf Gottfrid	3 Oct 1750	FM	
Älf, Samuel	15 Mar 1756	FM	
Älf, Samuel	6 Dec 1756	FM	
Älf, Samuel	19 Sep 1757	FM	
Älf, Samuel	31 Oct 1757	FM	
Älf, Samuel	undated	FM	
Älf, Samuel	5 Jun 1758	FM	
Älf, Samuel	25 Jun 1759	FM	
Älf, Samuel	undated	FM	
Älf, Samuel	17 Dec u.å.	FM	

Posse, Hedvig Ulrika, m. Törnflycht (1688–1762)

Recipient	Date	Corpus	Source
Törnflycht, Augusta (m. Wrede-Sparre)	29 Apr 1736	FF	RA, Börstorpssamlingen, E 3080
Törnflycht, Augusta (m. Wrede-Sparre)	15 Oct 1736	FF	
Törnflycht, Augusta (m. Wrede-Sparre)	24 Apr 1737	FF	
Törnflycht, Augusta (m. Wrede-Sparre)	4 May 1737	FF	
Törnflycht, Augusta (m. Wrede-Sparre)	7 May 1737	FF	
Törnflycht, Augusta (m. Wrede-Sparre)	12 May 1737	FF	
Törnflycht, Augusta (m. Wrede-Sparre)	15 Jun 1737	FF	
Törnflycht, Augusta (m. Wrede-Sparre)	3 Jul 1739	FF	
Törnflycht, Augusta (m. Wrede-Sparre)	23 Jul 1739	FF	
Törnflycht, Augusta (m. Wrede-Sparre)	9 Oct 1739	FF	

Recipient	Date	Corpus	Source
Törnflycht, Augusta (m. Wrede-Sparre)	23 Oct 1733	FF	
Törnflycht, Augusta (m. Wrede-Sparre)	12 Jan 1739	FF	
Törnflycht, Augusta (m. Wrede-Sparre)	30 Nov 1739	FF	

Sparre, Brita Stina, m. Törnflycht (1720–76)

Recipient	Date	Corpus	Source
Tessin, Ulrika Maria (m. Sparre)	19 Aug 1754	FF	RA, Börstorpssamlingen, E 3047
Tessin, Ulrika Maria (m. Sparre)	12 Aug 1757	FF	
Tessin, Ulrika Maria (m. Sparre)	27 Mar 1758	FF	
Tessin, Ulrika Maria (m. Sparre)	3 Apr 1758	FF	
Tessin, Ulrika Maria (m. Sparre)	13 Apr 1758	FF	
Tessin, Ulrika Maria (m. Sparre)	27 Apr 1758	FF	
Tessin, Ulrika Maria (m. Sparre)	16 Sep 1758	FF	
Tessin, Ulrika Maria (m. Sparre)	12 Dec 1758	FF	
Tessin, Ulrika Maria (m. Sparre)	8 Mar 1759	FF	
Tessin, Ulrika Maria (m. Sparre)	5 Apr 1759	FF	
Tessin, Ulrika Maria (m. Sparre)	11 Jun 1759	FF	
Tessin, Ulrika Maria (m. Sparre)	24 Jul 1759	FF	
Tessin, Ulrika Maria (m. Sparre)	8 May 1760	FF	
Törnflycht, Carl Fredrik	16 Mar 1758	FM	RA, Börstorpssamlingen, E 3097
Törnflycht, Carl Fredrik	20 Mar 1758	FM	
Törnflycht, Carl Fredrik	1 Aug 1758	FM	
Törnflycht, Carl Fredrik	2 Nov 1758	FM	
Törnflycht, Carl Fredrik	30 Jul 1759	FM	
Törnflycht, Carl Fredrik	27 Aug 1759	FM	
Törnflycht, Carl Fredrik	15 Oct 1759	FM	
Törnflycht, Carl Fredrik	9 Jul 1760	FM	
Törnflycht, Carl Fredrik	22 Jul 1760	FM	
Törnflycht, Carl Fredrik	15 Aug 1760	FM	
Törnflycht, Carl Fredrik	19 Aug 1760	FM	
Törnflycht, Carl Fredrik	29 Aug 1760	FM	

Stenbock, Beata, m. Sparre (1638–1712)

Recipient	Date	Corpus	Source
Lindschöld, Erik	20 Feb 1682	FM	RA, Ericsbergsarkivet, Autografsaml., vol. 202

Lindschöld, Erik	3 Dec 1682		FM
Lindschöld, Erik	12 Dec 1682		FM

Stenbock, Eva, m. Barnekow, (1710–1785)

Recipient	Date	Corpus	Source
Stenbock, Gustav Leonard	15 Jun 1733	FM	RA, Ericsbergsarkivet, Autografsaml., vol. 202
Stenbock, Gustav Leonard	31 Dec 1733	FM	
Stenbock, Gustav Leonard	18 Jan 1734	FM	
Stenbock, Gustav Leonard	21 Oct 1734	FM	
Stenbock, Gustav Leonard	23 Oct 1735	FM	
Stenbock, Gustav Leonard	10 Nov 1735	FM	
Stenbock, Gustav Leonard	28 Aug 1736	FM	
Stenbock, Gustav Leonard	19 Sep 1741	FM	
Stenbock, Gustav Leonard	4 Nov 1741	FM	
Stenbock, Gustav Leonard	May 1742	FM	

Stenbock, Magdalena Christina, m. De la Gardie (1730–1801)

Recipient	Date	Corpus	Source
Sparre, Brita Stina (m. Törnflycht)	undated	FF	RA, Börstorpssamlingen, E 3099
Sparre, Brita Stina (m. Törnflycht)	7 Jan 1772	FF	
Sparre, Brita Stina (m. Törnflycht)	1 Feb 1772	FF	
Sparre, Brita Stina (m. Törnflycht)	8 Mar 1772	FF	
Sparre, Brita Stina (m. Törnflycht)	18 Mar 1772	FF	
Sparre, Brita Stina (m. Törnflycht)	24 Apr 1772	FF	
Sparre, Brita Stina (m. Törnflycht)	30 May 1772	FF	
Sparre, Brita Stina (m. Törnflycht)	? Jun 1772	FF	
Sparre, Brita Stina (m. Törnflycht)	20 Jul 1772	FF	
Sparre, Brita Stina (m. Törnflycht)	31 Aug 1772	FF	
Sparre, Brita Stina (m. Törnflycht)	29 Jan 1773	FF	
Sparre, Brita Stina (m. Törnflycht)	undated	FF	
Sparre, Brita Stina (m. Törnflycht)	undated	FF	
Sparre, Fredrik	14 Jul 1751	FM	RA, Börstorpssamlingen, E 2974
Sparre, Fredrik	25 Jul 1751	FM	
Sparre, Fredrik	11 Aug 1751	FM	

Recipient	Date	Corpus	Source
Sparre, Fredrik	22 Aug 1751	FM	RA, Börstorpsamlingen, E 2974
Sparre, Fredrik	10 Dec 1751	FM	
Sparre, Fredrik	3 Jun 1751	FM	
Sparre, Fredrik	20 Jun 1755	FM	
Sparre, Fredrik	1 Dec 1762	FM	
Sparre, Fredrik	5 Dec 1762	FM	
Sparre, Fredrik	11 Dec 1762	FM	
Sparre, Fredrik	12 Jul 1783	FM	
Sparre, Fredrik	20 Jun 1784	FM	

Strömfelt, Beata Christina (1737–1820)

Recipient	Date	Corpus	Source
Strömfelt, Eva Charlotta	13 Jan 1762	FF	RA, Ericsbergsarkivet, Autografsaml., vol. 210
Strömfelt, Eva Charlotta	8 Sep 1762	FF	
Strömfelt, Eva Charlotta	12 Sep 1762	FF	
Strömfelt, Eva Charlotta	7 Oct 1762	FF	
Strömfelt, Eva Charlotta	15 Oct 1762	FF	
Strömfelt, Eva Charlotta	19 Oct 1762	FF	
Strömfelt, Eva Charlotta	4 Nov 1762	FF	
Strömfelt, Eva Charlotta	25 Nov 1762	FF	
Strömfelt, Eva Charlotta	23 Dec 1762	FF	
Strömfelt, Eva Charlotta	20 Jan 1763	FF	
Strömfelt, Eva Charlotta	10 Feb 1763	FF	
Strömfelt, Eva Charlotta	17 Feb 1763	FF	
Strömfelt, Eva Charlotta	24 Feb 1763	FF	
Strömfelt, Eva Charlotta	3 Mar 1763	FF	
Strömfelt, Eva Charlotta	10 Mar 1763	FF	
Strömfelt, Eva Charlotta	11 Apr 1763	FF	
Strömfelt, Eva Charlotta	16 May 1763	FF	
Strömfelt, Eva Charlotta	19 May 1763	FF	
Strömfelt, Eva Charlotta	26 May 1763	FF	
Strömfelt, Eva Charlotta	14 Sep 1763	FF	
Strömfelt, Eva Charlotta	9 Oct 1763	FF	
Strömfelt, Eva Charlotta	27 Oct 1763	FF	
Strömfelt, Eva Charlotta	26 Jan 1764	FF	

Tessin, Ulrika Maria, m. Sparre (1694–1765)

Recipient	Date	Corpus	Source
Sparre, Brita Stina (m. Törnflycht)	11 Oct 1741	FF	RA, Börstorpssamlingen, E 3100
Sparre, Brita Stina (m. Törnflycht)	19 Dec 1741	FF	
Sparre, Brita Stina (m. Törnflycht)	5 Feb 1742	FF	
Sparre, Brita Stina (m. Törnflycht)	12 Apr 1742	FF	
Sparre, Brita Stina (m. Törnflycht)	4 Aug 1746	FF	
Sparre, Brita Stina (m. Törnflycht)	4 Aug 1746	FF	
	to 12 Nov 1750		
Sparre, Brita Stina (m. Törnflycht)	4 Aug 1746	FF	
	to 12 Nov 1750	FF	
Sparre, Brita Stina (m. Törnflycht)	12 Nov 1750	FF	
Sparre, Brita Stina (m. Törnflycht)	13 Feb 1751	FF	
Sparre, Brita Stina (m. Törnflycht)	24 Feb 1751	FF	
Sparre, Brita Stina (m. Törnflycht)	31 Jul 1752	FF	
Sparre, Brita Stina (m. Törnflycht)	3 Jan 1753	FF	
Sparre, Brita Stina (m. Törnflycht)	28 Mar 1753	FF	

Törnflycht, Augusta, m. Wrede-Sparre (1714–1780)

Recipient	Date	Corpus	Source
Törnflycht, Carl Fredrik	26 Aug 1742	FM	RA, Börstorpssamlingen, E 3100

Westerskiöld, Regina, m. Estenberg (1698–1764)

Recipient	Date	Corpus	Source
Estenberg, Olof	7 Jan 1723	FM	RA, Stafsundsarkivet, Estenbergska saml., vol. 3 b, fasc. VII
Estenberg, Olof	7 Dec 1723	FM	
Estenberg, Olof	10 Dec 1723	FM	
Estenberg, Olof	28 Dec 1723	FM	
Estenberg, Olof	28 Apr 1740	FM	RA, Stafsundsarkivet, Estenbergska saml., vol. 5 b, fasc. IV
Estenberg, Olof	31 May 1740	FM	
Estenberg, Olof	30 Jun 1740	FM	
Estenberg, Olof	20 Aug 1740	FM	
Estenberg, Olof	15 Sep 1740	FM	
Estenberg, Olof	2 Jan 1740	FM	
Estenberg, Olof	11 Nov 1740	FM	

Recipient	Date	Corpus	Source
Estenberg, Olof	17 Dec 1740	FM	
Estenberg, Olof	2 Jan 1741	FM	
Estenberg, Olof	26 Jul 1741	FM	
Estenberg, Olof	27 Nov 1744	FM	
Estenberg, Olof	3 Dec 1746	FM	
Estenberg, Olof	24 Jan 1747	FM	
Estenberg, Olof	24 Feb 1747	FM	
Estenberg, Olof	8 Mar 1747	FM	
Estenberg, Olof	24 Feb 1748	FM	
Estenberg, Olof	20 Nov 1748	FM	
Estenberg, Per Olof	28 Oct 1726	FM	RA, Stafsundsarkivet, Estenbergska saml., vol. 4 b, fasc. IV
Estenberg, Per Olof	12 Jan 1727	FM	
Estenberg, Per Olof	18 Apr 1727	FM	
Estenberg, Per Olof	25 Sep 1727	FM	
Estenberg, Per Olof	3 Jun 1728	FM	
Estenberg, Per Olof	20 Jun 1728	FM	

Wrede, Agneta, m. Lillie (1674–1730)

Recipient	Date	Corpus	Source
Lillie, Axel Johan	2 May 1694	FM	RA, Börstorpssamlingen, E 2998
Lillie, Axel Johan	5 Jun 1694	FM	
Lillie, Axel Johan	13 Jun 1694	FM	
Lillie, Axel Johan	27 Jun 1694	FM	
Lillie, Axel Johan	4 Jul 1694	FM	
Lillie, Axel Johan	17 Jul 1694	FM	
Lillie, Axel Johan	8 Aug 1694	FM	
Lillie, Axel Johan	5 Sep 1694	FM	
Lillie, Axel Johan	15 Sep 1694	FM	

Estenberg, Per (1686–1740)

Recipient	Date	Corpus	Source
Estenberg, Olof	10 Dec 1723	MM	RA, Stafsundsarkivet, Estenbergska saml., vol. 3 b, fasc. VII

Gjörwell, Carl Christoffer (1731–1811)

Recipient	Date	Corpus	Source
Gjörwell, Brite Louise (m. Almqvist) (1)	6 Aug 1798	MF	Source 1. *Bibliotekarien C. C. Gjörwells familjebref*, ed. Oscar Levertin (Stockholm: n. pub., 1900)
Gjörwell, Brite Louise (m. Almqvist) (1)	28 Jan 1799	MF	
Gjörwell, Gustafva Eleonora (m. Lindahl) (1)	4 Jul 1790	MF	
Gjörwell, Gustafva Eleonora (m. Lindahl) (1)	31 May 1791	MF	
Gjörwell, Gustafva Eleonora (m. Lindahl) (1)	10 Dec 1793	MF	Source 2. *En stockholmskrönika ur C. C. Gjörwells brev: 1757–1778*, ed. Otto Sylwan (Stockholm: Bonniers, 1920)
Gjörwell, Gustafva Eleonora (m. Lindahl) (1)	1 Dec 1797	MF	
Gjörwell, Gustafva Eleonora (m. Lindahl) (1)	3 Apr 1798	MF	
Lidén, Johan Henrik (2)	24 Dec 1764	MM	
Lidén, Johan Henrik (2)	29 Jun 1773	MM	
Schönberg, Anders (2)	2 May 1774	MM	

Kellgren, Johan Henrik (1751–95)

Recipient	Date	Corpus	Source
Clewberg, Abraham Niclas	16 Nov 1770	MM	*Samlade skrifter*, vol. 6, ed. Otto Sylwan (Stockholm: Svenska vitterhetssamfundet, 1923)
Clewberg, Abraham Niclas	? Oct 1773	MM	
Clewberg, Abraham Niclas	? Feb 1774	MM	
Clewberg, Abraham Niclas	undated 1774	MM	
Clewberg, Abraham Niclas	17 Jan 1775	MM	
Clewberg, Abraham Niclas	10 Nov 1775	MM	
Clewberg, Abraham Niclas	17 May 1776	MM	
Clewberg, Abraham Niclas	28 Apr 1777	MM	
Clewberg, Abraham Niclas	7 Jul 1780	MM	
Clewberg, Abraham Niclas	3 Oct 1789	MM	

Thorild, Thomas (1759–1808)

Recipient	Date	Corpus	Source
Fougt, Elsa	? Jul 1791	MF	*Samlade skrifter*, vol. 6, ed. Stellan Arvidson, (Stockholm: Svenska vitterhetssamfundet, 1976–1980)
Fougt, Elsa	? Aug 1791	MF	
Fougt, Elsa	? Aug 1791	MF	
Göthe, Charlotta	23 Apr 1784	MF	

Hindström-Köllner, Gustava Margareta	19 Nov 1790	MF
Heurlin, Sven Erland	24 Jul 1780	MM
Heurlin, Sven Erland	17 Apr 1781	MM
Heurlin, Sven Erland	23 Feb 1782	MM
Hylander, Anders	30 Jun 1779	MM
Hylander, Anders	13 Mar 1781	MM

Letters, Subproject 3

Hedvig Elisabet Charlotta (1759–1818)

Recipient	Date	Corpus	Source
Fersen, Sophie von (m. Piper)	22 Dec 1777	FF	Riksarkivet, Stockholm (RA), Stafsundsarkivet, smärre enskilda saml., vols. 13–16
Fersen, Sophie von (m. Piper)	31 Dec 1777	FF	
Fersen, Sophie von (m. Piper)	23 Jan 1778	FF	
Fersen, Sophie von (m. Piper)	17 Aug 1778	FF	
Fersen, Sophie von (m. Piper)	22 Jun 1785	FF	
Fersen, Sophie von (m. Piper)	15 Aug 1797	FF	
Fersen, Sophie von (m. Piper)	16 Aug 1797	FF	
Fersen, Sophie von (m. Piper)	18 Aug 1797	FF	
Reuterholm, Gustaf Adolf	18 Jul 1789	FM	RA, Reuterholm-Adelgrenska samlingen, vol. 27
Reuterholm, Gustaf Adolf	3 Aug 1789	FM	
Reuterholm, Gustaf Adolf	6 Aug 1789	FM	
Reuterholm, Gustaf Adolf	20 Aug 1789	FM	
Reuterholm, Gustaf Adolf	30 Aug 1789	FM	
Reuterholm, Gustaf Adolf	25 Sep 1789	FM	

Lillienstedt, Charlotta Ulrika, m. Spens (1712–1793)

Recipient	Date	Corpus	Source
Törnflycht, Augusta (m. Wrede-Sparre)	3 May 1736	FF	RA, Börstorpssamlingen, E 3080
Törnflycht, Augusta (m. Wrede-Sparre)	undated 1736	FF	
Törnflycht, Augusta (m. Wrede-Sparre)	undated 1736	FF	
Törnflycht, Augusta (m. Wrede-Sparre)	undated 1736	FF	
Törnflycht, Augusta (m. Wrede-Sparre)	21 Oct 1736	FF	
Törnflycht, Augusta (m. Wrede-Sparre)	undated	FF	

Oxenstierna, Charlotta (1672–1727)

Recipient	Date	Corpus	Source
Oxenstierna, Eva (m. Stenbock)	29 Jun 1694	FF	RA, Ericsbergsarkivet, Fam. Stenbocks papper, vol. 57
Oxenstierna, Eva (m. Stenbock)	23 May 1696	FF	
Oxenstierna, Eva (m. Stenbock)	19 Jul 1696	FF	
Oxenstierna, Eva (m. Stenbock)	21 Jul 1696	FF	
Oxenstierna, Eva (m. Stenbock)	5 Aug 1696	FF	
Oxenstierna, Eva (m. Stenbock)	12 Aug 1696	FF	
Oxenstierna, Eva (m. Stenbock)	19 Aug 1696	FF	
Oxenstierna, Eva (m. Stenbock)	? Aug 1696	FF	
Oxenstierna, Eva (m. Stenbock)	13 Oct 1696	FF	
Oxenstierna, Eva (m. Stenbock)	14 Oct 1696	FF	
Oxenstierna, Eva (m. Stenbock)	2 Feb 1697	FF	
Oxenstierna, Eva (m. Stenbock)	2 Jun 1697	FF	
Oxenstierna, Eva (m. Stenbock)	6 Oct 1697	FF	
Oxenstierna, Eva (m. Stenbock)	24 Jan 1700	FF	
Oxenstierna, Eva (m. Stenbock)	4 Apr 1700	FF	
Oxenstierna, Eva (m. Stenbock)	5 Aug 1704	FF	
Stenbock, Magnus	19 Jun 1697	FM	
Stenbock, Magnus	22 Sep 1697	FM	
Stenbock, Magnus	6 Apr 1698	FM	
Stenbock, Magnus	16 Dec 1699	FM	
Stenbock, Magnus	14 Jun 1707	FM	

Sack, Hedvig Elisabet, m. Bielke (1708–1760)

Recipient	Date	Corpus	Source
Tessin, Carl Gustaf	6 Sep 1728	FM	RA, Ericsbergsarkivet, Autografsaml., vol. 181
Tessin, Carl Gustaf	24 Jan 1730	FM	
Tessin, Carl Gustaf	4 Aug 1731	FM	
Tessin, Carl Gustaf	17 Jul 1749	FM	
Tessin, Carl Gustaf	16 May 1753	FM	
Tessin, Carl Gustaf	19 Jun 1757	FM	
Tessin, Carl Gustaf	23 May 1758	FM	

Sparre, Brita Stina, m. Törnflycht (1720–1776)

Recipient	Date	Corpus	Source
Strömfelt, 'Ulla' (m. Sparre)	30 Oct 1757	FF	RA, Börstorpssamlingen, E 3075
Strömfelt, 'Ulla' (m. Sparre)	9 Mar 1758	FF	
Strömfelt, 'Ulla' (m. Sparre)	26 Feb 1760	FF	
Strömfelt, 'Ulla' (m. Sparre)	26 Feb 1762	FF	
Strömfelt, 'Ulla' (m. Sparre)	3 Jun 1762	FF	
Strömfelt, 'Ulla' (m. Sparre)	12 Apr 1763	FF	
Strömfelt, 'Ulla' (m. Sparre)	16 Jun n.a.	FF	
Strömfelt, 'Ulla' (m. Sparre)	28 May 1770	FF	
Törnflycht, Augusta (m. Wrede-Sparre)	17 Jun 1740	FF	RA, Börstorpssamlingen, E 3080
Törnflycht, Augusta (m. Wrede-Sparre)	19 Jul 1740	FF	
Törnflycht, Augusta (m. Wrede-Sparre)	25 Sep 1748	FF	
Törnflycht, Augusta (m. Wrede-Sparre)	29 Nov 1748	FF	
Törnflycht, Augusta (m. Wrede-Sparre)	10 Apr 1750	FF	
Törnflycht, Augusta (m. Wrede-Sparre)	10 Dec 1754	FF	
Tessin, Carl Gustaf	5 May 1739	FM	RA, Ericsbergsarkivet, Autografsaml., vol. 196
Tessin, Carl Gustaf	30 Nov 1739	FM	
Tessin, Carl Gustaf	1 Feb 1740	FM	
Tessin, Carl Gustaf	4 Oct 1740	FM	
Tessin, Carl Gustaf	18 Aug 1741	FM	
Tessin, Carl Gustaf	29 Aug 1769	FM	
Törnflycht, Carl	13 Jun 1746	FM	RA, Börstorpssamlingen, E 3097
Törnflycht, Carl	16 Jun 1746	FM	
Törnflycht, Carl	undated	FM	

Sparre, Charlotta Fredrika, m. von Fersen (1719–1795)

Recipient	Date	Corpus	Source
Sparre, Brita Stina (m. Törnflycht)	13 Aug 1739	FF	RA, Börstorpssamlingen, E 3080
Sparre, Brita Stina (m. Törnflycht)	2 Dec 1739	FF	
Sparre, Brita Stina (m. Törnflycht)	12 Oct 1740	FF	
Sparre, Brita Stina (m. Törnflycht)	7 Dec 1740	FF	
Sparre, Brita Stina (m. Törnflycht)	undated	FF	
Sparre, Brita Stina (m. Törnflycht)	26 Aug 1744	FF	
Strömfelt, 'Ulla' (m. Sparre)	30 Sep 1759	FF	RA, Börstorpssamlingen, E 3047

Recipient	Date	Corpus	Source
Strömfelt, 'Ulla' (m. Sparre)	24 Jul 17..	FF	
Strömfelt, 'Ulla' (m. Sparre)	26 Oct 1760	FF	
Strömfelt, 'Ulla' (m. Sparre)	20 Jun 1761	FF	
Strömfelt, 'Ulla' (m. Sparre)	17 Apr 1770	FF	
Strömfelt, 'Ulla' (m. Sparre)	13 May 1770	FF	
Tessin, Ulrika Maria (m. Sparre)	30 May 1740	FF	
Tessin, Ulrika Maria (m. Sparre)	24 Dec 1740	FF	
Tessin, Ulrika Maria (m. Sparre)	9 Apr 1741	FF	
Tessin, Ulrika Maria (m. Sparre)	23 Oct 1763	FF	
Tessin, Ulrika Maria (m. Sparre)	2 Aug 1764	FF	RA, Börstorpssamlingen, E 3061
Sparre, Carl	20 Feb 1746	FM	
Sparre, Carl	22 Apr 1746	FM	
Sparre, Carl	7 Jul 1746	FM	
Sparre, Carl	2 Jun 1747	FM	
Sparre, Carl	21 Aug 1747	FM	
Sparre, Carl	12 Dec 1749	FM	
Sparre, Carl	12 Sep 1757	FM	
Sparre, Carl	4 Jun 1758	FM	
Sparre, Carl	4 Feb 1759	FM	
Fredrik Sparre	29 Aug 1758	FM	RA, Börstorpssamlingen, E 2974
Fredrik Sparre	4 Jun 1767	FM	
Fredrik Sparre	9 Sep 1770	FM	
Fredrik Sparre	11 Jul 1773	FM	
Fredrik Sparre	8 Aug 1775	FM	
Fredrik Sparre	25 Sep 1789	FM	

Sparre, 'Ulla', m. Tessin (1711–1768)

Recipient	Date	Corpus	Source
Sparre, Brita Stina (m. Törnflycht)	3 Sep 1739	FF	RA, Börstorpssamlingen, E 3100
Sparre, Brita Stina (m. Törnflycht)	10 Mar 1740	FF	
Sparre, Brita Stina (m. Törnflycht)	25 Mar 1740	FF	
Sparre, Brita Stina (m. Törnflycht)	15 Apr 1740	FF	
Sparre, Brita Stina (m. Törnflycht)	27 Apr 1767	FF	
Strömfelt, 'Ulla' (m. Sparre)	17 Jun 1753	FF	RA, Börstorpssamlingen, E 3075

Strömfelt, 'Ulla' (m. Sparre)	14 Oct 1754	FF	
Strömfelt, 'Ulla' (m. Sparre)	18 Dec 1757	FF	
Strömfelt, 'Ulla' (m. Sparre)	? Jul 1758	FF	
Strömfelt, 'Ulla' (m. Sparre)	26 Sep 1761	FF	
Tessin, Ulrika Maria (m. Sparre)	? Jun 1737	FF	RA, Börstorpssamlingen, E 3047
Tessin, Ulrika Maria (m. Sparre)	31 Dec 1739	FF	
Tessin, Ulrika Maria (m. Sparre)	30 Jun 1740	FF	
Tessin, Ulrika Maria (m. Sparre)	28 Feb 1760	FF	
Törnflycht, Augusta (m. Wrede-Sparre)	21 Sep 1739	FF	RA, Börstorpssamlingen, E 3082
Törnflycht, Augusta (m. Wrede-Sparre)	25 Sep 1739	FF	
Törnflycht, Augusta (m. Wrede-Sparre)	15 Jan 1741	FF	
Törnflycht, Augusta (m. Wrede-Sparre)	14 Jul 1742	FF	
Törnflycht, Augusta (m. Wrede-Sparre)	10 Oct 1748	FF	
Törnflycht, Augusta (m. Wrede-Sparre)	15 Sep 1752	FF	
Törnflycht, Augusta (m. Wrede-Sparre)	22 Mar 1753	FF	
Törnflycht, Augusta (m. Wrede-Sparre)	5 Dec 1757	FF	
Törnflycht, Augusta (m. Wrede-Sparre)	? Feb 1759	FF	
Törnflycht, Augusta (m. Wrede-Sparre)	23 Apr 1764	FF	
Sparre, Fredrik	? Jun 1750	FM	RA, Ericsbergsarkivet, F. Sparres samling, vols. 11–12
Sparre, Fredrik	16 Sep 1752	FM	
Sparre, Fredrik	17 Jan 1760	FM	
Sparre, Fredrik	27 Jan 1760	FM	
Sparre, Fredrik	9 Dec 1765	FM	
Sparre, Fredrik	2 Jun 1766	FM	
Sparre, Fredrik	11 Jun 1766	FM	
Sparre, Fredrik	14 Feb 1768	FM	
Tessin, Carl Gustaf	undated	FM	RA, Börstorpssamlingen, E 3088
Tessin, Carl Gustaf	13 Jul 1724	FM	
Tessin, Carl Gustaf	10 May 1725	FM	
Tessin, Carl Gustaf	29 Jun 1726	FM	RA, Ericsbergsarkivet, C. G. Tessins saml. vols. 5–6
Tessin, Carl Gustaf	26 Dec 1730	FM	
Tessin, Carl Gustaf	5 Jan 1731	FM	
Tessin, Carl Gustaf	9 Oct 1731	FM	
Tessin, Carl Gustaf	26 Oct 1731	FM	
Tessin, Carl Gustaf	12 Feb 1732	FM	
Tessin, Carl Gustaf	16 Feb 1732	FM	

Recipient	Date	Corpus	Source
Tessin, Carl Gustaf	18 Jul 1732	FM	
Tessin, Carl Gustaf	22 Jul 1732	FM	
Tessin, Carl Gustaf	5 Jul 1733	FM	
Tessin, Carl Gustaf	5 Jan 1734	FM	
Tessin, Carl Gustaf	16 Jan 1734	FM	
Tessin, Carl Gustaf	20 Jan 1734	FM	
Tessin, Carl Gustaf	10 Jul 1741	FM	
Tessin, Carl Gustaf	28 Jul 1741	FM	

Strömfelt, 'Ulla', m. Sparre (1724–1780)

Recipient	Date	Corpus	Source
Sparre, Brita Stina (m. Törnflycht)	14 Mar 1761	FF	RA, Börstorpssamlingen, E 3100
Sparre, Brita Stina (m. Törnflycht)	27 Apr 1767	FF	
Sparre, Brita Stina (m. Törnflycht)	16 Feb n.a.	FF	
Sparre, Brita Stina (m. Törnflycht)	3 May 1770	FF	
Sparre, Brita Stina (m. Törnflycht)	23 Jul 1770	FF	
Sparre, Brita Stina (m. Törnflycht)	11 Oct 1773	FF	
Sparre, Brita Stina (m. Törnflycht)	30 Jul n.a.	FF	
Sparre, Brita Stina (m. Törnflycht)	undated	FF	
Sparre, 'Ulla' (m. Tessin)	12 Dec 1760	FF	RA, Ericsbergsarkivet, Autografsaml., vol. 210
Sparre, 'Ulla' (m. Tessin)	25 Aug 1761	FF	
Tessin, Ulrika Maria (m. Sparre)	2 Aug 1758	FF	RA, Börstorpssamlingen, E 3047
Tessin, Ulrika Maria (m. Sparre)	4 Apr 1760	FF	RA, Börstorpssamlingen, E 3062
Sparre, Carl	3 ? n.a.	FM	
Sparre, Carl	30 Jun 1756	FM	
Sparre, Carl	4 Jul 1756	FM	
Sparre, Carl	18 Aug 1757	FM	
Sparre, Carl	22 Aug 1757	FM	
Sparre, Carl	23 Feb 1758	FM	
Sparre, Carl	27 Feb 1758	FM	
Sparre, Carl	2 Mar 1758	FM	
Sparre, Carl	28 Nov 1758	FM	
Sparre, Carl	1 Dec 1758	FM	
Sparre, Carl	5 Dec 1758	FM	
Sparre, Carl	24 Mar 1770	FM	RA, Börstorpssamlingen, E 3064

Recipient	Date	Corpus	Source
Sparre, Carl	4 Apr 1770	FM	
Sparre, Carl	6 Aug 1770	FM	
Sparre, Carl	20 Jun 1773	FM	
Sparre, Carl	24 Jun 1773	FM	
Sparre, Carl	28 Jun 1773	FM	
Sparre, Carl	30 Jun 1778	FM	
Sparre, Carl	15 Aug 1778	FM	
Sparre, Fredrik	16 Nov 1757	FM	RA, Börstorpssamlingen, E 2976
Sparre, Fredrik	24 Nov 1757	FM	
Sparre, Fredrik	10 Dec 1757	FM	
Sparre, Fredrik	7 Oct 1759	FM	
Sparre, Fredrik	4 Nov 1759	FM	
Sparre, Fredrik	31 Jul 1778	FM	

Törnflycht, Augusta, m. Wrede-Sparre (1714–1780)

Recipient	Date	Corpus	Source
Sparre, Brita Stina (m. Törnflycht)	1 Mar 1740	FF	RA, Börstorpssamlingen, E 3100
Sparre, Brita Stina (m. Törnflycht)	15 Jul 1742	FF	
Sparre, Brita Stina (m. Törnflycht)	26 Nov 1743	FF	
Sparre, Brita Stina (m. Törnflycht)	14 Jul 1750	FF	
Sparre, Brita Stina (m. Törnflycht)	5 Dec 1750	FF	
Sparre, 'Ulla' (m. Tessin)	15 Aug 1739	FF	RA, Ericsbergsarkivet, Autografsaml., vol. 223
Sparre, 'Ulla' (m. Tessin)	11 May 1740	FF	
Sparre, 'Ulla' (m. Tessin)	26 Jun 1740	FF	
Sparre, 'Ulla' (m. Tessin)	19 Aug 1742	FF	
Sparre, 'Ulla' (m. Tessin)	16 Sep 1742	FF	
Sparre, 'Ulla' (m. Tessin)	27 Mar 1751	FF	
Sparre, Fredrik	24 Aug 1763	FM	RA, Börstorpssamlingen, E 2977
Sparre, Fredrik	15 Oct 176?	FM	
Sparre, Fredrik	28 Jul 177?	FM	
Sparre, Fredrik	18 Sep 1776	FM	
Sparre, Fredrik	3 Jan 1777	FM	
Sparre, Fredrik	30 Jul 177?	FM	
Sparre, 'Sigge'	25 Aug 1757	FM	RA, Börstorpssamlingen, E 3084
Sparre, 'Sigge'	12 Nov 1757	FM	
Sparre, 'Sigge'	2 Dec 1757	FM	

Recipient	Date	Corpus	Source
Sparre, 'Sigge'	13 Mar 1758	FM	
Sparre, 'Sigge'	11 Jul 1758	FM	
Sparre, 'Sigge'	10 Oct 1758	FM	
Wrede-Sparre, Axel	16 Sep 1735	FM	RA, Börstorpssamlingen, E 3079
Wrede-Sparre, Axel	8 Oct 1737	FM	
Wrede-Sparre, Axel	28 Aug 1740	FM	
Wrede-Sparre, Axel	1 Dec 1740	FM	
Wrede-Sparre, Axel	? Dec 1740	FM	
Wrede-Sparre, Axel	7 Jun 1741	FM	
Wrede-Sparre, Axel	8 Oct 1748	FM	
Wrede-Sparre, Axel	3 Nov 1748	FM	
Wrede-Sparre, Axel	10 Nov 1748	FM	
Wrede-Sparre, Axel	8 Dec 1748	FM	
Wrede-Sparre, Axel	19 Mar 1769	FM	

Sparre, Carl (1723–1791)

Recipient	Date	Corpus	Source
Sparre, Brita Stina (m. Törnflycht)	22 Sep 1740	MF	RA, Börstorpssamlingen, E 3100
Sparre, Brita Stina (m. Törnflycht)	21 Oct 1740	MF	
Sparre, Brita Stina (m. Törnflycht)	14 Mar 1745	MF	
Sparre, Brita Stina (m. Törnflycht)	22 Apr 1745	MF	
Sparre, Brita Stina (m. Törnflycht)	12 Aug 1745	MF	
Strömfelt, 'Ulla' (m. Sparre)	undated	MF	RA, Börstorpssamlingen, E 3070
Strömfelt, 'Ulla' (m. Sparre)	29 Jun 1756	MF	
Strömfelt, 'Ulla' (m. Sparre)	3 Sep 1760	MF	RA, Börstorpssamlingen, E 3072
Strömfelt, 'Ulla' (m. Sparre)	8 Sep 1760	MF	
Strömfelt, 'Ulla' (m. Sparre)	26 Sep 1761	MF	
Strömfelt, 'Ulla' (m. Sparre)	22 Jul 1771	MF	RA, Börstorpssamlingen, E 3074
Strömfelt, 'Ulla' (m. Sparre)	24 Jul 1771	MF	
Sparre, Fredrik	25 Sep 1749	MM	RA, Börstorpssamlingen, E 2972
Sparre, Fredrik	27 Sep 1749	MM	
Sparre, Fredrik	21 Oct 1749	MM	
Sparre, Fredrik	4 Jul 1777	MM	
Sparre, Fredrik	1 Sep 1779	MM	

Sparre, Fredrik (1731–1803)

Recipient	Date	Corpus	Source
Sparre, Brita Stina (m. Törnflycht)	1 Mar 1751	MF	RA, Börstorpssamlingen, E 3100
Sparre, Brita Stina (m. Törnflycht)	28 Apr 1751	MF	
Sparre, Brita Stina (m. Törnflycht)	13 May 1751	MF	
Sparre, Brita Stina (m. Törnflycht)	17 Apr 1755	MF	
Sparre, Brita Stina (m. Törnflycht)	25 Jul 1768	MF	
Sparre, Brita Stina (m. Törnflycht)	24 Sep 1773	MF	
Strömfelt, 'Ulla' (m. Sparre)	7 Nov 1757	MF	RA, Börstorpssamlingen, E 3075
Strömfelt, 'Ulla' (m. Sparre)	21 Nov 1757	MF	
Strömfelt, 'Ulla' (m. Sparre)	15 Jan 1761	MF	
Strömfelt, 'Ulla' (m. Sparre)	3 Dec 1770	MF	
Strömfelt, 'Ulla' (m. Sparre)	13 Dec 1770	MF	
Törnflycht, Carl	5 Aug 1756	MM	RA, Börstorpssamlingen, E 3097
Törnflycht, Carl	23 Sep 1758	MM	
Törnflycht, Carl	21 Oct 1759	MM	
Törnflycht, Carl	15 Nov 1759	MM	

Tessin, Carl Gustaf (1695–1770)

Recipient	Date	Corpus	Source
Sparre, 'Ulla' (m. Tessin)	30 Oct 1739	MF	*Tableaux de Paris et de la cour de France 1739–1742: lettres inédites de Carl Gustaf, comte de Tessin* ed. Gunnar von Proschwitz (Gothenburg: Acta) Universitatis Gothoburgensis, 1983
Sparre, 'Ulla' (m. Tessin)	1 Nov 1739	MF	
Sparre, 'Ulla' (m. Tessin)	27 Feb 1741	MF	
Sparre, 'Ulla' (m. Tessin)	9 / 29 Jun 1741	MF	
Sparre, 'Ulla' (m. Tessin)	1 Feb / 21 Jan 1742	MF	
Sparre, 'Ulla' (m. Tessin)	11 Feb / 31 Jan 1742	MF	
Strömfelt, 'Ulla' (m. Sparre)	9 Jul 1748	MF	RA, Börstorpssamlingen, E 3075
Strömfelt, 'Ulla' (m. Sparre)	6 Aug 1749	MF	
Strömfelt, 'Ulla' (m. Sparre)	5 Apr 1756	MF	
Strömfelt, 'Ulla' (m. Sparre)	5 Dec 1768	MF	
Härleman, Carl	19 Jun / 1 Jul 1740	MM	*Tableaux de Paris et de la cour de France 1739–1742: lettres inédites de Carl Gustaf...* ed. Gunnar von Proschwitz (Gothenburg: Acta) Universitatis Gothoburgensis, 1983
Härleman, Carl	11 / 22 Jul 1740	MM	
Härleman, Carl	22 Oct / 2 Nov 1740	MM	

Recipient	Date	Corpus	Source
Härleman, Carl	15 / 26 Dec 1740	MM	
Härleman, Carl	16 / 27 Jan 1741	MM	
Sparre, Fredrik	14 Nov 1752	MM	
Sparre, Fredrik	30 Nov 1752	MM	
Sparre, Fredrik	23 May 1763	MM	
Sparre, Fredrik	29 Oct 1764	MM	RA, Ericsbergsarkivet, F. Sparres samling, vol. 10

Wrede-Sparre, Axel (1708–1772)

Recipient	Date	Corpus	Source
Sparre, Brita Stina (m. Törnflycht)	9 Aug 1741	MF	RA, Börstorpssamlingen, E 3100
Sparre, Brita Stina (m. Törnflycht)	3 Jul 1763	MF	
Törnflycht, Augusta (m. Wrede-Sparre)	15 Jun 1741	MF	RA, Börstorpssamlingen, E 3081
Törnflycht, Augusta (m. Wrede-Sparre)	? Jun 1741	MF	
Törnflycht, Augusta (m. Wrede-Sparre)	16 Mar 1753	MF	
Törnflycht, Augusta (m. Wrede-Sparre)	16 May 1758	MF	
Törnflycht, Augusta (m. Wrede-Sparre)	13 Jun 1758	MF	
Törnflycht, Augusta (m. Wrede-Sparre)	16 Jun 1758	MF	
Törnflycht, Augusta (m. Wrede-Sparre)	4 Jul 1758	MF	
Törnflycht, Augusta (m. Wrede-Sparre)	7 Jul 1758	MF	
Törnflycht, Augusta (m. Wrede-Sparre)	14 Jul 1758	MF	
Sparre, Fredrik	16 Jun 1764	MM	RA, Börstorpssamlingen, E 2974
Sparre, Fredrik	29 Oct 1764	MM	
Sparre, Fredrik	16 Dec 1768	MM	
Sparre, Fredrik	1 Feb 1771	MM	

Letters, Subproject 5

Austen, Jane (1775–1817)

Recipient	Date	Corpus	Source
Austen, Anna, m. Lefroy (see also Lefroy)	29–31 Oct (?) 1812	FF	Jane Austen's Letters, ed. by R.W. Campbell (3rd rev edn, rev. by Deirdre Le Faye; Oxford: OUP, 1995)
Austen, Caroline	30 Oct 1815	FF	
Austen, Caroline	13 Mar 1816	FF	

Recipient	Date	Corpus	Source
Austen, Cassandra	14–15 Jan 1796	FF	
Austen, Cassandra	24 Oct 1798	FF	
Austen, Cassandra	28 Dec 1798	FF	
Austen, Cassandra	14 Jun 1814	FF	
Lefroy, Anna, b. Austen (see also Austen)	29 Nov 1814	FF	
Lefroy, Anna, b. Austen	30 Nov 1814	FF	
Lefroy, Anna, b. Austen	29 Sep 1815	FF	
Lloyd, Martha	12–13 Nov 1800	FF	
Lloyd, Martha	16 Feb 1813	FF	
Walter, Philadelphia	8 Apr 1798	FF	
Austen, Charles	6 Apr 1817	FM	
Austen, Francis	21 Jan 1805	FM	
Austen, Francis	22 Jan 1805	FM	
Austen, James-Edward	9 Jul 1816	FM	
Austen, James-Edward	16–17 Dec 1816	FM	
Austen, James-Edward	27 May 1817	FM	
Clarke, James Stanier	15 Nov 1815	FM	
Clarke, James Stanier	11 Dec 1815	FM	
Clarke, James Stanier	1 Apr 1816	FM	
Murray, John	23 Nov 1815	FM	
Murray, John	11 Dec 1815	FM	
Murray, John	1 Apr 1816	FM	

Baillie, Joanna (1762–1851)

Recipient	Date	Corpus	Source
Banister, Mrs	28 Mar 1814	FF	*The Collected Letters of Joanna Baillie* ed. Judith Bailey Slagle, 2 vols (Madison: Farleigh Dickinson University Press, 1999)
Berry, Mary	25 Dec 1805	FF	
Berry, Mary	2 Mar ?1806	FF	
Davy, Lady Jane	12 Oct 1816	FF	
Elliott, Anne	26 Oct 1809	FF	
Elliott, Anne	26 Feb 1810	FF	
Gordon, Anne Isabella 'Annabella', Baroness Byron, b. Milbanke (see also Milbanke)	1 Jul ?1816	FF	
Grahame, Mrs	2 Feb 1812	FF	

Recipient	Date	Corpus
Holtord, Margaret, m. Hodson	6 Jan 1815	FF
Milbanke, Anne Isabella 'Annabella', m. Gordon, Baroness Byron (see also Gordon)	3 Oct 1814	FF
Millar, Anne	8 Aug 1801	FF
Murdoch, Miss	17 Dec ?1806	FF
Erskine, William	4 Feb 1810	FM
Grahame, James	11 Mar 1810	FM
Hutchison, Rev.	13 Nov ?1807	FM
Lawrence, Sir Thomas	18 Jan 1812	FM
Lawrence, Sir Thomas	15 Jan 1816	FM
Mackenzie, Henry	12 Dec 1809	FM
Scott, Sir Walter	1808	FM
Scott, Sir Walter	4 Apr 1808	FM
Sotheby, William	12 Dec 1804	FM
Sotheby, William	26 Dec 1804	FM
Struthers, John	5 Dec 1811	FM
Thomson, George	18 Feb 1804	FM

Boscawen, Frances, b. Glanville (1719–1805)

Recipient	Date	Corpus	Source
Delany, Mary, b. Granville, formerly Mrs Pendarves (1)	20 Sep 1771	FF	Source 1. Cecil Aspinall-Oglander, *Admiral's Widow: Being the Life and Letters of the Hon. Mrs Edward Boscawen from 1761 to 1805* (London: Hogarth Press, 1942)
Delany, Mary, b. Granville, formerly Mrs Pendarves (1)	28 Jun 1772	FF	
Delany, Mary, b. Granville, formerly Mrs Pendarves (1)	14 Jul 1772	FF	
Evelyn, Julia, m. Sayer (see also Sayer) (2)	10 Aug 1737	FF	Source 2. Cecil Aspinall-Oglander, *Admiral's Wife: Being the Life and Letters of the Hon. Mrs Edward Boscawen from 1719 to 1761* (London: Longman, 1940)
More, Hannah (1)	5 Sep 1785	FF	
More, Hannah (1)	5 Aug 1795	FF	
Sayer, Fanny (1)	25 Feb 1783	FF	
Sayer, Julia, b. Evelyn (see also Evelyn) (2)	20 Nov 1755	FF	
Sayer, Julia, b. Evelyn (2)	25 Aug 1758	FF	
Sayer, Julia, b. Evelyn (2)	5 Sep 1758	FF	
Sayer, Julia, b. Evelyn (1)	4 Jan 1770	FF	

Recipient	Date	Corpus
Sayer, Julia, b. Evelyn (1)	17 Sep 1771	FF
Sayer, Julia, b. Evelyn (1)	11 Jul 1772	FF
Boscawen, Edward (2)	13 Aug 1746	FM
Boscawen, Edward (2)	18 Mar 1747	FM
Boscawen, Edward (2)	24 Mar 1747	FM
Boscawen, Edward (2)	18 Oct 1747	FM
Boscawen, Edward (2)	19 Oct 1747	FM
Boscawen, Edward (2)	3 Nov 1747	FM
Boscawen, Edward (2)	?1754	FM
Boscawen, Edward (2)	19 Oct 1757	FM
Boscawen, Edward (2)	undated	FM
Butler, Rev. William (1)	27 Jun 1797	FM
Falmouth, George Boscawen, 3rd Viscount (1)	31 Dec 1791	FM
Falmouth, George Boscawen, 3rd Viscount (1)	1 Jan 1800	FM

Burney, Frances 'Fanny', m. d'Arblay (1752–1840)

Recipient	Date	Corpus
Broome, Charlotte, b. Burney, formerly Mrs Francis (see also Francis) (1)	14 Aug 1798	FF
Burney, Elizabeth, b. Allen (1)	22 Jan 1796	FF
Burney, Esther (2)	Jul 1770	FF
Burney, Sarah, b. Rose (1)	1 Apr 1797	FF
Burney, Susanna Elizabeth (2)	after 10 Dec 1778	FF
Coussmaker, Catherine (2)	after 1 Dec 1778	FF
Francis, Charlotte, b. Burney, later Mrs Broome (see also Broome) (1)	after 19 Dec 1791	FF
Francis, Charlotte, m. Barrett (1)	6 Jul 1801	FF
Hales, Lady (2)	Dec 1778 or Jan 1779	FF
Thrale, Hester Lynch, b. Salusbury, later Mrs Piozzi (2)	14 Dec 1779	FF
Thrale, Hester Maria, m. Elphinstone, Viscountess Keith (1)	Jul 1798	FF
Waddington, Marianne (1)	7 Nov 1791	FF
Waddington, Marianne (1)	2 Aug 1793	FF

Source

Source 1. *The Journals and Letters of Fanny Burney* (Madame d'Arblay), 12 vols, ed. by Joyce Hemlow et al. (Oxford: Clarendon, 1972–84)

Source 2. *The Early Journals and Letters of Fanny Burney* ed. Lars E. Troide et al., 4 vols, (Oxford: Clarendon, 1987–2003)

Recipient	Date	Corpus
Broome, Ralph Sr. (1)	before 1 Mar 1798	FM
Burney, Charles Jr. (1)	2 Jul 1792	FM
Burney, Charles Sr.	10 Oct 1779	FM
Burney, Charles Sr. (1)	2 Oct 1792	FM
Burney, James (1)	before 11 May 1797	FM
Crisp, Samuel (2)	15 May 1775	FM
Crisp, Samuel (2)	2 Dec 1776	FM
Crisp, Samuel (2)	pmk 20 May 1779	FM
d'Arblay, Alexandre-Jean-Baptiste Piochard (1)	c.26 Sep 1793	FM
d'Arblay, Alexandre-Jean-Baptiste Piochard (1)	22 Oct 1796	FM
Johnson, Samuel (2)	16 Nov 1779	FM

Burney, Sarah Harriet (1772–1844)

Recipient	Date	Corpus	Source
Barrett, Charlotte, b. Francis	29 Jan 1811	FF	*The Letters of Sarah Harriet Burney*, ed. Lorna J. Clark (Athens, Ga: University of Georgia Press, 1995)
Barrett, Charlotte, b. Francis	1 Nov 1820	FF	
Broome, Charlotte, b. Burney, formerly Mrs Francis	7 Jun 1820	FF	
Burney, Sarah, b. Rose	4 Oct 1815	FF	
d'Arblay, Frances 'Fanny', b. Burney	6 May 1818	FF	
d'Arblay, Frances 'Fanny', b. Burney	before 3 Aug 1820	FF	
d'Arblay, Frances 'Fanny', b. Burney	7 Dec 1820	FF	
More, Mary	22 Oct 1798	FF	
Raper, Frances, b. Phillips	1807–10	FF	
Young, Martha, b. Allen	7 Oct 1793	FF	
Young, Martha, b. Allen	28 Oct 1796	FF	
Young, Mary	2 Aug 1793	FF	
Young, Mary	10 Oct 1796	FF	
Ayrton, William	3 Dec 1814	FM	
Burney, Charles Sr.	25 Oct 1798	FM	
Burney, Charles Jr.	1 Feb 1808	FM	
Burney, Charles Jr.	12 Feb 1808	FM	
Burney, Charles Jr.	26 Jan 1814	FM	
Burney, Richard Allen	7 Oct 1813	FM	

Colburn, Henry	24 Jan 1814	FM
Colburn, Henry	early 1816	FM
Huttner, Johann Christian	16 Jan 1809	FM
Huttner, Johann Christian	28 Feb 1809	FM
Huttner, Johann Christian	28 May 1809	FM
Huttner, Johann Christian	14 Nov 1809	FM

Lamb, Elizabeth, Viscountess Melbourne, b. Milbanke (1751–1818)

Recipient	Date	Corpus	Source
Bessborough, Henrietta Ponsonby, Countess of, b. Spencer	28 Jul 1815	FF	*Byron's 'Corbeau blanc': The Life and Letters of Lady Melbourne*, ed. Jonathan David Gross (Liverpool: Liverpool University Press, 1998)
Devonshire, Georgiana Cavendish, Duchess of, b. Spencer	Aug 1776	FF	
Devonshire, Georgiana Cavendish, Duchess of, b. Spencer	1780	FF	
Devonshire, Georgiana Cavendish, Duchess of, b. Spencer	27 Jun 1780	FF	
Devonshire, Georgiana Cavendish, Duchess of, b. Spence	24 Jul 1786	FF	
Huskisson, Mrs	Sep–Oct 1814	FF	
Lamb, Caroline, b. Ponsonby	13 Apr 1810	FF	
Milbanke, Anne Isabella 'Annabella', m. Gordon, Baroness Byron	21 Oct 1812	FF	
Milbanke, Anne Isabella 'Annabella', m. Gordon, Baroness Byron	25 Oct 1812]	FF	
Milbanke, Anne Isabella 'Annabella', m. Gordon, Baroness Byron	25 May 1814	FF	
Milbanke, Anne Isabella 'Annabella', m. Gordon, Baroness Byron	1 Dec 1814	FF	
Milbanke, Anne Isabella 'Annabella', m. Gordon, Baroness Byron	20 Dec 1814	FF	
Milbanke, Judith, Lady Milbanke, b. Noel	30 Jul 1805	FF	
Burney, Charles	2 Sep? after 1791	FM	
Fox, Henry	5 Dec 1804	FM	
George, Prince of Wales, later George IV		FM	

George, Prince Regent, later George IV
(see also George, Prince of Wales)

Recipient	Date	Corpus
Gordon, George, Lord Byron	4 Feb 1811	FM
Gordon, George, Lord Byron	24 Feb 1813	FM
Gordon, George, Lord Byron	15 Mar 1813	FM
Gordon, George, Lord Byron	24 Mar 1813	FM
Lamb, Frederick	20–21 Jan 1805 or earlier	FM
Lamb, Frederick	27 Feb 1815	FM
Lamb, George	13 Jul 1814	FM
Milbanke, Ralph	20 Mar 1791	FM
Unknown creditor	1799	FM

Piozzi, Hester Lynch, b. Salusbury, formerly Mrs Thrale (1741–1821)

Recipient	Date	Corpus	Source
Burney, Frances 'Fanny', m. d'Arblay	12 Jul 1784	FF	*The Piozzi Letters: Correspondence of Hester Lynch Piozzi, 1784–1821* (formerly Mrs Thrale) ed. Edward Alan Bloom and Lilian D. Bloom, 6 vols (Newark: University of Delaware Press, 1989–2002)
Byron, Sophia	11 Aug 1788	FF	
Lewis, Charlotte	20 Sep 1789	FF	
Lewis, Charlotte	18 Aug 1792	FF	
Owen, Margaret	c.12 Feb 1799	FF	
Pennington, Penelope Sophia, b. Weston (see also Weston)	24 Jan 1793	FF	
Pennington, Penelope Sophia, b. Weston	30 Jan 1793	FF	
Siddons, Sarah	27 Aug 1794	FF	
Thrale, Hester Maria, m. Elphinstone, Viscountess Keith	7 Jul 1787	FF	
Thrale, Hester Maria, m. Elphinstone, Viscountess Keith	13 Nov 1793	FF	
Weston, Penelope Sophia, m. Pennington (see also Pennington)	3 Apr 1789	FF	
Williams, Lady	18 Dec 1798	FF	
Williams, Margaret, of Bodelwyddan	28 Feb 1798	FF	
Chappelow, Leonard	7 Dec 1789	FM	
Chappelow, Leonard	15 Mar 1795	FM	

Drummond, Henry	after 19 May before 1 Jun 1792	FM
Johnson, Samuel	4 Jul 1784	FM
Johnson, Samuel	15 Jul 1784	FM
Lysons, Samuel	18 Jul 1788	FM
Lysons, Daniel	16 Mar 1794	FM
Lysons, Daniel	15 Feb 1795	FM
Lysons, Daniel	5 Jan 1796	FM
Ray, Robert	3 Jan 1798	FM
Weston, Jacob	10 Jan 1798	FM
Weston, Jacob	18 Dec 1798	FM

Wollstonecraft, Mary, m. Godwin (1759–1797)

Recipient	Date	Corpus	Source
Alderson, Amelia	11 Apr 1797	FF	*Collected Letters of Mary Wollstonecraft*, ed. Ralph M. Wardle (Ithaca: Cornell University Press, 1979)
Arden, Jane	c.4 Jun 1773–16 Nov 1774	FF	
Arden, Jane	17 Oct 1779	FF	
Barlow, Ruth	27 Apr 1794	FF	
Barlow, Ruth	20 May 1794	FF	
Barlow, Ruth	8 Jul 1794	FF	
Bishop, Eliza, b. Wollstonecraft	Nov/Dec 1785	FF	
Hays, Mary	c.Jan 1797	FF	
Wollstonecraft, Everina	12 eller 19 Jan 1784	FF	
Wollstonecraft, Everina	30 Oct 1786	FF	
Wollstonecraft, Everina	3 Mar 1787	FF	
Wollstonecraft, Everina	22 Mar 1797	FF	
Blood, George	4 Feb 1786	FM	
Cristall, Joshua	19 Mar 1790	FM	
Dyson, George	c.15 May 1797	FM	
Godwin, William	4 Oct 1796	FM	
Godwin, William	6 Jun 1797	FM	
Hamilton Rowan, Archibald	26 Jan 1796	FM	
Hamilton Rowan, Archibald	12 Sep 1796	FM	

Recipient	Date	Corpus	Source
Imlay, Gilbert	1 Jan 1794	FM	
Imlay, Gilbert	c.10 Oct 1795	FM	
Imlay, Gilbert	c.Mar 1796	FM	
Johnson, Joseph	13 Sep 1787	FM	
Roscoe, William	3 Jan 1792	FM	

Wordsworth, Dorothy (1771–1855)

Recipient	Date	Corpus	Source
Beaumont, Lady	24 Aug 1804	FF	*The Letters of William and Dorothy Wordsworth*, ed. Ernest de Selincourt and Alan M. Hill, 8 vols (2nd edn, Oxford: Clarendon, 1967–93)
Beaumont, Lady	28 Mar 1805	FF	
Beaumont, Lady	4 Nov 1805	FF	
Clarkson, Mrs Thomas	17 Jul 1803	FF	
Clarkson, Mrs Thomas	21 Nov 1803	FF	
Clarkson, Mrs Thomas	18 Mar 1805	FF	
Clarkson, Mrs Thomas	2 Apr 1805	FF	
Crackanthorpe, Mrs Christopher	21 Apr 1794	FF	
Hutchinson, Mary	12 Sep 1802	FF	
Hutchinson, Sara	14 Jun 1802	FF	
Marshall, Mrs John	29 Sep 1802	FF	
Pollard, Jane	9 Oct 1791	FF	
Pollard, Jane	5 Jun 1793	FF	
Coleridge, Samuel Taylor	22 May 1801	FM	
Coleridge, Samuel Taylor	9 Dec 1803	FM	
Coleridge, Samuel Taylor	29 Mar 1804	FM	
Ferguson, Samuel	22 Feb 1804	FM	
Poole, Thomas	4 Jul 1799	FM	
Wordsworth, Christopher	8 Dec 1797	FM	
Wordsworth, Christopher	27 Feb 1805	FM	
Wordsworth, John	25 Dec 1802	FM	
Wordsworth, John	30 Apr–1 May 1803	FM	
Wordsworth, Richard	9 Aug 1793	FM	
Wordsworth, Richard	17 Jul 1802	FM	
Wordsworth, Richard	4 Mar 1805	FM	

Wortley Montagu, Lady Mary, b. Pierrepont (1689–1762)

Recipient	Date	Corpus	Source
Bute, Mary Stuart, Countess of, b. Wortley Montagu	3 Oct 1758	FF	*The Complete Letters of Lady Mary Wortley Montagu*, ed. Robert Halsband, 3 vols (Oxford: Clarendon, 1965–67)
Calthorpe, Barbara, b. Yelverton	7 Dec 1723	FF	
Erskine, Lady Frances	11 Dec 1731	FF	
Hewet, Frances, b. Bettenson	Sep 1709	FF	
Hewet, Frances, b. Bettenson	Oct 1709	FF	
Justice, Anne	c.5 Jul 1710	FF	
Mar, Frances Erskine, Countess of, b. Pierrepont	31 Oct 1723	FF	
Mar, Frances Erskine, Countess of, b. Pierrepont	Apr 1727	FF	
Mundy, Philippa, m. Massingberd	25 Sep 1711	FF	
Oxford, Henrietta Harley, Countess of, b. Cavendish Holles	29 Nov 1747	FF	
Pomfret, Henrietta Fermor, Countess of, b. Jeffreys	Sep 1738	FF	
Stuart, Lady Frances	4 Sep 1758	FF	
Wortley, Anne	5 Sep 1709	FF	
Algarotti, Francesco	c.29 Sep 1736	FM	
Algarotti, Francesco	21 Oct 1736	FM	
Algarotti, Francesco	Dec 1736	FM	
Arbuthnot, John	Oct 1729	FM	
Stuart Mackenzie, James	1 Jun 1742	FM	
Stuart, Sir James	18 Oct 1758	FM	
Stuart, Sir James	4 May 1759	FM	
Wortley Montagu, Edward	14 Nov 1710	FM	
Wortley Montagu, Edward	c.8 Aug 1712	FM	
Wortley Montagu, Edward	15 Aug 1712	FM	
Wortley Montagu, Edward	c.24 Nov 1714	FM	
Wortley Montagu, Edward Jr.	3 Mar 1761	FM	

Boswell, James (1740–1795)

Recipient	Date	Corpus	Source
			Source
Denis, Marie Louise, b. Mignot (2)	25 Dec 1764	MF	Source 1. *The General Correspondence of James Boswell, 1766–1769*, ed. Richard C. Cole, 2 vols (Edinburgh: EUP, 1993–97)
Douglas, Margaret Douglas, Duchess of, b. Douglas (1)	13 Oct 1766	MF	
Northumberland, Elizabeth Percy, b. Seymour, Countess of, later Duchess of Northumberland (3)	27 Dec 1762	MF	Source 2. *Boswell on the Grand Tour: Germany and Switzerland, 1764*, ed. Frederick A. Pottle (London: Heinemann, 1953), 276–77
Thrale, Hester Lynch, b. Salusbury, later Mrs Piozzi (1)	5 Sep 1769	MF	
van Tuyll van Serooskerken, Isabella, 'Belle de Zuylen', 'Zélide', m. de Charrière (4)	26 Feb 1768	MF	
Dick, Sir Alexander (1)	23 Oct 1766	MM	Source 3. *Boswell's London Journal, 1762–1763*; ed. Frederick A. Pottle (London: Heinemann, 1950), 108–109
Erskine, Andrew (1)	25 Aug 1768	MM	
Mickle, William Julius (1)	27 Jun 1768	MM	
Smollett, Tobias (1)	14 Mar 1768	MM	Source 4. *Boswell in Search for a Wife: 1766–1769*, ed. Frank Brady and Frederick A. Pottle (Melbourne: Heinemann, 1957), 359–61
Wilkes, John (1)	6 May 1766	MM	

Garrick, David (1717–1779)

Recipient	Date	Corpus	Source
			Source
Abington, Frances	18 Jun 1774	MF	*The Letters of David Garrick*, ed. David M. Little and George M. Kahrl, 3 vols (London: Oxford University Press, 1963)
Burlington, Dorothy Boyle, Countess of, b. Savile	20 Jul 1749	MF	
Griffith, Elizabeth, b. Griffith	17 Feb 1770	MF	
Montagu, Elizabeth, b. Robinson	2 May 1772	MF	
More, Hannah	before 28 Jul 1776	MF	
Berenger, Richard	3 Mar 1770	MM	
Cox, Richard	before 16 Aug 1769	MM	
Devonshire, William Cavendish, 4th Duke of	10 Sep 1757	MM	
Fountain, Peter	31 Jul 1776	MM	
Garrick, George	1 Sep 1752	MM	

Johnson, Samuel (1709–1784)

Recipient	Date	Corpus	Source
Boothby, Hill	30 Dec 1755	MF	The Letters of Samuel Johnson, ed. Bruce Redford, 5 vols (Oxford: Clarendon Press, 1992–94)
Piozzi, Hester Lynch, b. Salusbury; formerly Mrs Thrale (see also Thrale)	8 Jul 1784	MF	
Porter, Lucy	6 Feb 1759	MF	
Thrale, Hester Lynch, b. Salusbury, later Mrs Piozzi (see also Piozzi)	19 Jun 1775	MF	
Thrale, Hester Maria, m. Elphinstone, Viscountess Keith	3 Sep 1783	MF	
Boswell, James	13 Jul 1779	MM	
Boswell, James	9 Sep 1779	MM	
Chesterfield, Philip Dormer Stanhope, 4th Earl of	7 Feb 1755	MM	
Orrery, John Boyle, 5th Earl of	9 Jul 1752	MM	
Taylor, John	17 Jun 1783	MM	

Pope, Alexander (1688–1744)

Recipient	Date	Corpus	Source
Blount, Martha	after 24 Nov 1714	MF	The Correspondence of Alexander Pope, ed. George Sherburn, 5 vols (London: Clarendon Press, 1956)
Blount, Teresa	7 Aug 1716	MF	
Cowper, Judith	17 Jan 1723	MF	
Marlborough, Sarah Churchill, Duchess of, b. Jennings	6 Aug 1743	MF	
Wortley Montagu, Lady Mary, b. Pierrepont	1720?	MF	
Bolingbroke, Henry St John, 1st Viscount	3 Sep 1740	MM	
Caryll, John	30 Apr 1713	MM	
Cromwell, Henry	21 Dec 1711	MM	
Oxford, Edward Harley, 2nd Earl of	3 Mar 1726	MM	
Swift, Jonanthan	15 Oct 1725	MM	

Walpole, Horace, 4th Earl of Orford (1717–1797)

Recipient	Date	Corpus	Source
Coke, Lady Mary, b. Campbell	15 Oct 1765	MF	*The Yale Edition of Horace Walpole's Correspondence*, ed. W.S. Lewis, 48 vols (London: Yale University Press, 1937–83)
Hervey, Mary, Lady, b. Lepell	10 Nov 1764	MF	
Hervey, Mary, Lady, b. Lepell	3 Sep 1765	MF	
Lennox, Louisa, Lady George Lennox, b. Ker	8 Sep 1766	MF	
Suffolk, Henrietta Howard, Countess of, b. Hobart, later Mrs/Lady Berkeley	6 Oct 1766	MF	
Hanbury Williams, Charles	26 Jun 1744	MM	
Lincoln, Henry Fiennes Clinton, 9th Earl of, later 2nd Duke of Newcastle	22 Jun 1743	MM	
Lincoln, Henry Fiennes Clinton, 9th Earl of, later 2nd Duke of Newcastle	?1743–1744	MM	
Selwyn, George	12 Aug 1772	MM	
Seymour Conway, Henry	27 Jun 1748	MM	

Letters, Subproject 6

Brentano, Sophie, b. Schubart (1770–1806)

Recipient	Date	Corpus	Source
Arnstein, Henriette	5 May 1798	FF	*Meine Seele ist bey euch geblieben. Briefe Sophie Brentanos an Henriette Arnstein*, ed. Karen Schenck zu Schweinsberg (Acta Humaniora; Weinheim; VCH, 1985).
Arnstein, Henriette	26 May 1798	FF	
Arnstein, Henriette	26 Aug 1798	FF	
Arnstein, Henriette	3 Oct 1798	FF	
Arnstein, Henriette	6 Oct 1798	FF	
Arnstein, Henriette	15 Oct 1798	FF	
Arnstein, Henriette	30 Mar 1799	FF	
Arnstein, Henriette	8 Aug 1799	FF	
Arnstein, Henriette	4 Nov 1799	FF	
Arnstein, Henriette	18 Jun 1800	FF	
Arnstein, Henriette	12 Aug 1800	FF	
Servière, Charlotte	28 Jul 1800	FF	

Recipient	Date	Corpus	Source
Servière, Charlotte	21 Aug 1800	FF	
Wieland, Christoph Martin	10 Oct 1799	FM	Briefe und Begegnungen: Christoph Martin Wieland, Sophie Brentano, ed. by Otto Drude (Acta Humaniora: Weinheim: VCH, 1989).
Wieland, Christoph Martin	17 Oct 1799	FM	
Wieland, Christoph Martin	15 Nov 1799	FM	
Wieland, Christoph Martin	18 Jan 1800	FM	
Wieland, Christoph Martin	7 Mar 1800	FM	

Gessner, Judith, b. Heidegger (1736–1818)

Recipient	Date	Corpus	Source
Gessner, the children Dorothea, Konrad, and Heinrich	20 Oct 1790	FF	Judith Gessner, die Gattin des Idyllendichters und Malers Salomon Geßner – Mit einer Auswahl ihrer Familienbriefe, ed. P. Leemann-Van Elck (Zürich: Orell Füssli, 1942)
Gessner Wieland, Charlotte	10 Jun 1801	FF	
Gessner-Zellweger, Dorothea	? Mar 1795	FF	
Gessner-Zellweger, Dorothea	02 May 1795	FF	
Gessner-Zellweger, Dorothea	11 Sep 1802	FF	
Gessner-Zellweger, Dorothea	28 Sep 1802	FF	
Gessner-Zellweger, Dorothea	19 Sep 1804	FF	
Gessner Zellweger, Dorothea	22 Apr 1795	FF	
Gessner, Heinrich	28 Nov 1802	FM	
Gessner, Heinrich	7 Sep 1788	FM	
Gessner, Konrad	30 Jun 1790	FM	
Zellweger, Johann Kasper	22 Sep 1790	FM	
Zellweger, Johann Kasper	1 Feb 1801	FM	
Zellweger, Johann Kasper	11 Jan 1795	FM	
Zellweger-Hirzel, Johannes	22 Feb 1796	FM	
Zellweger-Hirzel, Johannes	3 Jan 1796	FM	
Zellweger-Hirzel, Johannes	27 May 1796	FM	
Zellweger-Hirzel, Johannes	8 Dec 1799	FM	
Zellweger-Hirzel, Johannes	9 Feb 1800	FM	

Gottsched, Luise, b. Kulmus (1713–1762)

Recipient	Date	Corpus	Source
Gottsched, Caroline	4 Jun 1759	FF	Louise Gottsched – 'mit der Feder in der Hand': Briefe aus den Jahren 1730–1762, ed. Inka Kording (Darmstadt: Wissenschaftliche Buchgesellschaft, 1999)
Gottsched, Katharine Friderike	4 Jan 1752	FF	

Recipient	Date	Corpus
N.N., Mrs	undated 1743	FF
Runckel, Dorothee Henriette von	15 Jul 1756	FF
Runckel, Dorothee Henriette von	4 Feb 1758	FF
Runckel, Dorothee Henriette von	8 Jun 1758	FF
Runckel, Dorothee Henriette von	4 Mar 1762	FF
Schulz, Wilhelmine	9 Aug 1750	FF
Schulz, Wilhelmine	16 Mar 1756	FF
Seckendorf, Clara Dorothea von	11 Apr 1750	FF
Thomasius, Maria Regina	6 Sep 1749	FF
Werner, Anna Maria	undated 1737	FF
Werner, Anna Maria	? Feb 1754	FF
Zerbst, Caroline Wilhelmine Sophie von	4 Dec 1755	FF
Ziegler, Marianne von	13 Oct 1734	FF
Gottsched, Johann Christoph	20 Sep 1730	FM
Gottsched, Johann Christoph	7 Jan 1731	FM
Gottsched, Johann Christoph	11 Apr 1733	FM
Gottsched, Johann Christoph	undated 1734	FM
Gottsched, Johann Christoph	undated 1748	FM
Gottsched, Johann Heinrich	? Apr 1746	FM
Manteuffel, Ernst Christoph von	undated 1739	FM
N.N., Mr	undated 1740	FM
N.N., Mr	27 Apr 1744	FM
N.N., Mr	14 May 1758	FM
N.N., Mr	? Mar 1758	FM
Runckel, Adolf Ferdinand von	2 Sep 1753	FM
Runckel, Friedrich Wilhelm von	7 Mar 1755	FM
Schöpflin, Johannes Daniel		FM

Huber, Therese, b. Heyne, div. Forster (1764–1829)

Recipient	Date	Corpus	Source
Böhmer, Caroline (Schlegel-Schelling)	25 Feb 1794	FF	*Briefe: Band I, 1774–1803*, ed. Magdalene Hauser & Corina Bergmann-Törner (Tübingen: Niemeyer, 1999)
Carus, Caroline	? Oct 1803	FF	
Carus, Caroline	24 Sep 1802	FF	
Heyne, Georgina	10 Dec 1785	FF	
Heyne, Georgina	? Dec 1785	FF	

Recipient	Date	Corpus	Source
Hottinger, Regula	16 Nov 1793	FF	
Hottinger, Regula	10 Apr 1794	FF	
Mejer, Luise	23 Mar 1782	FF	
Mejer, Luise	5 May 1782	FF	
Mejer, Luise	10 Sep 1782	FF	
Mejer, Luise	19 Sep 1782	FF	
Mejer, Luise	9 Nov 1782	FF	
Mejer, Luise	30 Nov 1782	FF	
Mejer, Luise	20 Jan 1783	FF	
Mejer, Luise	2 Sep 1783	FF	
Simanowitz, Ludovike	? Sep 1799	FF	
Berruch, Friedrich Justin	11 May 1790	FM	
Blumenbach, Johann Friedrich	4 Aug 1782	FM	
Blumenbach, Johann Friedrich	20 Jan 1785	FM	
Bürger, Gottfrid August	14 Jan 1790	FM	
Carus, Friedrich August	20 Aug 1801	FM	
Herder, Johann Gottfrid	21 Jul 1786	FM	
Heyne, Christian Gottlob	29 Jan 1788	FM	
Reichard, Heinrich August Ottokar	30 May 1784	FM	
Soemmerring, Samuel Thomas	26 Apr 1784	FM	
Soemmerring, Samuel Thomas	15 Sep 1784	FM	
Soemmerring, Samuel Thomas	14 Aug 1786	FM	
Spener, Carl	21 Jan 1787	FM	
Spener, Carl	22 May 1788	FM	
Spener, Carl	31 Oct 1785	FM	

Klopstock, 'Meta' Margareta, b. Moller (1728–1758)

Recipient	Date	Corpus	Source
Cramer, Charlotte	2 Jan 1754	FF	*Es sind wunderliche Dinger, meine Briefe: Meta Klopstocks Briefwechsel mit Friedrich Gottlieb Klopstock und mit ihren Freunden 1751–1758*, ed. Franziska & Hermann Tiemann (Munich: Beck, 1980).
Cramer, Charlotte	11 Feb 1755	FF	
Schmidt, Elisabeth	? Sep 1758	FF	
Schmidt, Elisabeth	24 Aug 1754	FF	
Schmidt, Elisabeth	1 Sep 1754	FF	
Schmidt, Elisabeth	30 Dec 1754	FF	

Schmidt, Elisabeth	18 Feb 1756	FF
Schmidt, Elisabeth	4 Apr 1756	FF
Schmidt, Elisabeth	20 Aug 1757	FF
Schmidt, Elisabeth	? May 1755	FF
Moller-Dimpfel, Margaretha	5 Aug 1755	FF
Moller-Dimpfel, Margaretha	21 Nov 1755	FF
Moller-Dimpfel, Margaretha	6 Sep 1756	FF
Klopstock, Friedrich Gottlieb	13 Apr 1751	FM
Klopstock, Friedrich Gottlieb	8 Feb 1752	FM
Klopstock, Friedrich Gottlieb	18 Feb 1752	FM
Klopstock, Friedrich Gottlieb	1 May 1752	FM
Klopstock, Friedrich Gottlieb	15 Jul 1752	FM
Klopstock, Friedrich Gottlieb	15 Oct 1752	FM
Cramer, Johann Andreas	3 Jun 1753	FM
Gleim, Johann Wilhelm Ludwig	5 May 1753	FM
Giseke, Nicolaus Dietrich	28 May 1753	FM
Giseke, Nicolaus Dietrich	16 Aug 1753	FM
Giseke, Nicolaus Dietrich	18 Sep 1753	FM
Zornickel, Tobias	1 Apr 1758	FM

Pfalz, Liselotte von der (1652–1722)

[Elisabeth Charlotte of the Palatinate, Duchesse d'Orléans]

Recipient	Date	Corpus
Degenfeld, Amalie Elisabeth	4 Nov 1701	FF
Degenfeld, Amalie Elisabeth	30 Mar 1704	FF
Degenfeld, Louise	22 Apr 1706	FF
Degenfeld, Louise	16 Oct 1710	FF
Degenfeld, Louise	30 Apr 1713	FF
Degenfeld, Louise	1 Jul 1714	FF
Degenfeld, Louise	17 Sep 1719	FF
Karoline von Wales	13 Dec 1718	FF
Pfalz, Sophie von der	12 Jun 1701	FF
Pfalz, Sophie von der	7 Jul 1701	FF
Pfalz, Sophie von der	22 Aug 1709	FF

Source

Liselotte von der Pfalz: Elisabeth Charlotte, Duchesse d'Orléans, Madame: Briefe, ed. Annedore Haberl (Munich: Hanser, 1996).

Pfalz, Sophie von der	8 Apr 1712	FF
Pfalz, Sophie von der	6 May 1714	FF
Schaumburg-Lippe, Johanna Sophie von	23 Nov 1717	FF
Schaumburg-Lippe, Johanna Sophie von	30 Jan 1722	FF
Theodor von Neuhof, Baron Goertz	8 Jun 1719	FM
Braunschweig, Anton Ulrich von	9 Mar 1714	FM
Harling, Christian Friedrich von	21 Sep 1718	FM
Harling, Christian Friedrich von	24 Feb 1718	FM
Haxthausen, Christian August von	24 Oct 1694	FM
Leibniz, Gottfried Wilhelm	26 Sep 1715	FM
Lothringen, Leopold von	11 Oct 1699	FM
Pfalz, Karl Ludwig von der	6 Jun 1676	FM
Pfalz, Karl Ludwig von der	18 Jul 1683	FM
Pfalz, Karl Ludwig von der	17 May 1688	FM
Pfalz, Karl Ludwig von der	22 Nov 1677	FM

Roche, Sophie von La, b. Gutermann (1730–1807)

Recipient	Date	Corpus	Source
Keller, Caroline von	undated 1792	FF	*Ich bin mehr Herz als Kopf: Ein Lebensbild in Briefen Sophie von La Roche*, ed. Michael Maurer (Munich: Beck, 1983).
l'Espinasse, Elsy de	4 Mar 1787	FF	
Meyer, Barbara	? Mar 1753	FF	
Pobeckheim, Sophie von	21 Jun 1800	FF	
Roche, Elsy von La	6 Mar 1792	FF	
Roche, Elsy von La	17 Oct 1797	FF	
Solms-Laubach, Elise zu	25 Jun 1783	FF	
Solms-Laubach, Elise zu	30 Jan 1785	FF	
Solms-Laubach, Elise zu	20 Jan 1786	FF	
Solms-Laubach, Elise zu	7 Mar 1788	FF	
Solms-Laubach, Elise zu	14 Sep 1791	FF	
Zanthier, Charlotte von	24 Nov 1791	FF	
Zanthier, Charlotte von	10 Mar 1792	FF	
Bodmer, Johann Jacob	30 Jan 1753	FM	
Brentano, Clemens	11 Jul 1798	FM	
Dalberg, Wolfgang Heribert von	10 Mar 1779	FM	
Jacobi, Johann Georg	20 Jan 1786	FM	

Recipient	Date	Corpus
Jacobi, Johann Georg	8 Jul 1795	FM
Lavater, Johann Caspar	19 Feb 1784	FM
Ludwig X	20 Apr 1790	FM
Merck, Johann Heinrich	12 Feb 1776	FM
Merck, Johann Heinrich	24 Dec 1780	FM
Pfeffel, Gottlieb Konrad	13 May 1784	FM
Roche, Fritz von La	5 Nov 1780	FM
Roche, Fritz von La	31 Jan 1787	FM
Roche, Fritz von La	14 May 1787	FM
Roche, Fritz von La	27 Nov 1792	FM
Wieland, Christoph Martin	10 Nov 1760	FM
Wieland, Christoph Martin	25 Feb 1770	FM

Schlegel-Schelling, Caroline, b. Michaelis (1763–1809)

Recipient	Date	Corpus	Source
Böhmer, Philippine Augusta	21 Sep 1799	FF	'Lieber Freund, ich komme weit her schon an diesem frühen Morgen': Caroline Schlegel-Schelling in ihren Briefen, ed. Sigrid Damm (4th edn., Darmstadt: Luchterhand-Literaturverlag, 1988)
Gotter, Luise (b. Stieler)	7 Oct 1778	FF	
Gotter, Luise	23 Oct 1782	FF	
Gotter, Luise	8 Mar 1789	FF	
Gotter, Luise	24 Jan 1793	FF	
Gotter, Luise	11 Jul 1796	FF	
Gotter, Luise	11 Jul 1796	FF	
Gotter, Luise	24 Apr 1799	FF	
Gotter, Luise	? Jun 1799	FF	
Michaelis, Lotte	20 Mar 1786	FF	
Michaelis, Lotte	28 May 1786	FF	
Goethe, Johann Wolfgang	26 Nov 1800	FM	
Gotter, Friedrich Wilhelm	18 Mar 1793	FM	
Gotter, Friedrich Wilhelm	12 May 1793	FM	
Gotter, Friedrich Wilhelm	16 May 1793	FM	
Gotter, Friedrich Wilhelm	15 Jun 1793	FM	
Gotter, Friedrich Wilhelm	13 Jul 1793	FM	
Göschen, Georg Joachim	16 Dec 1797	FM	
Meyer, Friedrich Ludwig Wilhelm	1 Mar 1789	FM	

Recipient	Date	Corpus
Meyer, Friedrich Ludwig Wilhelm	15 Aug 1793	FM
Meyer, Friedrich Ludwig Wilhelm	9 Dec 1793	FM
Schelling, Friedrich Wilhelm Joseph	? Oct 1800	FM
Schelling, Friedrich Wilhelm Joseph	? Oct 1800	FM

Varnhagen, Rahel, b. Levin (1771–1833)

Recipient	Date	Corpus	Source
Boye, Mrs (4)	15 Apr 1801	FF	Source 1. *Rahel Varnhagen und ihre Zeit (Briefe 1800–1833)*, ed. Friedhelm Kemp (Munich: Kösel, 1968)
B., Mrs (4)	undated 1806	FF	
Friedländer, Rebecca (2)	15 Dec 1805	FF	
Friedländer, Rebecca (2)	27 Dec 1805	FF	Source 2. *Briefe an eine Freundin: Rahel Varnhagen an Rebecca Friedländer*, ed. Deborah Hertz (Cologne: Kiepenheuer & Witsch, 1988)
Friedländer, Rebecca (2)	? Dec 1805	FF	
Friedländer, Rebecca (2)	2 Jan 1806	FF	
Friedländer, Rebecca (2)	5 Jan 1806	FF	Source 3. *Rahel Varnhagen im Umgang mit ihren Freunden (Briefe 1793–1833)*, ed. Friedhelm Kemp (Munich: Kösel, 1967)
Friedländer, Rebecca (2)	? Jan 1806	FF	
Friedländer, Rebecca (2)	undated 1805	FF	
Humboldt, Caroline von (1)	7 Sep 1813	FF	Source 4. *Rahel Varnhagen. Briefe und Aufzeichnungen*, ed. Dieter Bähtz (Leipzig: Kiepenheuer, 1985)
Humboldt, Caroline von (3)	7 Dec 1813	FF	
Varnhagen, Rose (1)	25 Sep 1800	FF	
Varnhagen, Rose (4)	14 Dec 1800	FF	
Brinckmann, Karl Gustav von (3)	15 Jul 1794	FM	
Brinckmann, Karl Gustav von (4)	25 Jul 1794	FM	
Brinckmann, Karl Gustav von (3)	5 Feb 1795	FM	
Brinckmann, Karl Gustav von (3)	? Jul 1800	FM	
Veit, David (3)	18 Nov 1793	FM	
Veit, David (3)	18 Feb 1794	FM	
Veit, David (3)	10 Mar 1794	FM	
Veit, David (3)	16 Oct 1794	FM	
Veit, David (3)	15 Nov 1794	FM	
Veit, David (4)	12 Dec 1794	FM	
Veit, David (4)	21 Mar 1795	FM	
Veit, David (4)	28 Aug 1795	FM	

Forster, Georg (1754–1794)

Recipient	Date	Corpus	Source
Forster, Justine R.B. (1)	27 Sep 1782	MF	**Source** Source 1. *Georg Forsters Werke: Sämtliche Schriften, Tagebücher, Briefe. Bd. 13, Briefe bis 1783*; ed. Siegfried Scheibe (Berlin: Akademie-Verlag, 1978)
Gatterer, Philippine (1)	31 Dec 1778	MF	
Gatterer, Philippine (1)	? Jan 1779	MF	
Gatterer, Philippine (1)	15 Feb 1779	MF	
Heyne, Therese (2)	? Jul 1785	MF	Source 2. *Georg Forsters Werke: Sämtliche Schriften, Tagebücher, Briefe. Bd. 14, Briefe 1784–Juni 1787*, ed. Brigitte Leuschner (Berlin: Akademie-Verlag, 1978)
Campe, Joachim Heinrich (1)	5 Oct 1779	MM	
Nicolai, Christoph Friedrich (1)	15 Mar 1779	MM	
Spener, Johann Karl Philipp (1)	15 Mar 1779	MM	
Spener, Johann Karl Philipp (1)	30 Jan 1780	MM	
Spener, Johann Karl Philipp (2)	22 Aug 1785	MM	

Gellert, Christian Fürchtegott (1715–1769)

Recipient	Date	Corpus	Source
Biehle, Johanna Wilhelmine	10 Nov 1758	MF	**Source** C.B. Gellerts Briefwechsel. Bd. II, ed. John B. Reynolds (Berlin: de Gruyter, 1987)
Biehle, Johanna Wilhelmine	18 Dec 1758	MF	
Eckstädt, Erdmuthe Dorothea Magdalena Vitzthum von	15 Nov 1759	MF	
Schönfeld, Johanna Erdmuth von	25 Jan 1759	MF	
Schönfeld, Johanna Erdmuth von	28 Mar 1759	MF	
Buschmann, Ernst August	16 Aug 1759	MM	
Rochow, Friedrich Eberhard von	23 Jan 1759	MM	
Schlegel, Johann Adolf	23 Dec 1758	MM	
Wagner, Andreas	22 May 1759	MM	
Wagner, Andreas	8 Jun 1759	MM	

Herder, Johann Gottfried (1744–1803)

Recipient	Date	Corpus	Source
Flachland, Karoline (1)	13 Jul 1771	MF	**Source** Source 1. *Briefe: Gesamtausgabe, Bd. II, Mai 1771–April 1773*, ed. Wilhelm Dobbek and Günther Arnold (Weimar: Böhlau, 1977)
Flachland, Karoline (1)	10 Aug 1771	MF	
Heyne, Therese (1)	21 Feb 1772	MF	

Recipient	Date	Corpus	Source
Lippe-Detmold, Casimire zur (2)	16 Jul 1776	MF	Source 2. *Briefe: Gesamtausgabe, Bd.III, Mai 1773-September 1776,* ed. Wilhelm Dobbek and Günther Arnold (Weimar: Böhlau, 1978)
Raspe, Elisabeth (2)	23 Jan 1775	MF	
Hartnoch, Johann Friedrich (1)	? Aug 1771	MM	
Heyne, Christian Gottlob (1)	21 Feb 1772	MM	
Heyne, Christian Gottlob (1)	? Aug 1772	MM	
Lavater, Johann Kaspar (2)	30 Dec 1775	MM	
Merck, Johann Heinrich (1)	? Aug 1771	MM	

Klopstock, Friedrich Gottlieb (1724–1803)

Recipient	Date	Corpus	Source
Moller, Meta (2)	1 Jan 1752	MF	Source 1. *Werke und Briefe: Historisch-Kritische Ausgabe. Abteilung Briefe I. Briefe 1738–1750,* ed. Horst Gronemeyer et al. (Berlin: de Gruyter, 1978)
Moller, Meta (2)	4 Mar 1752	MF	
Schmidt, Maria Sophia (1)	3 Jul 1750	MF	
Schmidt, Maria Sophia (2)	14 Mar 1751	MF	
Schmidt, Maria Sophia (2)	28 Dec 1751	MF	Source 2. *Werke und Briefe: Historisch-Kritische Ausgabe. Abteilung Briefe II. Briefe 1751–1752,* ed. Horst Gronemeyer et al. (Berlin: de Gruyter, 1985)
Bodmer, Johann Jakob (1)	29 Jun 1750	MM	
Giseke, Nicolaus Dietrich (2)	20 Jul 1751	MM	
Gleim, Johann Wilhelm Ludwig (2)	13 Jan 1751	MM	
Schlegel, Johann Adolf (1)	21 Nov 1750	MM	
Schmidt, Johann Christoph (1)	1 Aug 1750	MM	

Wieland, Christoph Martin (1733–1813)

Recipient	Date	Corpus	Source
Bechtolsheim, Juliane Christiane von	14 Jan 1784	MF	*Wielands Briefwechsel Bd. 8 (Juli 1782–Juni 1785), Erster Teil: Text,* ed. Annerose Schneider (Berlin: Akademie-Verlag, 1992)
Bechtolsheim, Juliane Christiane von	27 Sep 1784	MF	
Herder, Maria Karoline	2 Apr 1784	MF	
Roche, Marie Sophie von La	29 Feb 1784	MF	
Roche, Marie Sophie von La	30 Apr 1784	MF	
Gleim, Johann Wilhelm Ludwig	9 May 1784	MM	
Heyne, Christian Gottlob	29 Nov 1784	MM	
Hillern, Justin Heinrich von	9 Aug 1784	MM	
Reich, Philipp Erasmus	3 Sep 1784	MM	
Reich, Philipp Erasmus	8 Nov 1784	MM	

About the Authors

Eva Hættner Aurelius is Professor of Comparative Literature at Lund University, Sweden. Her research has focused on, amongst many subjects, women's autobiographies before the twentieth century, including Queen Christina of Sweden's. She has also published on the history of literature written by Scandinavian women, and done research on the work of Swedish author Birger Sjöberg. Eva Hættner Aurelius is a Member of the Royal Swedish Academy of Letters, History and Antiquities, and Akademie der Wissenschaften zu Göttingen.

Hedda Gunneng is Associate Professor of Latin and senior lecturer in Medieval Studies at Gotland University. She is an experienced editor of medieval texts, in Latin as well as in Medieval Swedish. She has also published on Latin paleography and women's history. Her present research concerns the perception of the Middle Ages in computer games.

Elisabet Hammar is Associate Professor of French. She received her Ph.D. in Romance languages from Stockholm University. In her thesis she focused on language didactics studying how French was taught in Sweden before 1807 ('L'enseignement du français en Suède jusqu'en 1807') and its social counterpart ('La Française. Mille et une façons d'apprendre le français en Suède avant 1807'). She has since continued in the field of the history of language didactics and the history of pedagogics.

Jon Helgason is Ph.D. and Researcher in Comparative Literature at Lund University as well as an editor of the Swedish Academy Dictionary. In his thesis *Hjärtats skrifter: en brevkulturs uttryck i korrespondensen mellan Anna Louisa Karsch och Johann Wilhelm Ludwig Gleim (Schriften des Herzens: Briefkultur des 18. Jahrhunderts im Briefwechsel zwischen Anna Louisa Karsch und Johann Wilhelm Ludwig Gleim)* he examined the culture of letters and the emergence of the literary public sphere in Europe in the eighteenth century.

Marie Löwendahl has a Ph.D. in Comparative Literature at Lund University. Her research mainly concerns letter-writing in Sweden during the eighteenth century. As well as taking part of the research project 'Women's language', her dissertation, *Min allrabästa och ömmaste vän! Kvinnors brevskrivning under svenskt 1700-tal* (*My dearest and most tender Friend! Women's Letter-Writing in Eighteenth Century Sweden*), touches the subject of a supposed female style of letter-writing during the period. The main focus of her work is on letter-writing as a genre, and the concept of the letter being a type of writing best suited for women.

Lena Olsson has a Ph.D. in English literature at Lund University, and wrote her thesis on John Cleland's *Memoirs of a Woman of Pleasure*. Her research is focused on sexuality, gender, and popular literature in eighteenth-century England. Lena Olsson has edited Cleland's abridged *Memoirs of Fanny Hill* and the anonymous *The Genuine History of* [...] *Sally Salisbury*. She currently works as an independent scholar and authorized public translator from English into Swedish.

Börje Westlund is Associate Professor of Scandinavian languages at Stockholm University and former senior lecturer in Swedish at Linköping University and Södertörn University. He has a wide experience of editing medieval texts in Swedish as well as in Latin. Börje Westlund has published on runology, on Swedish and Icelandic palaeography, and Medieval text philology. His present research focuses on runology and eighteenth-century Swedish.